SCHOOLING DISADVANTAGED CHILDREN

Racing Against Catastrophe

Human history becomes more and more
a race between education and catastrophe.
— H. G. Wells, *The Outline of History*

SCHOOLING DISADVANTAGED CHILDREN

Racing Against Catastrophe

Gary Natriello
Edward L. McDill
Aaron M. Pallas

Teachers College, Columbia University
New York and London

Published by Teachers College Press, 1234 Amsterdam Avenue
New York, NY 10027

Library of Congress Cataloging-in-Publication Data
Natriello, Gary.
  Schooling disadvantaged children : racing against catastrophe /
Gary Natriello, Edward L. McDill, Aaron M. Pallas.
     p.   cm.
  Includes bibliographical references.
  ISBN 0-8077-3015-7 (alk. paper). — ISBN 0-8077-3014-9 (pbk. :
alk. paper)
    1. Socially handicapped children — Education — United States.
2. Federal aid to education — United States.   3. Educational
innovations — United States.   I. McDill, Edward L. (Edward Lamar)
II. Pallas, Aaron M.   III. Title.   IV. Title: Racing against
catastrophe.
LC4091.N39   1990   89-77441
371.96′7′0973 — dc20   CIP

ISBN 0-8077-3015-7
ISBN 0-8077-3014-9 (pbk.)

Printed on acid-free paper

Manufactured in the United States of America

97   96   95   94   93   92   91   90   8   7   6   5   4   3   2   1

Contents

Preface

Though we did not know it at the time, our work on the material in this volume began in 1984, when we were invited by the American Educational Research Association to prepare one of the papers the association was assembling to respond to the report of the National Commission on Excellence in Education. Our paper was to focus on an area omitted from the report of that commission, school dropouts. In 1984, with the attention of the educational community directed to issues of "excellence," there was little interest in students who might leave school prior to graduation.

As coauthors of that paper, we found that our previous experiences were quite complementary. Natriello had been studying the impact of organizational processes on students, with a particular interest in those processes that led students to become disengaged from the school. Pallas had conducted some of the first analyses of the High School and Beyond study (Sebring et al., 1987) and had a general interest in the impact of stratification processes on students. McDill had prepared major reviews of the impact of compensatory education programs (McDill, McDill, & Sprehe, 1969, 1972) and had longstanding interests in the organization of secondary schools. All of us were disappointed in the retreat of the federal government from a concern for educational equity and equal educational opportunity.

We prepared our paper and a series of subsequent articles that detailed the plight of dropouts and potential dropouts in U.S. schools. Shortly after that, Natriello was invited to serve as guest editor for a special issue of the *Teachers College Record* devoted to the topic of dropouts. It appeared in 1986 and called additional attention to the one-fourth of U.S. students who were not completing high school. As interest in dropouts grew and extended to disadvantaged students more generally, we received repeated requests to extend our original analyses, which had focused on the impact of the excellence movement reforms on potential dropouts.

We broadened our research on the conditions of potential dropouts to include the entire population of disadvantaged students. At the urging of policy makers and practitioners interested in developing solutions to the problems of dropout-prone and disadvantaged youth, we examined the impact of various programs developed to reduce dropping out.

Late in 1986 we were invited to prepare a background paper for the

Subcommittee on the Educationally Disadvantaged of the Committee for Economic Development (CED). Preparation of the paper gave us the opportunity to synthesize much of the work that we had been doing in various other places over the past several years. What began as a modest-sized paper soon grew into a report of several hundred pages. As we rushed to meet what was a reasonable deadline for the brief paper, but an almost impossible one for the growing report, it became clear that even the larger work would not give us the opportunity to cover all of the material that we felt was important when thinking about the educationally disadvantaged. The idea for the current volume grew out of our realization that there was still more to be said about this issue.

Over the next two years, we refined and extended the original background paper prepared for the CED into its present form. During that time we were pleased to become a part of a new federally funded research-and-development center, the Center for Research on Effective Schooling for Disadvantaged Students (CDS). Located at The Johns Hopkins University, it became the home for this project and for new projects devoted to making schools more responsive to the needs of disadvantaged students.

Although the present volume is a current statement of some of the most important information on the educationally disadvantaged, our hope is that it will quickly become out of date, for, as we will make clear, there is a great need for additional research on the disadvantaged. We hope that this volume and others like it signal not the end, but only the end of the beginning of a new era of research and policy making designed to ameliorate the condition of disadvantaged students in our schools.

Acknowledgments

The work on which this volume is based was supported by two distinct sources. The first is the Subcommittee on the Educationally Disadvantaged of the Committee for Economic Development (CED) of New York City, which commissioned us to prepare a background paper for their compelling report, *Children in Need: Investment Strategies for the Educationally Disadvantaged* (CED, 1987). The major modifications and expansion of that background paper, which constitute the present volume, were facilitated by the Center for Research on Effective Schooling for Disadvantaged Students (CDS) at The Johns Hopkins University, supported as a national research-and-development center by the Office of Educational Research and Improvement (OERI), U.S. Department of Education (Grant No. R117R90002). We are indebted to both CED and OERI for their support and encouragement in this work; however, the opinions expressed herein are ours and do not necessarily reflect the position or policy of either organization.

Special thanks are due to a number of colleagues from around the country who patiently answered questions and provided feedback on portions of the volume. These include Jomills Braddock, Joyce Epstein, Denise Gottfredson, Gary Gottfredson, John Hollifield, Nancy Karweit, James McPartland, and Robert Slavin of CDS; Sol Hurwitz and Sandra Hamburg of CED; Henry Levin of Stanford University; Russell Gersten of the University of Oregon; Joseph Grannis, Anna Neumann, and A. Harry Passow of Teachers College, Columbia University; and Ron Galbraith and Peter Sieger of Teachers College Press. Many others contributed to our thinking in less direct ways. Of course, any errors of omission or commission belong to us.

SCHOOLING
DISADVANTAGED
CHILDREN
Racing Against Catastrophe

Part I

WHO ARE THE EDUCATIONALLY DISADVANTAGED?

Interest in educationally disadvantaged youth has waxed and waned over the years as policy makers and educators have periodically devoted attention to the problems such youth present to our schools and to our society. In a curious way the current attention being paid to disadvantaged students is a result of their being ignored by the educational reform movement of the early 1980s. The 1983 report of the National Commission on Excellence in Education (NCEE), which signaled the start of that reform movement, made no mention of the plight of the disadvantaged. This failure capped a decade-long period of neglect of this population.

In the wake of the 1983 NCEE report, a number of those responding pointed out the failure to consider the disadvantaged in the recommendations of the commission (Edson, 1984; Howe, 1984; Stedman & Smith, 1983). Others began to study the likely impact of the recommendations on the disadvantaged (Alexander & Pallas, 1984). Much of this initial reaction focused on students who drop out of school. Concerns were raised that the kinds of policies recommended would make it more likely for certain students to leave school before graduation (McDill, Natriello, & Pallas, 1986; Natriello, 1987b). A number of individuals (Hahn & Danzberger, 1987; Rumberger, 1987) and organizations (U.S. General Accounting Office, 1986b, 1987c) issued reports calling attention to the dropout problem.

The initial concern over potential dropouts broadened, however, to include the school experiences of disadvantaged youth in general, whether they dropped out or remained in schools. Once again individuals (Levin, 1985) and organizations (Committee for Economic Development, 1987; Council of Chief State School Officers, 1988; Grant Foundation Commission on Work, Family, and Citizenship, 1988) issued reports calling attention to the problems. By the late 1980s the issue of disadvantaged students in U.S. public schools had returned to a position of prominence in the national dialogue on education that it had not enjoyed since the late 1960s.

It is our contention that the problems of disadvantaged students are the result of long-term conditions that are not susceptible to short-term solutions. Certainly they will not be solved during one of the relatively brief periods when they have a prominent place in the priorities of policy makers

(Downs, 1966). Consequently, it is very important to maintain a sufficient level of interest in and attention to the problems of the disadvantaged in our schools over a sustained period of time to begin to make some progress in improving the educational experiences of this group of youngsters.

Chapters 1 through 3 provide the basic information to support a long-term commitment to addressing the educational problems of disadvantaged students. Chapter 1 considers the different perspectives on disadvantaged students that have been popular over the last 35 years. It examines the interaction between the various definitions of the educationally disadvantaged and the policies formulated to address their problems. Chapter 2 describes the current conditions of the educationally disadvantaged by reviewing the indicators commonly used to identify the population. It also discusses the limitations of these indicators in providing insight into some of the more serious problems confronted by the disadvantaged. Chapter 3 highlights the need for sustained attention to the problems of disadvantaged students in our schools by projecting significant growth in the size of the disadvantaged population over the next generation if current conditions remain relatively stable. This growth in the numbers and proportions of disadvantaged students will present a challenge to our schools over the coming years.

The chapters in this part thus serve as a point of departure for the discussions of programs and policies in the remainder of the book. They are designed to call continuing attention to the most serious problem facing our schools today and in the foreseeable future.

1

Defining the Educationally Disadvantaged

Defining the educationally disadvantaged is a necessary and important element in any attempt to understand the problem of disadvantaged students in our schools. Yet the very decision to define this population could be interpreted as an attempt to place the blame for the educational problems disadvantaged children present on those who suffer the consequences of these problems the most, the students themselves. This act thus places us squarely in the midst of one of the many epistemological and ideological disputes that have characterized discourse on the disadvantaged during the last 35 years in U.S. society.

There are at least two sides to the dispute over the definition of some segment of the student population as disadvantaged. On one side are those who have argued that identifying the population experiencing problems in U.S. schools is a necessary step to solving those problems (Hammack, 1987; Morrow, 1987). Individuals holding this position contend that, in order to solve the problems of the schools, we must understand which subgroups of the total student population are most affected by the problems. On the other side are those who caution that defining a group of students as disadvantaged locates the problem in the students themselves rather than in the institutions that purport to serve them (Wehlage & Rutter, 1987). They argue that focusing attention on groups of students instead of on schools misdirects us away from the problems of the schools and ultimately from addressing the problems experienced by disadvantaged students.

A second problem connected with the identification of such youngsters is that it might set in motion a self-fulfilling prophecy that impedes the progress of disadvantaged individuals and groups (Grannis, 1975; Merton, 1948; Rist, 1970). Both students and their teachers might simply lower their expectations when students are identified as disadvantaged.

The issue of identification is more than just an academic dispute among scholars; it has quite practical implications as well. For example, some school districts have begun ambitious projects to identify and follow students likely to experience difficulties with the school program (Hammack, 1987). Indeed, a recurrent theme in recent reports on the problems in U.S. schools is the recommendation for early identification of such students (Committee for Economic Development, 1987), reflecting the position that such a step is necessary for solving the problems. Fearing the effects of the labeling process, however, some school districts, such as New York City, have deliberately refrained from collecting information on the racial and ethnic backgrounds of students (Perlez, 1987). At least in the case of New York City, this position has been reversed as minority groups have demanded that data on the school performance of minority youngsters be made available so that school officials might be forced to respond to these students' needs (Aspira, 1983).

The definition and identification of disadvantaged youth also influence educational policy. The way in which we define and conceptualize such groups shapes the policies and programs we develop to respond to the problems associated with them. If the problem is defined solely as one of student characteristics, as has been the case in the past, then the proposed solutions are not likely to involve changes in the institutions that serve disadvantaged youth. However, just because we have previously defined the disadvantaged as the source of their own educational problems is no reason to refrain from attempting a better definition today. Rather, the earlier shortcomings suggest a need to devote greater attention to careful definition and identification of such students in ways that are likely to lead to the development of appropriate solutions to their educational problems.

We think that it is important and useful to identify those students who are educationally disadvantaged, but only when the information will be used to alter the operation of the institutions that serve these students, to make such services more effective. Moreover, we believe that the improvements in institutions that might be developed from a greater understanding of the problems of disadvantaged youth are likely to benefit all youth.

In examining the changing conceptions of disadvantaged youth and the problems they present to the schools, we can distinguish at least four periods over the past 35 years during which distinct themes have characterized the nation's thinking on this subject. Although we discuss these themes as being associated with particular periods of time, in fact they have tended to overlap and exist simultaneously, with particular themes rising and falling as the dominant explanation for the problems of the disadvantaged. Moreover, all four themes continue to play some role in our thinking today.

THE DISADVANTAGED AS "CULTURALLY DEPRIVED" OR "SOCIALLY DISADVANTAGED"

The notion of cultural deprivation as both a defining characteristic and an explanation of the problems of disadvantaged students was the earliest and at one point the most popular perspective on these students during the last 35 years. Tracing the development of the term *culturally deprived* in the

1950s and 1960s, Friedman (1970) identifies the 1955 presidential address at the School Psychology division of the annual meeting of the American Psychological Association as the genesis of its common use. The address, entitled "Cultural Deprivation and Child Development," referred to "deprived homes," "deprived areas," and "emotional deprivation" (Friedman, 1970, p. 5) to explain the problems of children in the New York City schools.

In the late 1950s and early 1960s the term came into such widespread use that Riessman (1962) used it for the title of his book, *The Culturally Deprived Child,* because, as he explained, "it is the term in current usage" (p. 3). He did this despite the fact that he observed that it was not appropriate to think of people in lower socioeconomic groups as culturally deprived since "they possess a culture of their own, with many positive characteristics that have developed out of coping with a difficult environment" (p. 3). Despite Riessman's reservations, his use of the term contributed to its spread throughout the general public (Friedman, 1970). Appropriate or not, the idea of the culturally deprived child became a popular image.

The terms *culturally deprived* and *socially disadvantaged* represent the same perspective on disadvantaged youth, as the work of Havighurst makes clear. In answer to the question, "Who are the socially disadvantaged?" Havighurst (1965) notes that *disadvantage* is a relative term; that is, it is always in relation to some other child and some other kind of life. Havighurst goes on to discuss how a disadvantaged status may pertain to being "disadvantaged for living competently in an urban, industrial, and democratic society," adding that "the socially disadvantaged child is one who is handicapped in the task of growing up to lead a competent and satisfying life in American society" (p. 211).

Havighurst (1965) develops this definition further by providing examples of students who may be classified as socially disadvantaged, defining and describing them in terms of (1) family characteristics, such as a family that fails to expose the child to an elaborated language (Bernstein, 1960, 1961, 1962, 1964) and fails to set expectations regarding school-related activities such as reading; (2) personal characteristics such as inferior auditory or visual discrimination, or inferior judgment concerning time, number, and other basic concepts; and (3) social group characteristics such as low socioeconomic status and membership in a minority group that has experienced social and economic discrimination. Summing things up, Passow and Elliott (1967) note that those who speak in terms of the "socially disadvantaged" (e.g., Deutsch, 1960) see experiential deficits in early childhood as the cause of the condition.

Boocock (1980) and Hurn (1985) observe that some proponents of this perspective trace the problems of disadvantaged students not only to what we commonly understand as deprivation but also to early exposure to a "culture of poverty" that impairs their ability to profit from schooling. Such children are seen as deprived of a stimulating environment. Proponents of this interpretation (Brooks, 1966; Deutsch, 1963; Hunt, 1964; Riessman, 1963) argue that disadvantaged children are not exposed to environments that lead to the development of the skills necessary for the use of linguistic and mathematical symbols. Moreover, Boocock (1980) identifies features of the culture of poverty as including "fatalism, feelings of frustration and alienation from the larger society, a present- rather than future-time orientation, resulting in an inability to plan for the future, and preference for physical over mental activities and gratifications" (pp. 62–63). The consequences of this culture are particularly acute for children, since, as Lewis (1966) observes, the "family in the culture of poverty does not cherish childhood as a specially prolonged and protected stage in the life cycle" (p. 23).

The view that the disadvantaged are culturally deprived influenced the nature of the political and programmatic response to the problem in at least two major ways in the early 1960s. First, it determined the time targeted as most advantageous for intervention. Educational policies emphasized the preschool years as a critical time, especially ages 3 and 4, when programs of compensatory "planned enrichment" would serve to counteract the experiential inadequacies of the child's environment. If cultural deprivation were the result of a lack of appropriate early experiences in the family and community, then compensatory approaches should be developed to counteract such experiences.

A second development was the growth of federally supported programs designed to make this population more like middle-class Americans. As part of the War on Poverty, such programs were intended to "make over the poor" by educating them and changing their places of residence, personality traits, skills, and fertility patterns (Friedman, 1970). If the disadvantaged were deprived of a culture, they would be supplied with a middle class one. As the concept of cultural deprivation became widely accepted, it became a common explanation for the plight of the disadvantaged in U.S. society. Social programs to alleviate the problems of the downtrodden in the society were fashioned with this explanation as an initial assumption.

THE DISADVANTAGED AS "EDUCATIONALLY DEPRIVED"

The notion of cultural deprivation or social disadvantage places attention on the experiences of students that occur both prior to entry to school and outside of school during their careers as students. A second perspective on the plight of disadvantaged students suggests that much of the difficulty they experience is connected with schooling. Passow (1970) makes clear the differences between the two perspectives, but uses the term *educationally disadvantaged* to refer to the former position and the term *educationally deprived* to refer to the latter. He argues that

> A child is at a disadvantage if, because of social or cultural characteristics (e.g., social class, race, ethnic origin, poverty, sex, geographical location, etc.) he comes into the school system with knowledge, skills and attitudes which impede learning and contribute to a cumulative academic deficit. . . . The disadvantage may persist throughout school life and contribute to restricting later economic and social opportunities . . . a child is deprived if, for social, political, or cultural reasons, the "normal" facilities of the school system are available to him only in restricted form. [p. 16]

The distinction between these two perspectives is not simply the result of a sterile academic debate. Boocock (1980) and Hurn (1985) observe that there has been a bitter controversy over whether the sources of the poor educational performance of the disadvantaged lie in family background or the school program. Critics of the theory of cultural deprivation (Baratz & Baratz, 1970; Clark, 1965, 1972; Valentine, 1968) have argued that the problem lies in the inadequate schools disadvantaged students attend. Moreover, these critics charge that the cultural-deprivation theorists have misinterpreted cultural differences as cultural deficits and have, in effect, created an explanation for the problem which blames the victims.

Some of these critics, as noted earlier, have argued that lower-class children possess a culture of their own (Riessman, 1962). Baratz and Baratz (1970) believe that the disadvantaged are culturally different, not deficient, and that major social programs that assume such youngsters are culturally deficient are doomed to failure because they do not attempt to build on the strengths of the existing cultural forms. Valentine (1971) has criticized both the cultural-deficit model and the cultural-difference model and argued that "poor Afro-Americans — far from being either deficient or merely different in culture — often possess a richer repertoire of varied life styles than their ethnically non-descript social superiors" (pp. 8–9).

Others have dismissed the notion of cultural deprivation as an explanation of the problems of the disadvantaged because it fails to explain the variations in performance among students from the same community. Moreover, they charge, such a focus is too often used to excuse the failings of the educational system (Friedman, 1970). Baratz and Baratz (1970) argue that the widespread acceptance of the cultural-deprivation perspective sets in motion a process of institutional racism. Rist (1970) and Dornbusch (1974) have demonstrated the impact of this process as it operates through the lower expectations and lower standards held for students from traditionally disadvantaged groups. Bowles and Gintis (1976) have argued that the group of students we are referring to as disadvantaged are the product of economic processes in the larger society and that schools simply function to reinforce existing distinctions among different classes in society.

The implications for social and educational programs and policies that derive from the view that disadvantaged youth are educationally deprived are quite different from those derived from the view that they are culturally deprived. The focus of programmatic intervention is shifted to the school and other institutions that serve disadvantaged youth. Interventions in the preschool period are less important, since the primary difficulties experienced by these students occur when they confront major institutions of society such as the school. Moreover, interventions in the family and community may be seen as disrupting existing cultural patterns that strengthen both the communities and the individuals in them.

The distinction made between school-related and nonschool-related factors in discussions of culturally deprived versus educationally disadvantaged populations is reflected in the problem of defining intended beneficiaries in the recent congressionally mandated evaluation of Chapter I, the largest federal compensatory education program. The authors of that report (Kennedy, Jung, & Orland, 1986) note that there has been considerable debate since the inception of the program over who should be eligible to receive compensatory education—poor students regardless of their educational achievement or low-achieving students, regardless of their family's income. Kennedy et al. avoid this dilemma by reporting data related both to students who are poor and to those who have low achievement.

THE DISADVANTAGED AS "AT RISK"

More recent discussions of the disadvantaged have relied upon a new term to capture the problematic situation in which disadvantaged youth exist. This term, *at risk*, appears to connote different things to different observers. For some it suggests a view of youth who may be more likely than others to experience problems in school. For example, McCann and Austin (1988) observe that "the problem of 'students at risk' refers to students who, for whatever reason, are at risk of not achieving the goals of education, of not acquiring the knowledge, skills, and dispositions to become productive members of the American society" (p. 1). Others have discussed the problem in terms of students who are at risk of not graduating from high school (Beyer & Smey-Richman, 1988).

A general theme running throughout such uses of the term is its future orientation, referring to students who may be more likely to experience problems at some point in the future. This emphasis is usually related to proposals for efforts to identify such students before the problems become manifest. The implication is that at-risk students have certain characteristics that make it possible to identify them, but that these characteristics become problematic only in conjunction with events and conditions that have yet to unfold.

The idea that a condition of being at risk results from a combination of individual and environmental characteristics is traceable to the health literature (Grannis, 1989). This is consistent with a second connotation of the term, that is, that being at risk involves a differential susceptibility in which the environment becomes unnegotiable for certain individuals (Grannis, 1979).

Focusing on the interaction between individual and environmental characteristics requires a more refined specification of both types of factors, such as that suggested by Stodolsky and Lesser (1967). They argue that we must move beyond the common definition of disadvantaged status based on characteristics such as social class and ethnicity, to the identification of "environmental circumstances which are closely articulated with developmental processes and which vary considerably within and across social-class and ethnic lines" (p. 64). They claim that "particular clusterings of environmental circumstances known to be related to developmental processes would lead to identification of disadvantaged status in more complex but precise terms" (p. 64). This may be seen as one advantage of viewing the disadvantaged as being at risk.

There are other benefits to this perspective. By defining the disadvantaged population as possessing characteristics that make it susceptible to certain environmental conditions, we can avoid the conflict over whether the problem is located in the students and their family and community circumstances or in the schools. For example, a recent definition of the disadvantaged by Levin (1986) pays little attention to the distinction between "disadvantaged" and "deprived" that earlier seemed so important. He constructs a portrait of this group that links both school and nonschool experiences to the problem, arguing that "pupils defined as educationally disadvantaged lack the home and community resources to fully benefit from recent educational reforms as well as from conventional schooling practices" (p. 1). He specifies these disadvantages in terms of a number of factors such as poverty, cultural differences, and linguistic differences, and notes that they are especially concentrated among minority groups, immigrants, non-English-speaking families, and economically disadvantaged populations. This shift away from the school/nonschool controversy is striking. The view that Levin typifies is that educational disadvantages are a product of both kinds of factors.

But the perspective that views and labels disadvantaged students as being at risk is not without problems. Despite the implication that being at risk involves a differential susceptibility to environmental conditions, the term is routinely used to designate students who possess certain characteristics, without giving attention to the environmental conditions that might pose problems for these students. As Freedberg (1987) observes, "The danger is that the terms 'at risk' and 'minority' are rapidly becoming synonymous, perpetuating racial stereotypes that have handicapped minorities for decades" (p. 5M). More dramatically, Freedberg points out that the term *at risk,* "usually reserved for felons, rapists and other misfits who posed a danger to society" (p. 5M), is now being used to label 3-year-olds. Early identification might lead to the assignment of students to appropriate educational programs to help them overcome their problems and perform successfully in school, but it might also lead to the derogatory labeling of students and the self-fulfilling prophecy that consigns disadvantaged students to exposure to lower teacher expectations for their entire school careers. Moreover, unlike earlier terms that identified students with current problems, *at risk* suggests an ability to predict how students might turn out in the future, which could lead to problems for students who otherwise would not have experienced them.

The policy and programmatic implications of the at-risk perspective differ depending upon which interpretation of the term is used. If emphasis is placed on the interaction of individual and environmental characteristics, then the solution will be seen as the creation of more and different educational environments matched to the needs stemming from the individual characteristics of students. Thus, as we develop our understanding of the various types of susceptibility associated with students with different characteristics, we will be led to develop an equally varied set of educational programs and environments. We will be unlikely to prescribe the same infusion of middle-class culture suggested by the cultural-deprivation perspective or the strengthening of the traditional basic school programs suggested by the educational-deprivation perspective.

On the other hand, if emphasis is placed on identification of individual characteristics, the solution will be seen as early intervention. Unlike the early interventions suggested by the cultural deprivation perspective, however, the programmatic implications of the at-risk perspective argue for a modification of the educational environment of at-risk youth throughout their school careers. From this perspective the differential susceptibility of certain youth to environmental conditions is not something that can be remedied in a short-term program at a single stage in the life cycle.

THE DISADVANTAGED AS "YOUTH"

The labeling problems associated with the view of disadvantaged students as being at risk stem primarily from the political need to designate some relatively small segment of the student population as most in need of additional resources. This necessity arises in the face of limited funds. Yet there are alternative conceptualizations of disadvantaged status that are not constrained to a small segment of the total youth population.

Perhaps the broadest definition of the educationally disadvantaged is suggested by Fantini and Weinstein (1968), who argue that the disadvantaged include "all those who are blocked in any way from fulfilling their human potential" (p. 5). Fantini and Weinstein go on to locate the responsibility for the disadvantaged in our social institutions: "Failure in human goal attainment is therefore a reflection of institutional failure and, until our social institutions in general, and the schools in particular, are equipped to satisfy these goals, full human development is thwarted" (p. 5).

This perspective essentially defines the entire population or at least the entire youth population as potentially disadvantaged. By not identifying any one segment of the population as being disadvantaged, this type of conceptualization places the whole burden of addressing the problems of disadvantaged youth on an examination of the institutions that are intended to support and develop young people.

The perspective that all youth face problems that place them at a disadvantage in the society is represented in the work of the Panel on Youth of the President's Science Advisory Committee (Coleman et al., 1974). Their report reviews the problems faced by youth and by the broader society as it tries to integrate youth. These problems are portrayed as the result of society's task of attempting to socialize new members.

Two contemporary analyses of the problems of youth focus on the withdrawal of adult assistance with the socialization process for youth. Uhlenberg and Eggebeen (1986) examine changes in the well-being of white American adolescents between 1960 and 1980. They note that during this period the living conditions of adolescents actually improved, when measured in terms of the proportion living in poverty, the number of siblings with whom individuals must share the economic and social resources of the family, and the educational attainments of parents. At the same time the amount and proportion of government resources devoted to the problems of youth increased quite dramatically. However, the well-being of American youth has declined precipitously in several areas. Uhlenberg and Eggebeen argue that the academic achievement of American young people has declined since about 1960 and that their moral behavior, when measured in terms of criminal activity, alcohol and drug use, sexual activity, pregnancy and venereal diseases, and mortality rates, has deteriorated.

Uhlenberg and Eggebeen (1986) explain the deteriorating status of youth in the face of increases in the resources American society has been willing to devote to youth by arguing that there has been a "declining commitment of parents to their children over the past several decades" (p. 35). Citing changes in reported parental attitudes toward their children and changes in behavior patterns such as the increasing numbers of women entering the labor force and the increasing numbers of couples who are unwilling to stay married, these authors conclude that young people are likely to have less contact with their parents than did previous generations. However, Furstenburg and Condon (1987), drawing on more extensive data, conclude that "the trends in adolescent behavior are less clear-cut . . . and that the causal link to divorce and maternal employment is not well-supported by the data" (p. 3).

An argument to that of Uhlenberg and Eggebeen is advanced by Coleman and Hoffer (1987), who discuss the family resources to which children are exposed in terms of the difference between disadvantaged families and deficient families. They define "disadvantaged" family backgrounds as those marked by low income and low education levels, that is, those with relatively little human capital. These families fit the traditional notion of the disadvantaged. In contrast, they identify "deficient" family backgrounds as those in which children have little access to their parents, no matter what the levels of parental human capital. Such deficiencies may be structural; that is, they may be the result of the physical absence of family members, such as might occur in single-parent families or in families in which both parents work outside the home. But deficiencies may also be functional in nature; that is, they may involve the absence of strong relations between young people and their parents, even when they are physically present. Such functional deficiencies may arise when the children are heavily involved in relationships with other youth to the exclusion of their parents or when parents are heavily involved in relationships with other adults to the exclusion of their children.

Coleman and Hoffer (1987) point out that, whether the deficiencies are structural or functional, such families lack social capital, which is composed of the cross-generational relations among family members that make for strong family units. As they note, in the absence of sufficient social capital, the human capital of the parents may be irrelevant to the educational growth of the child.

The policy implications of viewing the disadvantaged as youth in general are quite different from those suggested by the other three perspectives. First, the youth perspective suggests the need for action on a broad scale that might affect all young people in the United States. Second, it seems to argue for a basic rethinking of how the society treats its young people as an initial step in ameliorating their problems. Such a reexamination raises the possibility that a more deliberate youth policy might be developed.

A WORKING DEFINITION

Our own definition of "educationally disadvantaged" borrows from the definitions of earlier analysts, but places them within an emerging understanding of education as a process that takes place both inside and outside of schools. Following Bailyn (1960), Cremin (1976), and others (see Clifford, 1985), we view educational experiences as coming not only from formal schooling, but also from the family and the community. Students who are educationally disadvantaged have been exposed to insufficient educational experiences in at least one of these three domains. While the first awareness of the consequences of such experiences may surface in the schools, where student performance is formally assessed, the source of the problem may rest with the school and/or with the family and the community in which the student is reared.

There are several implications of this definition that deserve special comment. First, families and communities may be viewed as educationally deficient without necessarily being socially deficient. For example, a strong, loving family may simply be unequipped to provide an educationally stimulating environment for its children. This may stem from cultural differences that make experiences in the family incompatible with those in U.S. schools or from economic limitations that leave families without sufficient resources beyond those necessary for survival.

Second, the deficiencies in any and all of these three domains may continue as students mature and move through the school system. Previous notions that children from poor families can be provided special services (e.g., Head Start) that bring them up to their grade level, and can then be released to move through schools on their own seem to suggest that, once students are in school, schools can do the entire job of educating students. Our view of schools as one of several educating institutions that simultaneously affect an individual's growth suggests that remediation cannot be confined to the school alone.

Finally, our definition of the educationally disadvantaged allows for variation in the disadvantaged population. Some students will have suffered from a lack of appropriate formal educational experiences, others will have suffered from a lack of intellectual experiences in the family, and still others will have suffered from a lack of educational experiences in the community. These three types of deficiencies may all manifest themselves in the same way on standard measures of academic achievement, but realizing the several possible sources of the deficiencies will sensitize us as we move to identify the size and location of the educationally disadvantaged population.

2

Current Conditions of the Educationally Disadvantaged

Whatever definition of "educationally disadvantaged" one employs, it is not possible to measure the number of educationally disadvantaged children precisely. We must rely instead on a series of rather gross indicators, which produce broad categories that tend to contain varying numbers of children who typically perform poorly in school. These categories are used by policy makers and educators to characterize populations of students and to plan educational programs. Nevertheless, almost everyone would agree that while these categories are useful for discussing the needs of groups of children, they are less than precise means for characterizing the educational fate of individual children.

THE DISADVANTAGED AND THEIR FAMILIES, SCHOOLS, AND COMMUNITIES

Our consideration of indicators of educational disadvantage focuses on the characteristics of individuals. This is mainly because there are some data, albeit imperfect, on the distribution of these risk factors in the U.S. school-aged population, making these the only such indicators for which it is plausible to make any projections at all. But, in highlighting the characteristics of individuals and their families, we do not intend to discount the importance of schools and communities. Our choice of indicators is driven more by the availability of data than by doubts about the influence of schools and communities on children's scholastic development.

With regard to communities, for instance, Wilson (1987) argues persuasively that the plight of the inner-city underclass stems from a weakening of basic social institutions attributable to prolonged joblessness in inner-city neighborhoods. He argues that the concentration of joblessness in such neighborhoods has created a social isolation, sequestering inner-city families from role models who can show that steady employment is an achievable goal and that there is a link between schooling and adult life chances. In the absence of sustained contact with the middle- and working-class families that used to inhabit such inner-city neighborhoods, the means for motivating young people to strive for success in school and work are diminished.

Clearly, then, it would be desirable to measure the concentration of poverty and joblessness in the neighborhoods in which U.S. children reside. Wilson (1987) shows that in 1980, among poor people residing in the five largest U.S. cities, poor blacks and Hispanics were much more likely to be living in high poverty concentration neighborhoods than were poor whites. Even a measure of poverty status, then, may obscure important contextual effects produced by living in high-poverty areas—effects that touch on virtually all aspects of a growing child's life in and out of school.

While it is clear that children living in poorer communities do not score as highly on standardized tests as children living in more affluent communities, it is hard to judge how much of an effect to attribute to the neighborhood itself. Jencks and Mayer (1988) have reviewed the literature on the effects on cognitive skills of living in a poor neighborhood or going to a school attended primarily by poor children. They conclude that there is little convincing evidence that living in a poor neighborhood or going to a poor school has a substantial effect on children's cognitive growth. These effects may exist, but the current studies are simply suggestive.

We also believe that schools are an important influence promoting or retarding the educational success of young people. But the major sources of advantage or disadvantage probably are within schools, rather than located in differences among schools. It is extremely difficult to quantify what makes a good school. The attributes of schools that are relatively easy to measure are for the most part not related in any systematic way to the outcomes of schooling. Hanushek (1981) shows that school resources like per-pupil expenditures; number of library books; teacher salaries, experience levels, and credentials; condition of physical plant; and pupil/teacher ratios have no consistent effects on the net outputs of schools. While the literature suggests that going to one school rather than another has modest effects on cognitive achievement (Jencks & Brown, 1975; McDill & Rigsby, 1973), what happens to a student within a given school is more important than which elementary or secondary school a student attends.

We note especially the sorting of students in elementary and secondary schools into ability groups and curricular tracks as a mechanism that can perpetuate or exacerbate educational disadvantages. At the elementary school level, Barr and Dreeben (1983) show how the nature of classroom reading instruction is responsive to the characteristics of reading groups. Children in groups with different mean aptitudes are instructed at different paces, are exposed to differing numbers of new words, and spend different amounts and proportions of classroom time on various instructional tasks. At both the elementary and secondary levels, the content, pacing and quality of instruction typically differ across instructional groups.

At the secondary level, different curriculum tracks are associated with different patterns of course taking, which are related to differing levels of standardized test performance (Gamoran, 1987). Low-track students also are exposed to slower and less complex classroom work, to lower teacher expectations, and to different peer relationships than students in higher tracks (Gamoran & Berends, 1987; Oakes, 1985).

In sum, then, we recognize the importance of families, schools, and communities in providing environments that can either enhance or disturb a child's opportunity for success in school. Most of the available data that help to describe these environments, however, are on characteristics of families or households, since these are the predominant units of data collection. In the section that follows, we examine several indicators of educational disadvantage and look at how they are distributed in the United States today.

INDICATORS OF DISADVANTAGE

We shall consider five key indicators associated with the educationally disadvantaged: racial/ethnic identity, poverty status, family composition, mother's education, and language background. All are correlated with poor performance in school, although not always for commonly understood or agreed-upon reasons. Where possible, we document the educational consequences of being at risk due to each one. These indicators are not independent, so that a child likely to be classified as educationally disadvantaged on the basis of one is more likely to be so classified on the basis of the others. Children classified as educationally disadvantaged on the basis of several indicators are at the greatest risk of educational failure.

Not all poor children are educationally disadvantaged, nor are all minority children, nor are all children from single-parent households. On average, though, each of these measurable characteristics is associated with low levels of educational achievement. Measures such as poverty status, racial/ethnic group identity, and family composition may signal not only limitations on family resources in support of education, but also limitations on the resources available to students from their schools and their communities. Some indicators, such as poverty, may be associated with inadequate resources for education in all of the major educating institutions to which young people are exposed: the family, the school, and the community.

Race and Ethnicity

Racial/ethnic group is perhaps the best-known factor associated with the educationally disadvantaged. Historically, members of minority groups typically have failed to succeed in schools at the same levels as the majority of the white group. There is a vast amount of evidence documenting the lower performance of black and Hispanic children in schools relative to white children.* Recent results from the National Assessment of Educational Progress (NAEP), for instance, have shown that the reading, writing, and mathematics skills of black and Hispanic children are substantially below those of white children, at ages 9, 13, and 17 (Applebee, Langer & Mullis, 1988; Beaton, 1986; Dossey, Mullis, Lindquist & Chambers, 1988; NAEP, 1985).

The Mathematics Report Card for the 1986 NAEP characterized students' mathematics performance in five proficiency levels (Dossey et al., 1988). Level 150 represents mastery of simple addition and subtraction facts, while level 200 represents beginning skills and understanding, including basic multiplication and division facts, and manipulation of two-digit numbers. Level 250 indicates understanding of basic operations, one-step word problems, and the ability to compare information from graphs and charts. Level 300 involves mastery of moderately complex procedures and reasoning, including decimals, fractions, and simple linear equations. Finally, level 350 represents the ability to solve multi-step problems, work with exponents and square roots, and solve algebraic equations and inequalities. Among 9-year-olds, 79.2% of white children were performing at the level of beginning skills and understanding, while only 53.3% of black children and 58.7% of Hispanic children had attained that level. This pattern persists among older children as well. More than three-quarters (78.7%) of white 13-year-olds performed at the level of basic operations and beginning problem solving, while only about one-half (49.4% and 55.2%, respectively) of black and Hispanic 13-year-olds had developed those skills. Among 17-year-olds, more than one-half (58.0%) of white youth were performing at the level of moderately complex procedures and reasoning, whereas only about one-quarter (21.7% and 26.8%, respectively) of black and Hispanic youth had attained that level of proficiency (Dossey et al., 1988).

A similar pattern is observed for reading achievement (Applebee et al., 1988), although we will not reproduce the figures here. For both reading and mathematics performance, the gaps between white children, on the one hand, and black and Hispanic, on the other, are substantial in elementary school, junior high or middle school, and high school. In fact, the average 17-year-old black student is performing only slightly better than the average

---

*Throughout this chapter, and the one that follows, the categories "white" and "black" refer mainly to non-Hispanic whites and non-Hispanic blacks, respectively. We are implicitly treating white, black and Hispanic as mutually exclusive categories, with whites and blacks of Hispanic origin considered Hispanic in the various tabulations we report. While we recognize that this is far from ideal, as a practical matter it simplifies our presentation considerably.

13-year-old white youth on standardized reading and math tests (Applebee et al., 1988). Hispanic 17-year-olds score slightly higher than black youth of the same age in mathematics, but about the same in reading.

The NAEP results pertain to children who are enrolled in the nation's public and private schools, so they may actually underestimate the gap in educational achievement between white and nonwhite children and youth, because Hispanic and black youth are less likely to complete high school than white youth. The High School and Beyond (HSB) study (Sebring et al., 1987), a nationally representative sample of approximately 30,000 high school sophomores enrolled in more than 1,000 high schools across the country in the spring of 1980, documented that black and Hispanic youth were more likely to leave high school before completion than white youth (Peng, 1983). In that study, 18% of Hispanic 1980 sophomores and 17% of black 1980 sophomores were not enrolled in high school in the spring of 1982, compared to 12.2% of white 1980 sophomores. The HSB figures probably are low estimates of high school dropout rates for these youth in the early 1980s. This is an artifact of the study design, which called for initially surveying students in the spring of their sophomore year of high school. Some, perhaps a great many, students drop out of school prior to the spring of their sophomore year; moreover, it may be that these early dropouts are disproportionately black and Hispanic. If, as we believe, early dropouts are more likely to be black and Hispanic, then the HSB estimate of the differences in dropout rates among racial/ethnic groups may understate the magnitude of the gap.

This, in fact, is what is implied by data from the October 1986 Current Population Survey (Bruno, 1988). At that time 13.9% of white respondents aged 22 to 24 neither were enrolled in school nor were high school graduates. This compares to 17.3% of the black respondents of the same age and 38.2% of the Hispanic respondents. The high school dropout problem clearly is most serious among the U.S. Hispanic population, but black youth, especially black males, also are less likely to have graduated from high school than white youth.

In 1988 the U.S. population under age 18 numbered approximately 63.6 million people. Of that total, approximately 70.4%, or 44.8 million children, were whites. About 15.1%, or 9.6 million children, were blacks, and 10.8%, or 6.8 million children, were Hispanic youth. An additional 3.8%, or 2.4 million children, were identified as some other racial group (usually Asian or Pacific Islander). This latter group typically is not regarded as being as educationally disadvantaged as the population of black and Hispanic children. Thus, in 1988 approximately 16.4 million children, or 26% of the population under age 18, would be considered educationally disadvantaged, using racial/ethnic identity as a broad indicator.

Diversity of the Hispanic Population. In describing the Hispanic population, we do not intend to suggest that this population is homogeneous (Portes & Truelove, 1987). According to 1988 Census figures, 62.3% of those identified as Hispanic reported being of Mexican origin. An additional 12.7% reported Puerto Rican origin, and 11.5% described their origin as Central or South American. A smaller fraction (5.3%) was of Cuban origin, and 8.1% reported other Hispanic origin, which includes those from Spain, or those who identify themselves generally as Hispanic, Spanish, Spanish-American, or Latino (U.S. Bureau of the Census, 1988a).

There are substantial social and economic differences among the Hispanic subgroups. Those of Mexican and Puerto Rican origin are substantially younger than those of Cuban, Central and South American, and other Hispanic origin. Just over a third of the Mexican and Puerto Rican populations are 15 years old or younger, compared to one-sixth of those of Cuban origin, and about a quarter of those of Central and South American and other Hispanic origin (U.S. Bureau of the Census, 1988a). In addition, the fertility rates of Hispanic females vary by subgroup, with those of Mexican-origin women exceeding those of women identified with the other Hispanic subgroups (Bean, Swicegood, & King, 1985). About 1 in 6 Mexican-origin families had six or more persons, but only about 1 in 30 Cuban-origin families was this large (U.S. Bureau of the Census, 1988a).

The composition of Hispanic families in the United States also differs across Hispanic subgroups. In March of 1988, Cuban and Mexican families were much more likely to be married-couple families than were Puerto Rican families (approximately 75% of Cuban and Mexican families, compared to 51.6% of Puerto Rican families). About two-thirds of Central and South American and other Hispanic families were married-couple families. Approximately 44% of Puerto Rican families had a female householder with no husband present (U.S. Bureau of the Census, 1988a). Mexican families also were larger on average than those of the other subgroups.

The Hispanic population in the United States is much less educated than the non-Hispanic population. Here too, though, some Hispanic subgroups are much better off than others. Among young adults aged 25 to 34 in 1988, only slightly more than half of persons of Mexican origin had completed at least 4 years of high school, while more than four-fifths of the Cuban and other Hispanic origin young adults and about two-thirds of the Puerto Rican and Central and South American young adults had done so (U.S. Bureau of the Census, 1988a).

The various U.S. Hispanic subgroups also differ in their labor-force participation and employment rates. Just over half of those of Puerto Rican origin aged 16 years or older were in the civilian labor force in 1988, compared to nearly three-quarters of those of Central and South American origin and about two-thirds of those of Mexican, Cuban, and other Hispanic origin. Among both males and females in the labor force, those of Cuban and Central and South American origin were much less likely to be unemployed than those of Mexican, Puerto Rican or other Hispanic origin. Overall, only 3% of those of Cuban origin and 5% of those of Central and South American origin 16 years of age or older were unemployed in 1988, compared to 9% of those of Puerto Rican and other Hispanic origin and 10% of the Mexican-origin population. As the total percent unemployed among persons 16 years and over in 1988 was about 6%, Hispanics of Cuban and Central and South American origin were less likely than the average American to be unemployed, while those identified with the other Hispanic subgroups were considerably more likely to be unemployed in 1988 (U.S. Bureau of the Census, 1988a).

Not surprisingly, these differences we have described translate into differences in poverty rates among the various Hispanic subgroups. Families from each of the Hispanic subgroups are more likely to be living in poverty than non-Hispanic families, but Puerto Rican families are much worse off than the other Hispanic groups. In 1987, 38% of families of Puerto Rican origin were living below the poverty line, compared to 26% of families of Mexican and other Hispanic origin, 19% of families of Central and South American origin, and 14% of Cuban-origin families. Families of Puerto Rican origin thus were nearly three times more likely to be living in poverty in 1987 than Cuban-origin families, and twice as likely as families of Central and South American origin (U.S. Bureau of the Census, 1988a).

These social and economic differences among Hispanic subgroups point to the diversity in the Hispanic population. They probably are correlated with differing family, community and schooling resources, which in turn place the different subgroups at differing levels of risk of failure in school. While we recognize the magnitude of these differences, as a practical matter we are limited in taking account of them by current conventions in the collection and reporting of data. We return to this problem in greater detail in Chapter 7; for now, though, we merely note that our implicit treatment of Hispanics in the United States as a homogeneous group reflects the availability of data far more than anything else.

Diversity of the Black and Asian-American Populations. We also believe that the black and Asian-American populations are quite diverse, with respect to their histories and cultures, their current socioeconomic achievements, and their prospects for success in U.S. schools. Lumping these distinct groups together no doubt obscures very real differences in the family, school, and community resources available to them. Here, too, we are handcuffed by the lack of adequate data differentiating these populations. Data collections typically are even less sensitive to variations in the black and Asian-American populations than they are to variations in the Hispanic population.

Poverty

A major commonly accepted reason that Hispanic and black children are educationally disadvantaged is because they are more likely to live in households with incomes below the poverty line. In fact, economic status and educational achievement are significantly linked. Children living in families with incomes below the poverty line are nearly twice as likely to be retained in a grade as children in nonpoverty-stricken families (Bianchi, 1984). Grade retention is both a reflection of low school achievement and a predictor of later academic difficulty. Children who are retained in a grade are substantially more likely to drop out of school before graduation (Pallas, 1987; Sherman, 1987). It therefore is no surprise that children from poor families also are more likely to drop out of high school. Stedman, Salganik and Celebuski (1988) found that, in 1980, among U.S. high school sophomores participating in the High School and Beyond study (Sebring et al., 1987), 24% of those in the lowest fifth of the income distribution had dropped out of high school by 1982, while only 11% of students in the other four-fifths of the distribution had dropped out. The lowest-income students thus were twice as likely to have dropped out of school.

There is a moderately strong association between poverty status and performance on standardized tests, but we have no direct evidence to support this contention. In spite of the great interest in the correlation between poverty and academic achievement, few studies measure both. We can report on the next best thing: differences in standardized test scores for children living in poorer and more affluent neighborhoods, taken from Applebee et al.'s (1988) analysis of data from the National Assessment of Educational Progress (NAEP). We recognize that such data may confound family effects with community effects, but they do illustrate the effects of living in poverty conditions.

Applebee et al.'s report on reading proficiency from the 1986 assessment contrasted two extreme community types, advantaged urban and disadvantaged urban. Students in advantaged urban communities attended schools in or around cities with a population greater than 200,000, where a high proportion of the residents were in professional or managerial jobs. In contrast, the students in disadvantaged urban communities also attended schools in or around cities having a population greater than 200,000, but in these communities a high proportion of the residents were receiving government assistance or were not regularly employed.

The 1986 reading proficiency scores were scaled so that the average score across 9-, 13-, and 17-year-olds was 50, with a standard deviation of 10 (Applebee et al., 1988). The average reading proficiency score of 9-year-old students in disadvantaged urban communities was 31.9, while the average among 9-year-olds in advantaged urban communities was 41.2. Students in disadvantaged communities thus are already nearly a standard deviation behind their more advantaged peers by age 9. A standard deviation difference in performance is relatively large. If reading proficiency is approximately normally distributed, then we can think of a difference of this magnitude as representing the difference between the 50th percentile and the 16th percentile. In other words, the average 9-year-old living in a disadvantaged urban community was scoring at about the 16th percentile of the distribution of reading proficiency among 9-year-olds living in advantaged urban communities.

The differences in proficiency levels between advantaged urban and disadvantaged urban students are only slightly smaller at ages 13 and 17 (Applebee et al., 1988). The average score for advantaged urban 13-year-olds was 51.6, while that for disadvantaged urban 13-year-olds was 43.8. The difference between the means of the two groups was thus about eight-tenths of a standard deviation. Contrasting 17-year-olds in advantaged and disadvantaged urban communities produced about the same difference, as 17-year-olds in advantaged urban neighborhoods scored, on average, 59.5, while those in disadvantaged urban neighborhoods had an average score of 51.2.

Another way of gauging the magnitude of these group differences is to compare them across age groups. The average 13-year-old in a disadvantaged urban community scored only about a quarter of a standard deviation higher than the average 9-year-old in an advantaged urban community. Moreover, the average 17-year-old in a disadvantaged urban setting scored at about the same level as a typical 13-year-old residing in an advantaged urban area (Applebee et al., 1988). These performance gaps are quite large.

In 1987 approximately 20% of all children under 18 years of age lived in families below the poverty line. This represents 12.4 million children in poverty. Minority children were much more likely to be living in poverty than white children. While the poverty rate for white children was approximately 12%, for black youngsters the rate was nearly 46%, and for Hispanic children the rate was about 40%. Although blacks and Hispanics comprised approximately one-quarter of the under-18 population in 1987, they represented about one-half of the children in poverty (U.S. Bureau of the Census, 1988c).

Single-Parent Families

Family structure is closely linked to poverty. Ellwood (1988) shows that long-term poverty is characteristic of single-parent households. His analysis of data from the Panel Study of Income Dynamics (Survey Research Center, 1981) indicates that, among children who grew up in the 1970s, nearly three-quarters (72.6%) who spent at least some time in a single-parent family lived in poverty at least part of the time. More than a third (37.8%) of these children spent at least 4 years of their first decade in poverty, and one in five (21.8%) lived in poverty for 7 or more of their first 10 years. In contrast, children living continuously in a two-parent, male-headed family have but a 20% chance of living in poverty at least 1 year in their first decade, and only a 2% chance of being poor continuously from birth to age 10.

Family structure also is related to educational outcomes (Milne, Myers, Rosenthal, & Ginsburg, 1986; Shinn, 1978). Children living in single-parent families have been found to score lower on standardized tests and receive lower grades in school, and to be more likely to drop out of high school. This conclusion is borne out by our own analysis of the 1986 NAEP reading and math proficiency data. For example, third-grade children living in homes lacking either their mother or father scored considerably lower than other third graders living in homes with both parents present. Children who reported that their father did not live in their home scored more than half a standard deviation lower in 1986 reading proficiency than children with a father present. Children in homes where their mother was not present performed even worse; such third graders scored more than seven-tenths of a standard deviation lower than children with a mother present. When these shortfalls are expressed in grade equivalents, our best guess is that third-grade children in homes lacking at least one parent were at least a year behind in reading proficiency when compared to other third graders living with both parents.

We find differences of similar magnitude for mathematics proficiency. Our tabulations of mathematics proficiency from the 1986 NAEP show that approximately 50% of third graders reporting that their father did not live in their home scored above level 200, beginning skills and understanding. Roughly 71% of those third graders who reported that their father was present surpassed that level. The lack of a mother in the home is an even more important disadvantaging characteristic. While 69% of the third graders with a mother present scored above level 200 in mathematics proficiency, only about 43% of those without a mother living in their home attained level 200.

Children in single-parent families also are almost twice as likely to drop out of high school than children from two-parent families. Stedman et al.

(1988), using the High School and Beyond data describing 1980 high school sophomores, found that 22.4% of children from single-parent families dropped out of high school, compared to 12.0% of those children from two-parent families. While part of this gap no doubt reflects the socioeconomic differences between solo-parent and two-parent households, family structure probably is an important advantaging or disadvantaging factor in its own right.

About 46 million children, or 72.7% of those under 18 years old, were living in families with both parents present in 1988. About 13.5 million children lived in households with just a mother present. In addition, 1.8 million children lived in households with just a father present, and about the same number lived in households with neither parent present (U.S. Bureau of the Census, 1989).

Family structure also is correlated with racial/ethnic origin. Minority children are much more likely to live in a single-parent family than are white children. In 1988, approximately three-fifths of black children, and just over one-third of Hispanic children, were living in single-parent or neither-parent families. In contrast, less than one-fifth of white children under 18 years of age were living in single-parent families in 1988 (U.S. Bureau of the Census, 1989).

Poorly Educated Mothers

Our view that education is a process that occurs in families, schools, and communities focuses some attention on the family and home environment. Mothers' characteristics are especially important in structuring the educational environment in the home. Mothers who are more highly educated themselves have more knowledge of their children's schooling, have more social contact with school personnel, and are better managers of their children's academic careers (Baker & Stevenson, 1986; Stevenson & Baker, 1987). Children of highly educated mothers do better in school, and stay in school longer, than children whose parents have not completed high school.

For example, children of poorly educated mothers score lower on standardized tests than children whose parents obtained higher levels of schooling. This is true at every age, but again we use data from third graders participating in the 1986 NAEP to illustrate this point. Third grade children whose mothers had not completed high school scored approximately 34.6 on the 1986 reading assessment, while third graders whose mothers had completed high school or obtained more schooling scored about 39.3. Children with poorly educated mothers thus score about six-tenths of a standard deviation below children with more highly educated parents in reading proficiency.

The effect of maternal education on how well young people do in school also is pronounced when we consider mathematics proficiency. Of the third-grade children participating in the 1986 NAEP, only 46% of those whose mothers had not completed high school scored above level 200, beginning skills and understanding, on the mathematics proficiency test. But nearly three-quarters (73%) of those children whose mothers were at least high school graduates had attained that level of skill mastery.

Maternal education also is related to the likelihood of dropping out of high school. Barro and Kolstad (1987) document that children in families where the mother has not completed high school are two to three times more likely to drop out of high school than those in families where the mother has obtained more schooling. Their tabulations of data from the High School and Beyond 1980 sophomore cohort show that nearly one-quarter of the youths whose mothers had not completed high school dropped out before graduation, while only half as many of those whose mothers had completed high school or obtained some college dropped out of high school. Only about 7% of the youths whose mothers had graduated from college or obtained even more schooling dropped out of high school between 1980 and 1982.

About one in every five children aged under 18 in 1987 lived with mothers who had not completed high school, representing a total of 12.7 million children. These children were disproportionately black and Hispanic. Among black youth living in families where the mother was present, nearly 30% had mothers who had not finished high school. And among Hispanic children living in families with mothers present, over 50% had mothers who were not high school graduates. The educational attainments of white mothers are much higher. Approximately 87% of the white children living in families with the mother present had mothers who had at least completed high school (U.S. Bureau of the Census, 1988b).

Limited English Proficiency

Students whose primary language is not English, or who have limited English proficiency, face special obstacles to success in school. There is little agreement on how to define or measure the size of the population with limited English proficiency. The Bilingual Education Act of 1984 defined an individual as "limited English proficient" (LEP) if that individual (1) comes from a home environment where a language other than English is the one most relied upon for communication and (2) has sufficient difficulty in understanding, speaking, reading, and writing English to deny the individual the opportunity to learn successfully in all-English classrooms (U.S. General Accounting Office, 1987a). In practice, though, it is difficult to operationalize these conditions.

Regardless of how limited English proficiency is assessed, by most criteria students defined as limited English proficient are at a substantial disadvantage in U.S. classrooms. Nor is this shortfall limited to verbal skills, as succeeding even in science and mathematics courses may require the ability to communicate well in English. This indicator of educational disadvantage also highlights the importance of family and community factors, as well as school influences. Parents who do not speak English may be severely hampered in their ability to help their children with their schoolwork or in their ability to manage their children's school career.

Data from the 1986 NAEP provide some evidence of the educational achievements of children with limited English proficiency. Our own unpublished tabulations of third graders' responses indicate that children who are exposed to or speak a language other than English at home score lower in both reading (in English) and math than their peers. In reading, for instance, the average score of third graders who speak a language other than English at home at least some of the time is approximately 36.7, while for third graders who speak only English at home, the average score is about 38.5. The difference in performance between the two groups represents about two-tenths of a standard deviation (relative to all third graders). Our best guess is that a difference of this size puts third-grade children who speak a language other than English at home at least some of the time about half a year behind other third graders who speak only English at home. A similar gap is observed in mathematics proficiency. Of the third graders who speak a language other than English at home at least some of the time, about 59% scored above level 200, beginning skills and understanding. But, among those third-grade children who speak only English at home, approximately 69% scored above level 200. Even in mathematics performance, then, language usage can be consequential.

The differences are somewhat larger when we move beyond a simple question of whether children ever speak a language other than English at home to consider the frequency with which languages other than English are spoken at home. Third-grade children who report that a language other than English is often spoken at home are sharply disadvantaged in both reading and mathematics proficiency relative to their peers whose predominant home language is English. In reading, for instance, children who say that a language other than English is often spoken at home score about half a standard deviation lower than children who say that a non-English language is spoken sometimes or never. Our best guess is that these children are already more than a full year behind their peers in reading proficiency in the third grade.

The situation is much the same for the mathematics proficiency of children who report that a language other than English is often spoken at home. Approximately 44% of such third graders scored over level 200 in mathematics proficiency, compared to nearly 69% of third graders in homes where other languages are sometimes or never spoken who scored at or above this level. This difference also appears large enough to place third graders in homes where languages other than English are often spoken a year behind their peers in mathematics proficiency.

In addition to these test score differences, there is sketchy evidence that children from minority-language backgrounds are more likely to drop out of high school than children from homes where English is spoken exclusively. Salganik and Celebuski (1987) report that, among sophomores in the High School and Beyond study, those from homes where only a non-English language was spoken were more than twice as likely to drop out of high school as students from homes where English was the sole or primary language spoken.

The U.S. Department of Education has produced an estimate of the number of school-aged children with limited English proficiency, based on the number of children scoring at or below the 20th percentile on a national English language proficiency test and demonstrating a dependence on their native language. The Department assessed dependence with a series of 11 indicators of dependency, such as whether a child speaks a non-English language at home, or whether a non-English language is the first or second household language. If a certain number of these indicators applied to a child, then that child was defined to be dependent on his or her native language.

The estimated number of LEP children is highly sensitive to the number of indicators of dependency (U.S. General Accounting Office, 1987a). If the criterion is the presence of 5 indicators of dependency, then the estimated number of school-aged (ages 5 to 17) LEP children in 1986 is 1.7 million children. If the slightly more stringent criterion of 6 indicators is used, the estimated number shrinks appreciably, to 1.2 million children. Conversely, defining dependency as the presence of at least 1 of the 11 indicators boosts the estimated size of the school-aged LEP population in 1986 to 2.6 million children.

The General Accounting Office has concluded that there is no easy way to validate the Education Department's estimate of the size of this population in the United States. The GAO's own surveys of the 50 states and the District of Columbia suggest that there were about 1.5 million LEP students nationwide in 1986. But, since these state reports are dependent on school district self-reports, they probably are an underestimate of the true size of the population, as not all districts report these data to their states, and some districts may undercount their LEP students (U.S. GAO, 1987a). The most cynical interpretation of undercounting is that failing to identify students with limited English proficiency releases a school district from the obligation of providing expensive and/or controversial programming to serve those students.

GEOGRAPHIC DISTRIBUTION OF THE DISADVANTAGED

The educationally disadvantaged are not distributed randomly throughout the country. Different risk factors are concentrated in different parts of the country. The major geographic centers of educationally disadvantaged students are central cities, rural areas, the South, and the Southwest.

The poverty rate is highest in central cities and rural areas. While the overall poverty rate for children in 1983 was about 22%, the rate in central cities of metropolitan areas was 31%. The rate for children in nonmetropolitan (mainly rural) areas was 24%. In contrast, the poverty rate for children living in noncentral (mostly suburban) portions of metropolitan areas was only 13%.

The fact that the poverty rate is highest in large central cities suggests that this is where the poor are concentrated. In fact, however, only slightly more than a third (35%) of the poor lived in large cities in 1980, and an additional 19% lived in the suburban neighborhoods of large cities (Ellwood, 1988). Only 7% of the poor lived in central-city neighborhoods where the poverty rate is 40% or higher. The fact that more poor people live in rural areas, small towns, and small metropolitan areas than live in large central cities surely defies the conventional wisdom. We would not want to trivialize ghetto poverty, but it represents only one facet of the poverty problem.

Poverty rates do not vary substantially across regions of the country. The highest regional poverty rate for children, 24.3%, is in the South; the lowest regional rate, 20.2%, is found in the Northeast and Mid-Atlantic region (U.S. House of Representatives, 1985).

The Hispanic population is mainly concentrated in a few states. As of March 1988, slightly more than one-third (33.9%) of the nation's Hispanic population resided in California, while more than one-fifth (21.3%) lived in Texas, about one in nine (10.9%) lived in New York, and 7.6% lived in Florida (U.S. Bureau of the Census, 1988a). These four states thus represented nearly three-quarters (73.7%) of the total number of Hispanics in the United States. Other states with substantial proportions of the total U.S. Hispanic population include Illinois (4.1%); New Jersey (3.3%); and the southwestern states of Arizona, Colorado, and New Mexico (8% among them).

The black population is largely concentrated in the South and in central cities. The largest numbers of blacks enrolled in public elementary and secondary schools in 1980 were in New York, Texas, Illinois, and California. Other states with sizable numbers include Florida, Georgia, North Carolina, and Louisiana (Grant & Snyder, 1986).

Family structure patterns vary both according to the region of the country and whether the area is predominantly rural or urban. The regional variations are not large. According to census data, 17.1% of U.S. children under age 18 were living in one-parent families in 1980, the last year for which detailed data have been published (U.S. Bureau of the Census, 1986b). This proportion was slightly higher in the Middle Atlantic, South Atlantic and Pacific states, and somewhat lower in the westernmost Midwest and Rocky Mountain states. At the state level, the extremes are formed by New York, where 21.8% of all children under 18 were living in one-parent families in 1980, and North Dakota, where the figure was just 9.5%.

Contrasting New York and North Dakota suggests that there might be substantial differences between urban and rural areas, as New York and the other Middle Atlantic states are more urbanized than North Dakota and the other western states. In fact, central cities do have very different family structure patterns than do suburban and rural (nonmetropolitan) areas. Children living inside central cities were almost twice as likely to be living in female-headed households with no husband present as children living outside central cities in suburban and rural areas. There were, however, no differences between suburban and rural locations in the proportion of female-headed families with no husband present in 1980 (U.S. Bureau of the Census, 1986a).

Published data on the geographic distribution of children whose mothers have not completed high school are scarce. The Census Bureau does, however, publish data from the Current Population Survey on the educational attainments of women of childbearing age (18 to 44 years old). Based on the 1981 figures (Bruno, 1984), women in this age group residing outside of central cities are somewhat more likely to have completed high school than similarly aged women living in central cities or nonmetropolitan areas. As with other risk factors, children living in suburbs appear to be somewhat better off than children living in heavily urban or rural areas.

Regional variations in the educational attainments of women of childbearing age boil down to the South versus the rest of the country. About 85% of the women aged 18 to 44 living in the Northeast, Midwest, and West report having completed high school. In contrast, only about 78% of similarly aged women residing in the South report finishing high school. Here, too, the evidence is cumulative that children living in the South are more likely to be exposed to educational risk factors than children living elsewhere in the country.

Although we were unable to obtain data on the geographic distribution of children with limited English proficiency that conform closely to the current federal definitions, we can report on some older data (Milne & Gombert, 1983) on students with a primary language other than English (PLOTE). Such students are concentrated in the Northeast and Southwest; in fact, more than two-thirds of the PLOTE population is in just three states: California, Texas, and New York. California and Texas each have more than one-quarter of the nation's PLOTE students. Smaller numbers of PLOTE students are found in New Jersey, Arizona, Florida, and New Mexico. A majority (55%) of PLOTE students are enrolled in central cities, about one-quarter are in suburban portions of metropolitan areas, and only about one-fifth attend schools in nonmetropolitan areas.

ESTIMATING THE SIZE OF THE DISADVANTAGED POPULATION

Despite the imprecise nature of the available indicators of the educationally disadvantaged population, it is clear that substantial numbers and troubling proportions of U.S. children may be classified as educationally disadvantaged. Figure 2.1 shows our estimates in recent years of the propor-

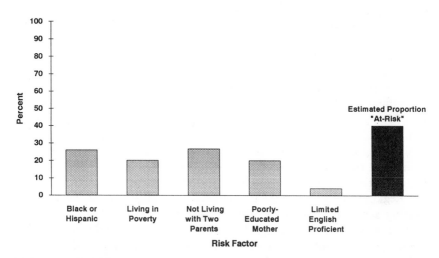

FIGURE 2.1 Estimated Proportion of the U.S. Population Under Age 18 at Risk of School Failure, 1988

tion of the population aged under 18 that can be classified as educationally disadvantaged on the basis of the five indicators we have considered in this chapter. With the exception of limited English proficiency, between one-fifth and about one-quarter of these children may be classified as educationally disadvantaged on the basis of a single indicator. Of course, as we noted earlier, these indicators are not totally redundant, so that any single indicator underestimates the size of the educationally disadvantaged population. A conservative estimate is that at least 40% of these children are at risk of failure in school on the basis of at least one of these five disadvantaging factors. Based simply on racial/ethnic origin and family structure alone, we know that approximately 40% are disadvantaged, since 25% of the 0–17 population are black or Hispanic, and an additional 14% are whites living in single-parent or neither-parent families. Given that the under-18 population was roughly 63.6 million in 1988, we estimate that at least 25 million of these children were educationally disadvantaged.

We may see the extent to which the five risk factors in Figure 2.1, taken singly, underestimate the extent of the educationally disadvantaged population by comparing (1) the proportions of children predicted to be at risk in terms of one of the indicators with (2) the proportion of children who may be currently classified as disadvantaged in terms of achievement. There are, of course, different criteria for what constitutes low achievement at a particular grade level. Few standardized tests provide scores that can be easily translated into concrete levels of proficiency that a lay public can understand.

The National Assessment of Educational Progress has taken steps to present student performance levels in ways that are anchored to specific knowledge and skills. The recent report on the 1986 reading assessment (Applebee et al., 1988) describes student performance on the written responses to reading passages as inadequate, minimal, satisfactory, or elaborated. A minimal response either did not answer the question or made irrelevant, inappropriate, or overgeneralized comments. A satisfactory response to the questions posed included an interpretation or generalization and one appropriate reason for the response, while an elaborated response went beyond a single reason (Applebee et al., 1988). The authors describe these criteria as relatively lenient, as even a response scored "elaborated" did not require a lengthy or carefully reasoned response.

For one passage, administered to students in grades 3, 7, and 11, only one-fifth of the 3rd graders were able to respond in a satisfactory way. Fewer than half of the 7th graders, and fewer than two-thirds of the 11th graders, were scored "satisfactory" or better in their written responses. The results were quite a bit worse on the other passage administered to each of the three grade levels. This second task involved relating a passage to the student's everyday experiences and making a simple comparison. On this task, *none* of the 3rd graders were able to produce a satisfactory comparison, and only .2% of the 7th graders were able to do so. Only 2.5% of the 11th graders were able to make a satisfactory comparison, and only 11.5% made even a minimal comparison.

As noted earlier in this chapter, NAEP has also characterized mathematics proficiency into five levels representing tangible differences in knowledge and skills. In 1986, more than one-quarter (26.1%) of the 9-year-old students surveyed had not yet mastered level 200, beginning skills and understanding. These students could not successfully subtract one two-digit number from another, nor recognize that three nickels and one dime were the same amount of money as a quarter. Approximately the same proportion of 13-year-olds in 1986 had not reached level 250, basic operations and beginning problem solving. These students could not subtract one three-digit number from another; nor multiply a two-digit number by a one-digit number; nor even judge which was worth the most: 11 nickels, 6 dimes, or 1 half-dollar. About one-half of the 17-year-olds participating in the 1986 NAEP mathematics assessment had not yet reached level 300, moderately complex procedures and reasoning. These students could not compute the area of a rectangle, nor identify the radius of a circle, nor tell that 87% of 10 is less than 10.

Thus, while most of the background indicators show that about 20% to 25% of children can be classified as disadvantaged on a single indicator, NAEP reading tests show that about 35% to 40% of students can be classified as educationally disadvantaged. This figure is quite close to our rough guess of the total proportion of children who bear at least one of the five indicators of disadvantage we have considered. Of course, as already indicated, the educationally disadvantaged population is not randomly distributed. Some schools and classrooms will have far fewer than this proportion of disadvantaged students, while others will have a far greater share. But if the figures reviewed thus far present a severe problem for today's schools, they only begin to suggest the size of the educationally disadvantaged population in the future.

3

Projected Changes in the Educationally Disadvantaged Population

In this chapter we use current and projected data provided by the U.S. Bureau of the Census to examine expected changes in the school-aged population between 1988 and 2020. In Chapter 2 we used current and recent data to identify patterns of disadvantage among black, white, and Hispanic youth at this time. Using these current patterns, we can project future patterns based on the anticipated number of black, white, and Hispanic youth in the future.

For example, if, as we saw in Chapter 2, Hispanic children have a high probability of living in poverty, and if there will be many more Hispanic children in the future, we would expect to find more children living in poverty in the future. Our analysis quantifies the logic of this argument, by reporting the projected number of children over the next 30 years who bear the five disadvantaging characteristics we considered in Chapter 2 (being black or Hispanic, living in poverty, not living with both parents, having a poorly educated mother, or having limited proficiency in English).

Ideally, we would construct our projections directly from future estimates of the number of children with these characteristics, rather than indirectly through changes in the racial/ethnic composition of the school-aged population. However, because projections of social and economic characteristics are very prone to error, as these factors can change quickly over time, we base our estimates on U.S. Bureau of the Census projections of the population by age and racial/ethnic group for selected years between 1980 and 2080 (Spencer, 1986, 1989). These estimates are updated from those we reported in Pallas, Natriello, and McDill (1989).

METHODOLOGICAL ASSUMPTIONS IN ESTIMATING THE HISPANIC POPULATION OF THE FUTURE

In this section we discuss several assumptions that underlie our projections, as well as some of their limitations. There are four complications in estimating the number of Hispanics in the future. We will discuss each in turn.

The first is the way that the Census Bureau typically reports population counts. Census estimates by race and Spanish origin typically are reported separately, where persons of Spanish origin may be of any race. Simply adding up the numbers of whites, blacks, and Hispanics thus counts twice those persons who identify themselves as both white and Hispanic or black and Hispanic. We resolved this problem by developing three mutually exclusive working categories, which we use throughout our projections: Hispanic, non-Hispanic white, and non-Hispanic black. To do this, we estimated the number and proportion of non-Hispanic whites and non-Hispanic blacks, based on cross-tabulations of race by ethnicity from the 1980 Census, and applied these proportions to the projections for blacks and whites reported by Spencer (1989).

The second complication is choosing plausible assumptions about the determinants of change in the Hispanic population in the future. The Census Bureau's projections are based on several assumptions regarding fertility, mortality, and migration rates. For each racial/ethnic group, 30 data series are produced, based on varying combinations of low, middle, and high levels of fertility, mortality, and migration. Of these, the most commonly used series are (1) those assuming high levels of all three factors, (2) those assuming medium levels of all three, and (3) those assuming low levels of all three.

We have chosen the high series projections for Hispanics, because we believe that these fertility and immigration rates are more plausible than the corresponding rates in the middle series. For instance, the middle series projections for Hispanics do not allow for undocumented immigration. As Spencer (1986) reports:

> Net immigration in the middle series also includes an assumption that there will be no permanent undocumented immigration in the future. This is probably not correct, but it is consistent with the Census Bureau's national population estimates and projections done before 1986. Until then, no allowance was made for undocumented immigration because there were no adequate measures of the component. As is true of our base-year population and fertility assumptions, the result of our net immigration assumptions is likely to make these projections of the Hispanic population somewhat conservative. [p. 28]

A third complication is the impact of the Immigration Reform and Control Act passed by Congress in 1986. It is not yet clear what the short- or long-term impact of this legislation will be on the annual number of undocumented immigrants. Consequently, it is very difficult to judge what the implications of this legislation will be on the size of the Hispanic population in the future.

Fourth, the projections of the Hispanic population may be based on current data that underestimate the true size of the Hispanic population in the United States. The Census projections stem from estimates provided by the Current Population Survey (CPS), which, like the decennial Census, fails to cover the Hispanic population completely. Fay, Passel, and Robinson (1988), reporting on the Census Bureau's attempts to assess the undercount in the 1980 Census, concluded that the available evidence implied that Hispanics were undercounted by approximately 6%. If we assume a similar undercount in the CPS, the projections that extrapolate from current data may understate the size of the Hispanic population in the future.

All in all, then, we believe that the high series projections of the Hispanic population of the future are appropriate for our calculations. In fact, the most recent Census statistics indicate that the current estimated size of the school-aged Hispanic population lies between the middle and high series projections. The middle series projected that the size of the Hispanic population under age 20 would be 7.4 million in 1988, whereas the high series projected that there would be 8.1 million (Spencer, 1986). In March 1988 the Current Population Survey estimate of the number of Hispanics under 20 years old was 7.5 million. While this figure is closer to the 1988 middle series projection than the 1988 high series projection, the assumption of a 6% undercount in the CPS boosts the 1988 estimate of the number of U.S. Hispanics in this age group to 8.0 million, about the same as the 1988 high series projection.

While we employ the high series projections for Hispanics, for whites and blacks we use the series which assumes a high level of immigration and medium levels of fertility and mortality. This is because the most recent projections reported by the Census Bureau do not report Hispanics separately from whites and blacks (Spencer, 1989). Since we are assuming relatively high levels of immigration in the Hispanic population, we extend that to the white and black population, as most of that projected immigration represents the net migration of the Hispanics included in the white and black projections.

We must emphasize that the projections we report are simply estimates based on a set of assumptions about social, economic, and educational conditions in the future. Some of these assumptions no doubt are more plausible than others. The patterning of our projections is thus more important than the precise numbers we report. We have no way to gauge the accuracy of our specific projections, so we will not be surprised if they are off the mark. Still, we are confident that they are suitable for making an informed estimate about what the future holds for American education and the magnitude of the challenges our society will face in coping with the changing landscape.

TRENDS IN THE SCHOOL-AGED POPULATION

The single most important factor in the school-aged population of the future is the expected increase in both the number and proportion of traditionally disadvantaged young people. The U.S. population aged under 18 is expected to increase by about 4% between 1988 and 2020, as the number of children in this age group rises from 63.6 million in 1988 to 66.4 million in 2020. The overall increase represents two quite different forces. First, the number of white youngsters is expected to decline by about 27% over this period. Second, the number of Hispanic children will nearly triple, increasing from 6.8 million in 1988 to 18.6 million in 2020. The expected increase in the Hispanic youth population of 11.7 million nearly offsets the expected decline of 12.2 million in the white population.

The anticipated changes in the number of blacks and people of other races are not nearly as striking as those of the white and Hispanic groups. The population of black youth under the age of 18 is expected to rise from 9.6 million in 1988 to 10.5 million in 2020, an increase of 9%. Moreover, while the population of other groups is projected to nearly double, this represents an absolute increase of just 2.3 million children over the 1988 population.

Figure 3.1 shows the projected racial and ethnic group distribution of the under-18 population from 1988 to 2020. This figure shows quite clearly that white children form a declining share of the school-aged population, while Hispanic children form an ever-increasing share. In 1988, about 70% of the school-aged population were whites. This share is expected to decline

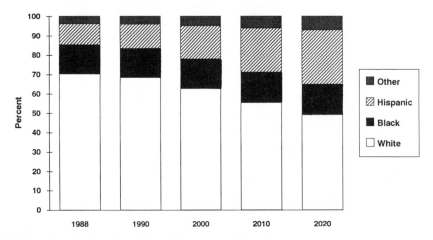

FIGURE 3.1 Projected Racial/Ethnic Composition of the U.S. Population Under Age 18, 1988–2020

to 49% in the year 2020. By contrast, in 1988, Hispanics comprised nearly 11% of the under-18 population, whereas by 2020, this figure is expected to be approximately 28%.

The proportions of blacks and children of other races in the U.S. school-aged population are expected to increase slightly from 1988 to 2020. The fraction of blacks is anticipated to rise from around 15% to about 16%, and the proportion of other racial groups from roughly 4% to 7%. While these changes are comparatively slight, they do contribute to the remarkable transformation of the American youth population. While about 7 in 10 children in 1988 were whites, only about 1 in 2 will be in 2020. While only 1 in 9 children in 1988 was Hispanic, more than 1 in 4 children will be in 2020.

The projected change in the racial/ethnic composition of the school-aged population implies a substantial increase in the size of the educationally disadvantaged population. We have already shown that racial and ethnic group status are correlated with several other indicators of the educationally disadvantaged population. There is, unfortunately, little reason to expect those correlations to disappear over the next 40 years; in fact, they may not change very much at all. Thus, assuming a constant relationship between racial/ethnic group identity and poverty, as the number and proportion of black and Hispanic children increase, so too will the number and proportion of children in poverty.

The figures for this trend, projected forward from 1987 to 2020, are shown in Figure 3.2. Over this 33-year period, the number of children in poverty is expected to rise from 12.4 to 16.5 million, an increase of 33%. The change in the actual proportion of children in poverty is not as dramatic, rising from about 20% of all children in 1987 to about 26% of all children in

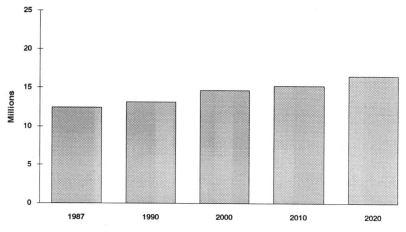

FIGURE 3.2 Projected Number of U.S. Children in Poverty, 1987–2020 (in millions)

2020. But focusing on the change in the proportion of children in poverty over time neglects the fact that the number of children is increasing substantially over time. It probably is more important to be aware that our educating institutions will need to serve 4 million more children in poverty in the year 2020 than they served in 1987.

Similar trends are observed for the other indicators of the educationally disadvantaged population as well. Projections of the number of children not living with both parents are shown in Figure 3.3. The figure is expected to increase from 16.9 million in 1987, to 19.9 million in 2020, a rise of roughly 18%. Our projections indicate that many more children will be living in families without both parents present in the future than are doing so today.

We also anticipate a sharp increase in the number of children living with mothers who have low levels of educational attainment. Figure 3.4 shows projections of the number of children living with mothers who have not completed high school, from 1987 to 2020. The number of such children is projected to increase by more than 5 million over the period 1987 to 2020, from 12.7 to 17.9 million. This change represents a 41% increase in the number of children living with poorly educated mothers.

Earlier we noted that the vast majority of U.S. children whose primary language is not English are Hispanic. As the Hispanic population expands, we expect a corresponding increase in the numbers of children whose primary language is not English. Our projections assume that the children of second-generation Hispanics will suffer the same language-related disadvantages that their parents experienced, an assumption that may not hold if the Hispanic population is assimilated into the mainstream of American society.

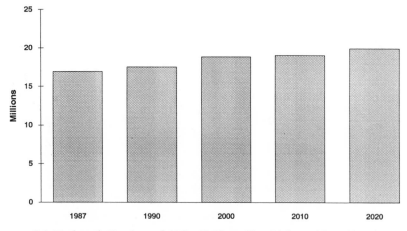

FIGURE 3.3 Projected Number of U.S. Children Not Living with Both Parents, 1987–2020 (in millions)

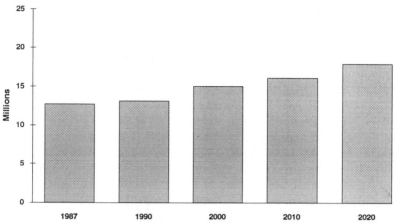

FIGURE 3.4 Projected Number of U.S. Children with Mothers Not Completing High School, 1987–2020 (in millions)

These projections thus are conservative from the standpoint of possible changes in society, but they are not conservative for dramatizing our point about the growing numbers of disadvantaged youth. Figure 3.5 shows anticipated changes, from 1986 to 2020, in the number of children speaking a primary language other than English. Among those under age 18, about 2.3 million were estimated to be PLOTE students in 1986. This number is projected to more than double, approaching 5.5 million by 2020. The proportion of children who speak a primary language other than English is anticipated to rise from under 4% in 1986 to about 8% by 2020.

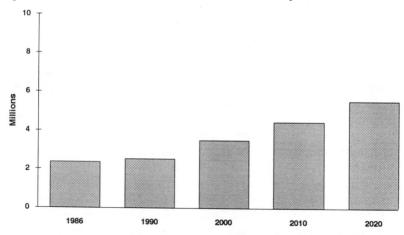

FIGURE 3.5 Projected Number of U.S. Children with a Primary Language Other Than English, 1986–2020 (in millions)

LONG-TERM CONSEQUENCES AND
COSTS TO THE NATION

Failure to educate the educationally disadvantaged adequately may have catastrophic consequences for the social and economic well-being of this country. We have already seen a spate of blue-ribbon commissions document the "crisis" in American education. The National Commission on Excellence in Education, in its 1983 report, *A Nation at Risk,* linked what it termed the "rising tide of mediocrity" in our schools to America's position in the world economy, especially relative to other countries believed to have superior education systems, such as Japan. Many of the other reports also claimed a relationship between investments in education and economic productivity (Committee for Economic Development, 1985; 1987).

In spite of widely held assumptions about the relationship between education and economic productivity, the research literature in this area provides relatively weak evidence for the power of schooling to enhance the economy (Natriello, 1987a). Among individuals, it is clear that persons obtaining more schooling earn more income (Jencks et al., 1979; Mincer, 1974). Economists take this as evidence that individuals with more schooling are more productive, although there are other processes that could produce the same correlation.

The relationships observed among individuals need not apply to the United States as a whole; that is, the expansion of education in the United States may not have a net effect on national economic growth. One of the most sophisticated studies to explore this hypothesis is Walters and Rubinson's (1983) analysis of the effects of educational expansion on economic output in the United States between 1890 and 1969. They found that, since 1933, increases in the number of persons enrolled in and graduating from high school have been associated with higher levels of national economic output 20 years later. They likewise discovered a link between the number of doctorates awarded and increased economic output ten years later. But they also reported that increases in college enrollments between 1933 and 1969 had no effect on national economic output. Neither the number of bachelor's nor master's degrees conferred was related to national economic output. The results thus only partially support the view of educational expansion as an important contributor to national economic productivity, and even those effects that they did find were rather small.

Even if the link between schooling and economic growth is tenuous, we believe that investments in education and the educationally disadvantaged are likely to have payoffs at least as great as other forms of investment this society may undertake. It is perhaps impossible to quantify precisely what the returns to such an investment might be, but we are confident that the economic and social benefits to investing in the schooling of the educationally disadvantaged greatly exceed the costs of those investments.

Some of the evidence for this conviction is based on recent summaries of cost-effective programs for children. One of the most widely cited is a staff report of the House Select Committee on Children, Youth and Families (U.S. House of Representatives, 1988). The key elements of an earlier version of this study were reported in the Committee for Economic Development's 1987 statement, *Children in Need*.

The House Select Committee (U.S. House of Representatives, 1988) reviewed the evidence on the effects of various programs for infants, children, and youth and, where possible, cited the results of cost/benefit analyses of these programs, showing the expected dollar savings associated with each program for a given dollar investment. The Committee's report considered infant and neonatal programs such as the Special Supplemental Food Program for Women, Infants and Children (WIC); prenatal care; and Medicaid Early Periodic Screening, Diagnosis, and Treatment (EPSDT) services. The report also studied childhood programs such as Childhood Immunization, Head Start preschool, elementary and secondary education programs such as Chapter I and Education for All Handicapped Children, and youth employment and training programs such as Job Corps and the Job Training Partnership Act (JTPA).

Each of the programs discussed in the Committee's report (U.S. House of Representatives, 1988) has demonstrable benefits for infants, children, or youth. We review several of these programs in Chapters 4, 5 and 6. The short-term benefits of some of these programs are relatively straightforward to calculate. For instance, infants born to mothers who did not receive early prenatal care are more likely to have low birthweights, which has immediate and predictable consequences for the cost of infant health care. The Institute of Medicine (1985) concluded that each dollar invested in early prenatal care can reduce the cost of infant care by more than three dollars.

For other programs, however, the short-term and long-term economic benefits are largely a matter of speculation, in part due to the difficulty in attaching dollar figures to the results. For instance, the House Select Committee's report (U.S. House of Representatives, 1988) claims that compensatory education can reduce the likelihood that a disadvantaged student will need to repeat a grade. From this the report concluded that an investment of $500 for a year of compensatory education can save $3,700, the average cost of a year of elementary or secondary school in 1987, by boosting students' achievement gains enough for them to be promoted to the next grade. As many students participating in compensatory education programs are held back anyway, this is obviously far too optimistic an estimated return for the dollars invested in compensatory education.

Nathan (1988) has argued that almost all cost/benefit analyses of demonstration projects need to be circumspect in their claims. He contends that the true costs and benefits of social and educational programs typically are unmeasured, or measured so poorly as to be almost useless. Both costs and benefits may be very difficult to quantify; moreover, few analyses truly allow for the assessment of long-term benefits, relying instead on tenuous assumptions about the future behaviors of individuals and institutions, and even flimsier conjectures about the costs of those behaviors.

Nathan (1988) calls for program evaluation research to focus on the measured impacts of programs, and to avoid quantifying the costs and benefits of programs in ways that obscure the speculative assumptions that typically drive such analyses. We could not agree more. In spite of our warnings, though, we wish to carry out a small exercise designed to underscore the potential costs of ignoring the problem of schooling the educationally disadvantaged population adequately. The figures we cite in concluding this chapter are primarily illustrative, and in no sense should what follows be thought of as a precise approach to estimating the relevant costs and benefits.

Costs of the High School Dropout Problem

Elsewhere (McDill et al., 1986) we have described the economic costs of the high school dropout problem. This group forms a large portion of the total population of educationally disadvantaged youth. A great many high school dropouts are educationally disadvantaged, by our definition, but there are other educationally disadvantaged youth with special needs who are unlikely to succeed as adults without educational intervention. Our estimates of the magnitude of the costs of the dropout problem should thus be seen as a lower limit on the costs of ignoring the educationally disadvantaged.

In our earlier study (McDill et al., 1986), we compared the estimated lifetime earnings of high school graduates and high school dropouts. According to the U.S. Bureau of the Census (1983), the lifetime earnings gap between male high school graduates and males who did not complete high school is approximately $260,000; the earnings gap between female high school graduates and noncompleters is about $170,000 over the life cycle. We estimated that about one-half of these differences in lifetime earnings could be attributed to the effects of dropping out of school. On average, then the economic cost of dropping out is about $100,000 in foregone lifetime earnings for each dropout.

In recent years, about 500,000 students per year have left junior high or high school before graduation, never to return to complete high school.

Each year, then, the estimated cost to the nation of the dropout problem is approximately $50 billion in foregone lifetime earnings alone. Also associated with this cost are foregone government tax revenues, greater welfare expenditures, poorer physical and mental health of our nation's citizens, and greater costs of crime, as well as a variety of social costs to which it is difficult to attach dollar figures (Catterall, 1985; Levin, 1972).

Our projections have indicated that the size of the educationally disadvantaged population is increasing rapidly over time. As the number of such youth rises, the costs to the nation will increase considerably. We recognize that our estimates of these costs are crude; nevertheless, we are confident that, whatever the actual figures are, the cost is extremely high, a dollar figure too large to comprehend fully.

We are not suggesting, however, that the nation throw money at schools. It is quite possible that some of our educational goals can be met by reallocating existing educational resources, a strategy discussed in Chapter 8. As the following chapters document, though, reallocating existing educational resources is unlikely to be sufficient to deal with the growing problem. We have argued that the costs associated with failing to educate the educationally disadvantaged adequately are likely to outweigh the costs of appropriate educational reforms. The next part of this book begins to explore the range of possible reforms, stressing existing programs ranging from infancy through young adulthood.

Part II

EDUCATIONAL AND SOCIAL PROGRAMS DESIGNED TO ADDRESS THE PROBLEMS OF THE DISADVANTAGED

The civil rights movement of the 1950s and 1960s led to *de jure* equality of educational opportunity for minority groups in American society. However, the movement did not result in minority students or those from low-income families taking full advantage of these legally defined rights, because a sizable percentage of them entered school with intellectual and social deficits or disadvantages that precluded academic success (McDill, McDill, & Sprehe, 1969, 1972; Passow, 1970). At the local and national levels, large-scale efforts were launched in the 1960s to "compensate" for the poverty or race-related deficiencies in the cognitive and social skills of these students.

The federal government was most prominent in the compensatory education movement of this era, investing very large sums of money in programs mandated first through the War on Poverty and through the Office of Economic Opportunity, followed quickly by Title I of the Elementary and Secondary Education Act of 1965, which immediately became the largest compensatory program in existence and has remained so until the present.

Although the compensatory education movement was, from the beginning, avowedly sociopolitical in nature, it had a substantial social science base in the theoretical and empirical research of scholars such as Basil Bernstein (1961), Benjamin Bloom (1964), Jerome Bruner (1961), Martin Deutsch (1967), and J. McVicker Hunt (1961), all of whom had concentrated considerable effort on understanding how environmental deprivation, linked to poverty and/or minority status, adversely affects the intellectual and socioemotional development of young children (Passow, 1970). Their ideas and social involvement had a major impact on the origins and course of the compensatory education movement. As noted by White (1970), compensatory education's social agenda has been dictated "not by grass roots demands but by the social diagnostician" (p. 164), or, as McDill et al. (1972) described it, by "the professional reformer who operates out of an academic environment and who manifested during the 1960s a growing desire to take an active hand in remaking American education" (p. 142).

Agencies and individual researchers implementing and assessing these programs over the past two decades have attempted to obtain valid evidence on the extent of their effectiveness. Our objective in Chapters 4 through 6 is to review and assess the scientific and educational utility of this body of knowledge for valid conclusions about the efficacy of educational interventions in counteracting the effects of educational and social disadvantages. More specifically, in this effort we employ information from these studies, the quality of which is very uneven, first to provide a brief review of the rationale, implementation, and evaluation of some of the most important of these programs at both the national and local levels; and second to abstract policy implications from this critique for improving the education of disadvantaged students.

Most of our attention here is focused on large federal efforts, since the primary thrust for compensatory education in the past two decades has come from federal agencies with mandates created by President Lyndon Johnson's War on Poverty. In confronting these two tasks we use a developmental or maturational approach to critique programs in maternal and child health and at the preschool, elementary, and secondary levels of schooling. This is the approach adopted in earlier assessments by McDill et al. (1969, 1972), by Levine and Havighurst (1984), and more recently by Saks (1984), and it has been prominent in a variety of theories of cognitive and psychosocial development applied to the education of disadvantaged children for the past three decades.

4

Preschool Programs

In this chapter we review and evaluate in some depth programs for students prior to elementary school. "Young children have been popular targets for community interventionists because of their conviction that the younger the children, the more flexible and easily changed they are . . . and the more cost effective the intervention will be" (Alexander & Malouf, 1983, p. 950).

Although elementary and secondary schooling are the most widely accessible services nationwide, there is growing concern about the provision of adequate education and education-related services prior to enrollment at the elementary level. In fact, some experts in the area of preschool education argue persuasively that a national momentum is under way for universal preschool education ("Committee asks," 1989; Zigler, 1987; Zimiles, 1985). Such concern extends not only to what are traditionally viewed as preschool programs, but also to those designed for the care of very young children and their mothers (Lesser, 1985). It is becoming increasingly clear that efforts to enhance the social, intellectual, and physical development of children, beginning early in their lives, offer an important opportunity for success (Lazar, 1983; Lesser, 1985; Woodhead, 1988; Zigler, 1987). In stressing the importance of early intervention, however, we are not arguing that early childhood is the only period during which compensatory education can be effective, a view that prevailed in the 1960s (McDill et al., 1972). On this issue we concur with Bereiter's (1971) stance: "But if it is true that an effective kindergarten program can overcome differences in preschool experience, then it may also be true that an effective first-grade program can overcome differences in kindergarten experience, and so on up to some unknown point where the weight of past experience tips the scales" (p. 19). Zigler (1987) recently expressed a similar sentiment: "Every age in a child's life is a major age. We must be just as concerned for the 6-year-old, the 10-year-old, and the 16-year-old as we are for the 4-year-old" (p. 257). But Woodhead (1988) is the most emphatic in warning about the tendency in some social and behavioral science circles to overemphasize the merits of early childhood intervention:

> In the long run, the scientific value of this body of research lies in its power to illustrate the inadequacy of such an appealing view of the role of early childhood intervention in attaining the goals of social policy. On the one hand, that view places unrealistic emphasis on the early years as a period for effecting

permanent individual change through educational and social programs. On the other hand, it distracts attention from other concurrent and subsequent processes in community and school that interact with experiences in the early years to determine long-term patterns of development. Accordingly, a first responsibility of social science advocacy is to avoid perpetuating and indeed to actively seek to counteract the tendency in public debate to adopt simple deterministic views of the scope for intervention in human development. [p. 452]

With these caveats in mind, we consider a range of maternal and child health and preschool compensatory programs.

MATERNAL AND CHILD HEALTH PROGRAMS

Programs to promote the health and well-being of mothers and children have long existed in the United States (Lesser, 1985). Support for such programs has come with judgments about the limited capacity of poor parents (Mason, Wodarski, & Parham, 1985). Since 1980 support for maternal and child health programs has been curtailed (Lesser, 1985; Miller, 1983). The growing recognition of the importance of early intervention in solving the problems of disadvantaged students has led quite expectedly to renewed interest in programs to promote prenatal health, assist teenage mothers, provide services to families, and enhance the general health of children.

There is striking evidence for the link between the health of expectant mothers and the long-term physical and intellectual well-being of their children. For example, Rantakallio (1979, 1983) reports that the children of mothers who smoked during pregnancy were shorter, more prone to respiratory diseases, and had poorer mean ability in school than children whose mothers did not smoke during pregnancy. Other studies have looked beyond the prenatal period. Lubchenco, Delivoria-Papadopoulos, and Searles (1972) and Littman and Parmelee (1978) report on the inverse relationship of problems in the prenatal and infancy periods, respectively, to measures of later healthy child development. Edwards and Grossman (1979) and Wolfe (1985) have reported on the positive relationship between health and cognitive development in children. Children who begin life with problems such as low birthweight may have low IQs throughout their lives. Several studies have shown the provision of good child care by the mother to be a significant predictor of later IQ (Broman, Nichols, & Kennedy, 1975; Werner, Bierman, & French, 1971). Moreover, health problems in childhood are likely to interfere with school attendance and, ultimately, with school performance (Weitzman, Klerman, Lamb, Menary, & Alpert, 1982; Wolfe, 1985).

Despite evidence from these and other studies of the relationship between maternal and child health and the long-term consequences for children in and out of school, the national picture of infant health is not encouraging. For example, the Children's Defense Fund (Hughes, Johnson, Simons, & Rosenbaum, 1986), reporting on the status of two indicators of maternal and child health — low birthweight and premature birth — concluded that conditions are becoming worse. One out of every 8 black infants and 1 out of every 18 white infants was born at low birthweight in 1983. One out of every 10 Hispanic infants was born at low birthweight in 1982, the last year for which national statistics were available. In 1983 1 out of every 6 black infants and 1 out of every 12 white infants was born prematurely, and in 1982 1 out of every 8 Puerto Rican infants and 1 out of every 9 Mexican-American infants was born prematurely.

Although these statistics are disturbing, they are not surprising when considered in the context of the recent reversal in the trends regarding prenatal care. Hughes et al. (1986) reported that in 1983 the percentage of women receiving late or no prenatal care increased after a decade of steady decline. A 1987 study by the U.S. General Accounting Office found that, in 20 of the 32 communities included in the study, 50% or more of the interviewed Medicaid recipients and uninsured women had insufficient prenatal care. Moreover, those who were most likely to obtain insufficient prenatal care were those who were uninsured, poorly educated, black or Hispanic, in their teen years, and living in the largest urban areas (U.S. GAO, 1987b). In view of the lack of adequate prenatal care, perhaps it should not be surprising that the United States leads Western countries in the percentage of infants born too soon or too small and therefore at risk of long-term developmental problems.

A particularly difficult aspect of the maternal health problem is the large number of teenage mothers in the United States. Because of the drop in the age of menarche and the increase in the number of sexually active teenagers, this country has experienced a dramatic increase in the number of children born to teenage mothers during the last 20 years (Bell, Casto, & Daniels, 1983). The Children's Defense Fund (Hughes et al., 1986) provides a description of the current state of teen pregnancy:

> In 1983 births to teen mothers were 13.7 percent of all births, representing about 500,000 births. Births to teens younger than age fifteen represented 0.3 percent of all births nationally. Babies born to young mothers (less than twenty years of age) are disproportionately likely to be born at low birthweight. In 1983, babies born to teenagers represented 13.7 percent of all births, but 20 percent of all low

birth weight births. Thus, the risk of pregnancy outcome is related inversely to age. Babies born to mothers younger than fifteen years of age are more than twice as likely to be born at low birthweight than those born to mothers twenty to twenty-four years old. They are also more than three times as likely to be born at very low birthweight (3.5 pounds or less). Young mothers were the least likely to receive early prenatal care. Only 54 percent of all teen mothers began care in the first trimester, and among black teen mothers the proportion dropped to 47 percent. Furthermore, while nationally 6 percent of pregnant women of all ages received little or no prenatal care, 12 percent of mothers younger than twenty years old receive no care before the seventh month of pregnancy or receive no care at all. [p. 39]

Teenage mothers, those women most in need of good prenatal care, are least likely to receive it (McCormick, Shapiro, & Starfield, 1984). Moreover, the children of teenage mothers, the very children often most in need of good child care, are often the least likely to receive it. Although research suggests that the most important factor for overcoming perinatal stress is the child care provided by the mother, teenage mothers are frequently not in a position to provide such care, since they often lack knowledge of proper nutrition, medical care, and child-rearing practices and find themselves in stressful circumstances (Bell et al., 1983). Perhaps as a result, the limited evidence available suggests that male children born to teenage parents are at a developmental disadvantage in preschool and elementary school, compared to children born to older mothers (Baldwin & Cain, 1981; Broman, 1981; Brooks-Gunn & Furstenberg, 1985; Furstenberg & Brooks-Gunn, 1985; Marecek, 1979). These developmental deficits increase over time, so that by adolescence children of teen mothers are more than twice as likely as children of older mothers to have repeated a grade and twice as likely to misbehave in school. These differences persist even when the effects of family background are controlled (Furstenberg & Brooks-Gunn, 1985).

Programs to enhance maternal and child health take a variety of forms. Perhaps the most widespread programs with an impact in this area are Medicaid, Aid to Families with Dependent Children (AFDC) and the Supplemental Food Program for Women, Infants, and Children (WIC). These programs appear to be cost-effective in reducing infant mortality and long-term developmental deficits. The Children's Defense Fund (Hughes et al., 1986) reports that, for every dollar spent on comprehensive maternity care, $11 can be saved over the lifetime of a child. The Institute of Medicine (1985) found that, for each dollar spent on prenatal care, $3.38 would be saved in the first year of the child's life. Schramm (1985) concludes that each dollar spent for nutritional supplements for pregnant women under the WIC program results in $.83 savings in Medicaid costs in the first month of a child's life alone. The U.S. GAO (1987b), in a study of California's OB

Access Pilot Project, a program to provide comprehensive prenatal care to Medicaid-eligible women, concluded that the benefit-to-cost ratio of the program ranged between 1.7 and 2.6 to 1, over the short run, and might be greater in the long run.

Despite such positive returns on maternal and child health programs, these programs are not reaching their intended beneficiaries. The Children's Defense Fund (Hughes et al., 1986) reports that in 1985 Medicaid reached only 46% of poor and nearly poor children, a reduction of 19% in children reached a decade earlier. The same Children's Defense Fund report shows that in only 18 states do AFDC and related Medicaid benefit levels exceed 50% of the federal poverty level. Moreover, no state served more than 50% of all mothers and children eligible for nutritional benefits under the WIC program, and 8 states served fewer than 30%.

There are a variety of local programs to aid mothers and children (e.g., Campbell, Breitmayer, & Ramey, 1986; Delatte, Orgeron, & Preis, 1985; Palmer, 1981; Seitz, Rosenbaum, & Apfel, 1985; Strobino et al., 1986). Such programs differ in their basing mode (e.g., whether they are school, community, or medically based), their intervention strategy (e.g., medical services, education for parents, education for children, family support), and their experience with implementation problems. It is difficult to quantify the effects of these programs, as the evaluations of them, with few exceptions, have suffered from methodological problems (Klerman, 1979; McDonough, 1984). Although no single approach to intervention can be recommended over another (McDonough, 1984), programs to enhance the health of mothers and children appear to be well worth the investment of resources. Certainly it makes little sense to support the type of compensatory educational services we discuss next if the basic health of these disadvantaged children is neglected.

NATIONAL PRESCHOOL COMPENSATORY EDUCATION PROGRAMS

Preschool is the maturational level that has received the most attention and resources over the past two decades. This is not surprising, given the popular notion which originated in the 1960s among compensatory experts that there is a critical developmental period for children during the first 3 to 5 years of life which has a profound impact on their intellectual and social development (Bloom, 1964; Hunt, 1961; White, 1970). The late economist Daniel Saks (1984) is an example of a more recent avowed proponent of the "get 'em while they're young" perspective: "Pre-school programs illustrate how important the developmental view of schooling is. Small differences in performance in early years of schooling cumulate over a student's early life to produce dramatic differences in performance of young adults. This is like compound interest" (p. 67).

A number of preschool intervention programs varying on dimensions such as cost per pupil, intensity of treatment, type of treatment, duration of treatment, age of pupils, and degree of parental involvement have been established. Without doubt the most visible and politically popular preschool program for disadvantaged children is Head Start. As noted by Zigler and Berman (1983), the importance of Head Start is a result of its scope and unique role as the first national intervention effort for preschoolers. It was launched in 1965 under the administrative authority of the Office of Economic Opportunity, with a multifaceted mission to provide a diverse array of child development services, including enhancement of the child's intellectual and academic skills, improvement of the child's physical health, improvement of the child's socioemotional development, involvement of the family in the child's development, and improvement of the family's functioning as a social unit. Initiated as a summer program, it soon became a year-round effort and now typically provides 2 years of services to a majority of its participants. Head Start had provided services to more than 8.5 million children by 1983, with an annual federal appropriation of more than $900 million (McKey et al., 1985). By 1987 it had served a total of approximately 10 million children (Levine & Havighurst, 1989).

Because there were few systematic studies of Head Start in its first 3 years of operation, no one knew how effective the program was. Thus, in 1968 the Westinghouse Learning Corporation, in collaboration with Ohio State University (Granger et al., 1969), conducted a national assessment of Head Start for the Office of Economic Opportunity, to determine to what extent the program, *at the national level,* had affected the socioemotional and cognitive growth of its client pupils. The study quickly became controversial in terms of its methodology (ex post facto design) and narrowness of scope (restricted to cognitive and intellectual outcomes) and the reliability and validity of criterion variables. Despite a spate of criticisms revolving around these issues, the following overall conclusion by the authors regarding the impact of Head Start seems justified (McDill et al., 1972; White, 1970; Williams & Evans, 1969):

> In sum, Head Start children cannot be said to be appreciably different from their peers in the elementary grades who did not attend Head Start in most aspects of cognitive and affective development measured in this study, with the exception of the slight, but nonetheless significant, superiority of full-year Head Start children on certain measures of cognitive development. [Granger et al., 1969, p. 8]

As noted by Cicirelli (1984), one of the authors of the Westinghouse study, *"it* [the study] *did not conclude that Head Start was a failure"* (p. 915), even though several influential critics of the evaluation misinterpreted its conclusions to that effect. Cicirelli goes on to make a telling point which we believe should serve as fundamental advice to the architects and implementers of all compensatory programs: "It [the study] concluded that Head Start had not been implemented in *sufficiently intensive fashion* to determine whether or not it could succeed in attaining its goals" (p. 915, italics added).

Numerous evaluations of local Head Start programs have been conducted since the Westinghouse assessment, "with some showing significant impact of Head Start and others indicating no impact or even a negative impact" (McKey et al., 1985, p. 2). It was not until recently, however, that a second national assessment of the magnitude and visibility of the Westinghouse study appeared. In 1985 CSR, Inc., of Washington, DC, published the findings of its comprehensive critique of all reports and evaluation studies (published and unpublished) of Head Start since its inception in 1965. As the authors of the report noted, CSR did the analysis in an attempt to determine the effects of Head Start on "children's cognitive development, socioemotional development and health as well as the impact on participant families and local communities" (McKey et al., 1985, p. 3). Thus, in contrast to the earlier Westinghouse evaluation, which involved primary data gathering from student participants in local Head Start projects, the ambitious CSR analysis involved the synthesis of all existing results from more than 200 separate evaluation studies of Head Start over the 20 years of its existence. Narrative review methods were applied to synthesize 64% of the studies, whereas the remaining 36% were subjected to the statistical technique of meta-analysis (McKey et al., 1985).

CSR's overall conclusions about the effects of Head Start as a preschool intervention effort were more optimistic than earlier large-scale efforts. By this we mean that Head Start appears to have statistically significant and educationally meaningful[1] short-term effects on cognitive and socioemotional development (i.e., self-esteem, social behavior, and achievement motivation) and perhaps more persistent effects on the physical health, motor development, and nutrition of participants. These significant and meaningful effects prepare students to succeed in school (i.e., develop social competence to adapt more easily to school life). Further, there are appreciable effects on families' use of those community institutions (health services, education, and the economic environment) that are viewed as functionally interdependent with local compensatory education programs.

However, this positive outlook for Head Start is tempered by the "fade-out" phenomenon. Results frequently show that the treatment and control groups are comparable in cognitive and socioemotional performance by the end of the first year of regular school. This "washing out" or "leveling off" of cognitive and affective gains for disadvantaged students in compensatory programs, as they progress through later grades, has been a widespread and persistent problem for the past two decades (Bronfenbrenner, 1975; Cicirelli, 1984; Granger et al., 1969; Levine & Havighurst, 1984; McDill et al., 1969, 1972; Stallings & Stipek, 1986). The Westinghouse evaluation of Head Start in 1969 also emphasized the problem of fade-out effects and advocated lengthier and more academically intensive treatment programs to deal with them. The 1985 Head Start evaluation by CSR, which compared program effects from studies conducted before 1970 with those conducted after 1970, adopted a similar view. CSR found that the average effect for the first 2 years after leaving Head Start was greater for studies conducted after 1970 and speculated that, "Head Start program changes made in the 1970's, such as converting summer Head Start to full year programs, initiating training and technical assistance efforts, implementing Head Start Performance Standards and launching the Child Development Associate credential, may be having positive effects on cognitive performance" (McKey et al., 1985, p. 20).

Gamble and Zigler (in press) strongly criticize the CSR meta-analysis of Head Start for being methodologically flawed. They claim that the failure of the CSR researchers to discard evaluation studies that were poorly designed and/or conducted precludes scientifically valid conclusions being drawn concerning long-term gains in the cognitive and affective development of Head Start children. These authors, relying on the advice of methodological experts such as Cronbach (1982) and Campbell and colleagues (Campbell & Boruch, 1975; Campbell & Erlebacher, 1970), argue that CSR should have abandoned their meta-analytic approach and instead have attended to "variations in quality and content of programs as well as specifics of research design" (p. 12) by relying most heavily on those 6 of the 32 studies of Head Start programs that had comparable treatment and control groups.

One cannot quarrel with the position that the validity of findings from research syntheses depends on carefully scrutinizing individual evaluation studies to eliminate those that fail to meet minimal methodological standards and placing more emphasis on those assessments with the highest quality designs. Further, as documented by Slavin (1986b), meta-analyses of educational evaluations have often been guilty of failing to make such distinctions, which has led to unwarranted conclusions being drawn from such overarching efforts. Thus, in principle, we are prepared to accept Gamble and Zigler's (in press) criticisms of the meta-analytic segment of the CSR review of the literature on Head Start evaluations. To insist, however, that the methodological flavor of the CSR study obviates its scientific utility is to throw the baby out with the bath water in our view. Despite the weaknesses of CSR's meta-analysis, its conclusion that the initial positive effects of Head Start did not persist is, as we clearly demonstrate in this chapter, a consistent finding in numerous evaluation studies of Head Start and other compensatory programs over the past quarter of a century. In the case of the CSR effort, it appears that the findings are sufficiently robust to offset design and analytical weaknesses. Finally, it should be pointed out that the CSR results (from both its meta-analysis and narrative review components) are not incompatible with the conclusion of Zigler (1973) of a dozen years earlier regarding the degree and nature of effectiveness of the Head Start program:

> Whether Head Start is seen as a success or a failure is determined by the factors one chooses to weigh in making such an assessment. Thus, if Head Start is appraised in terms of its success in universally raising the IQ's of poor children, and maintaining these IQ's over time, one is tempted to write off Head Start as an abject failure. On the other hand, if one assesses Head Start in terms of the improved health of tens of thousands of poor children who have been screened, diagnosed, and treated, Head Start is clearly a resounding success. [p. 3]

LOCAL PRESCHOOL COMPENSATORY
EDUCATION PROGRAMS

During the late 1950s, the 1960s, and into the decade of the 1970s, a vast array of local early childhood programs emerged, most of which received at least some federal support (McDill et al., 1972). They varied on a host of characteristics such as age of entry of children into the program, duration and intensity of treatment or intervention, quality and number of instructional personnel, type of curricula and materials, and extent of parental involvement (Lazar, Hubbell, Murray, Rosche, & Royce, 1977). Here we provide a brief overview and assessment of a very limited number of the most visible models. Our intent is not to be representative in our choice of programs that have emerged in the past three decades. Rather, we attempt merely to illustrate the types of longitudinal approaches and outcomes that have been developed to narrow the gap in intellectual and socioemotional growth between the advantaged and disadvantaged segments of our child population.

Two of the early approaches that have persisted for more than two decades (either in original or modified form) and are widely viewed as outstanding examples of preschool interventions are the Bereiter-Engelmann

(1966) Academic Preschool Program and the High/Scope Perry Preschool Program (Weikart, 1971). These two models are exemplary in that they specified clearly defined objectives and curricula, systematic schedules and procedures for implementation, and longitudinal evaluations with random assignment of subjects to experimental and control groups.

Bereiter-Engelmann Academic Preschool Program

The Bereiter-Engelmann (B-E) program originated in the early 1960s at the University of Illinois in the Institute for Research on Exceptional Children. The underlying psychological theory for the program has been referred to as "Skinnerian operant conditioning" (Stallings & Stipek, 1986, p. 738) or "behaviorist" (Schweinhart, Weikart, & Larner, 1986b, p. 18). Bereiter (1986a) strongly denies that the theoretical perspective is Skinnerian; rather he views it "as a rationalist approach of concept teaching" (p. 290).

The objectives of the program were to teach language, reading, and arithmetic to preschool children of low socioeconomic background (Bereiter & Engelmann, 1966). Students received equal amounts of instruction in each curricular area based on task analysis, and specific learning objectives and instructional methods were developed to achieve the basic goals. The methods involved the specification of well-defined concepts and operations for each skill area, with a heavy emphasis on constructions and intensive drills in predetermined sequences. In short, the B-E approach was strongly cognitive in orientation and not designed to foster the socioemotional skills of preschoolers, which made it stand apart from other more holistic models developed in the 1960s era. As a consequence, "it was cheered by behavioral psychologists, jeered by cognitive developmentalists. The latter group felt it unwise or even criminal to subject young children to such narrowly focused activities" (Stallings & Stipek, 1986, p. 738). This disagreement still rages today, as will be seen later.

The early evaluations of the B-E program by both its originators and others revealed consistent cognitive gains (reported in McDill et al., 1969) that did not fade out after 2 years of exposure. However, as Beller (1973) notes, by the end of the first grade the differences between treatment and control groups on tests of academic performance essentially disappeared. Partly as a consequence, the B-E program was modified by Siegfried Engelmann and Wesley Becker at the University of Oregon for use in teaching reading, math, and language to students in grades K through 3 and was labeled DISTAR (Direct Instruction System for Teaching and Remediation). Since this is essentially an elementary school intervention program, we will discuss it in the next chapter.

High/Scope Perry Preschool Program

The High/Scope preschool curriculum evolved from the Ypsilanti-Perry Preschool Project, which was one of the prototypical efforts of the early 1960s. It was developed by David Weikart and Lawrence Schweinhart, and is described as an open-framework model with cognitive/developmental underpinnings derived from Piagetian theory (Schweinhart et al., 1986b). In this approach the teacher and preschool child jointly plan and initiate activities and actively work together. Teachers initiate developmentally appropriate experiences (Schweinhart & Weikart, 1986a) in the classroom that reflect the long-range goals of the program, which are

> to develop children's ability to use a variety of skills in the arts and physical movement; to develop their knowledge of objects as a base of educational concepts; to develop their ability to speak, dramatize, and graphically represent their experiences and communicate these experiences to other children and adults; to develop their ability to work with others, make decisions about what to do and how to do it, and plan their use of time and energy; and to develop their ability to apply their newly acquired reasoning capacity in a wide range of naturally occurring situations with a variety of materials. [National Diffusion Network, 1986, p. J-6]

The plan-do-review sequence is designed to encourage children to achieve these cognitive, social, and affective goals by involving them in decision making and problem solving on a continuing basis. Thus, the primary role of the teacher is to be supportive of the children and to encourage them to achieve beyond the original plan, in each of the three domains.

Children in the High/Scope program attend classes in half-day sessions, 5 days per week over the entire school year. Systematic efforts are made to involve parents in the program through home visits on a weekly basis. One of the program's major strengths is its longitudinal design (with random assignment to experimental and control groups), which has provided systematic follow-up evidence thus far to age 19 on a large number of intellectual, academic, and social outcomes for an early cohort in the program. For example, after 2 years of preschool, the treatment group had appreciably higher IQ scores, but these differences faded by the end of Grade 2. Although both groups were well below national norms on several tests of academic achievement at age 14, the treatment group scored significantly, but only slightly, higher on each of them. Further, the experimental subjects were considerably less likely to be placed in special education programs, to be retained in grade, or to become high school dropouts than were the controls.

At age 19 the treatment group was significantly more likely than the control group to be functionally literate, enrolled in a postsecondary institution, and employed; and less likely to have been on welfare or arrested (Berrueta-Clement, Schweinhart, Barnett, Epstein, & Weikart, 1984). Several reviewers of preschool programs (Committee for Economic Development, 1985; National Diffusion Network, 1986; Stallings & Stipek, 1986) have viewed these results as impressive. Further, cost/benefit analysis of the program by the developers (Schweinhart & Weikart, 1986b) indicate a benefits-to-costs ratio of almost 6 to 1 per participant, which has led to the conclusion that "one year of the program is an extraordinary economic buy" (Committee for Economic Development, 1985, p. 44).

Despite these impressive differences between experimental and control groups in the High/Scope experiment, one should not lose sight of the fact that, by ordinary social and national norms, the experimental group remained seriously disadvantaged in adolescence and young adulthood. For example, at age 14 they scored 12 points below national norms on the California Test of Basic Skills. At age 19, 22% of them reported they had been arrested; as a cohort, they had spent an average of 8 years in special education classes; 35% had dropped out of school; 52% were currently unemployed; and only 45% supported themselves financially (Schweinhart & Weikart, 1980).

High/Scope Versus Bereiter-Engelmann

Recently, a major debate has erupted in both the professional literature and the mass media between proponents of the High/Scope program and those of the Bereiter-Engelmann approach, concerning purported differences in the two programs' ability to prevent nonconforming behavior in adolescence. This sharp disagreement is of sufficient educational and social policy significance to merit attention here. The exchange was precipitated by a publication by Schweinhart et al. (1986b) that concluded that, at age 15, important differences existed among a sample of 54 subjects who at ages 3 or 4 had been randomly assigned for 1 or 2 years to one of three distinct preschool curricula in Ypsilanti, Michigan, between 1967 and 1970. The three programs were described by the authors as the "DISTAR model,[2] the High/Scope model, and a model in the nursery school tradition" (Schweinhart et al., 1986b, p. 17). Outcomes evaluated in the study include IQ and academic achievement at several times during subjects' school careers, and self-reports at age 15 (Grade 9) of delinquency and other measures of social behavior. At age 8 no significant differences existed among the three treatment groups in achievement (measured by California Achievement Tests), and at age 15 no such differences were found among them on IQ. However, by this age appreciable differences had occurred across the groups on several self-reported measures of social behavior. "According to these data the DISTAR group engaged in twice as many delinquent acts as did the other two curriculum groups, including five times as many acts of property violence and twice as many acts of drug abuse and such status offenses as running away from home" (Schweinhart et al., 1986b, p. 34). Other measures of nonconformity were also more prevalent among the DISTAR group, such as poorer family relations, less participation in sports, and lower educational expectations. However, no significant differences were found on self-reported arrest rates even though almost half of the total sample claimed to have been arrested by age 15. The authors conclude that the "preschool DISTAR experiences did not actually harm the child's social development" (p. 42). However, they assert that their findings suggest several policy considerations, including two that are provocative:

1. Formal academic programs such as DISTAR may fail to produce the desired social behavior consequences in students.
2. Teacher-directed learning models such as DISTAR should be rigorously scrutinized and evaluated since such approaches may be ineffective in reducing children's later social nonconformity.

Predictably, some of the developers and implementers of the Bereiter-Engelmann and DISTAR models reacted negatively to the findings and conclusions from this study, which were widely interpreted in the press as linking highly structured academic preschool programs to later problems of personal and social adjustment for students placed in them. For example, Fred M. Hechinger (1986) made the following sensationalized assertion in the *New York Times:* "While such [highly structured] programs have been shown to raise academic performance, they appear often to lead to antisocial behavior, delinquency, and even violence later on" (p. C8). In the *Baltimore Sun* a front-page article on April 22, 1986 carried the headline "Preschool Academic Push Linked to Later Social Problems" (Englund, 1986, p. 1a).

The responses of B-E and DISTAR proponents (Bereiter, 1986a; Gersten, 1986) were specific and detailed and focused on issues such as the adequacy of the samples, the low reliability and validity of self-reported measures of delinquency, and the relatively small differences among the three programs as implemented. Schweinhart, Weikart, and Larner (1986a) produced a rejoinder to these criticisms in which they attempted to clarify what they believed were misinterpretations and distortions on the critics' part concerning these issues. Finally, they provided what they considered to be a meaningful interpretive link between conceptual and implementation differences among the preschool curricula and later adolescent social behavior, which strongly implied that direct-instruction approaches in preschool programs "may be harming young children" (p. 311).[3]

It is our judgment that the evidence and reasoning offered by Schweinhart and colleagues in this disagreement do not justify their strong conclusions from tentative empirical results concerning the likely harmful effects of direct-instruction preschool models on the later social adjustment of children. The flaws uncovered by their critics are in a number of instances persuasive. For example, there is a substantial literature in juvenile delinquency on the weaknesses of self-reported indicators of official juvenile misbehavior (Empey, 1978; Hindelang, Hirschi, & Weis, 1979; Hirschi, Hindelang, & Weis, 1982; Kleck, 1982; Tittle, Villemez, & Smith, 1982). In the volume by Berrueta-Clement et al. (1984) that reports on the effects of the High/Scope preschool program on various areas of development in young adulthood, the authors present information on subjects' official involvement with the criminal justice system, including police and court records, juvenile delinquency records, and adult crime records. The only comparisons made therein are between subjects enrolled in the High/Scope program and a control group that did not have any preschool experience. These comparisons reveal that, overall, the preschool subjects have less contact with the criminal justice system than the control group. However, the following comment by Schweinhart et al. (1986a) suggests that data on subjects' official involvement with the criminal justice system were not available for the direct-instruction and traditional nursery school curriculum groups in the 1986 study: "We would like to supplement the curriculum study's self-report data with data from institutional records and plan to do so in the next step of the research" (p. 306).

Another weakness of the curriculum study by Schweinhart et al. (1986b) is the sex imbalance between the direct-instruction group (56% male) and the High/Scope group (39% male). This disparity, in conjunction with the use of delinquency scales that focus primarily on male delinquency acts, could account for most if not all of the differences in delinquency rates between the High/Scope and direct-instruction groups, a point also emphasized by other critics (Bereiter, 1986a, 1986b; Gersten, 1986).

Further, we are concerned about strong policy inferences being drawn from an exploratory study of only 18 students per treatment group in a single midwestern community, particularly when data are elicited from subjects of low socioeconomic backgrounds with poor verbal skills. Official counts of delinquency taken from police and juvenile court records might have provided more convincing evidence.

Finally, Schweinhart et al.'s (1986b) study suffers from "proof by juxtaposition" (Lindesmith & Strauss, 1950, p. 597), in that they posited a causal link between two sets of phenomena widely separated in time (curricular experience in preschool and juvenile misbehavior) with no evidence presented on a host of other *intervening* educational or social experiences—risk factors that could be critical in explaining variations in delinquency. For example, one important risk factor during elementary school is not liking school (Gottfredson, 1985; Hirschi, 1969). Can it be established that direct-instruction students are more likely to become alienated or psychologically disengaged from school than those in the High/Scope program? On the other hand, successful academic performance in elementary school is widely accepted as a school factor that insulates students from delinquency. Are High/Scope students more likely in elementary or middle school to perform better academically than those in the direct-instruction curriculum? Schweinhart et al.'s (1986b) own evidence shows no differences in achievement scores between the two groups at the end of second grade.

Even Zigler (1987), who generally lauds the High/Scope Perry Preschool Program, criticizes the study on a number of methodological grounds, including (1) the sample is not representative of disadvantaged children; (2) the experimental and control groups are not comparable on the variable of maternal employment; (3) there is a confounding of the effects of educational intervention and efforts of staff to maintain an intact sample; (4) assignment of subjects to experimental and control groups was not completely random; and (5) the cost/benefit analysis overstates the benefits of the educational treatment. Zigler concludes his critique of the High/Scope program by advocating the following:

> I would like to see the outcome of the High/Scope model when mounted by people with less expertise than those employed in the Perry Project. Furthermore, evaluations of any intervention should be conducted by researchers not involved in the development of the model being evaluated (Zigler & Berman, 1983). Given the pervasiveness of self-fulfilling prophecies (Merton, 1948; Rosenthal & Jacobson, 1968), this caveat represents merely a common sense concern. [Zigler, 1987, p. 255]

Without doubt, the most trenchant criticism of both the substance and methods of the curriculum study of Schweinhart et al. (1986b) we have located is that of Gottfredson (1987), made in a review of a variety of preschool programs. He concludes that "the results of this small and irresponsibly-reported study, unless replicated in large sample research, are at best regarded as a fluke" (p. 43). Farrington (1987) in turn criticizes Gottfredson for being "excessively harsh" (p. 80) and strongly disagrees with Gottfredson's conclusion that the Perry results are irresponsibly reported. Nevertheless, Farrington does conclude that Schweinhart et al.'s (1986b) results are "tentative and provocative rather than definitive" (p. 82).

After reviewing the curriculum study by Schweinhart et al. (1986b) and the reactions of others to it, we believe that the former have generated a hypothesis concerning the relationship of preschool experiences to adolescent deviant behavior, not a scientifically verified set of results. To produce such demanding results requires a well-articulated and empirically replicated causal model that clearly specifies linkages among (1) preschool experiences; (2) later social and educational experience, performance, and behavior; and (3) adolescent outcomes. To draw either "policy implications" or "policy considerations" (Schweinhart et al., 1986b, p. 43) in the absence of such a verified causal scheme is not defensible on either scientific or educational policy grounds.

Other Longitudinal Preschool Program Analyses

There are two additional important longitudinal preschool analyses that have treatment and control groups and which emerged in the 1960s and have persisted into the 1980s. One is a component of the Parent Education Program developed at the University of Florida, Gainesville, by the late Ira Gordon and colleagues. The other is Louise Miller and Rondeall P. Bissell's study of four distinct Head Start programs in Louisville, Kentucky which began in the 1968–1969 academic year.

Gordon's Parent Education Program provided home intervention and, in year 2, home learning centers (HLCs), which were established to provide instruction to both parents and children from age 3 months to 3 years. Children's academic and social development were assessed through age 11 (Jester & Guinagh, 1983). The program concentrated on enhancing the personal and cognitive development of the child and also increasing the mother's self-esteem and her belief that she could influence her destiny and that of her child. The program trained paraprofessional home visitors to work with each mother on a weekly basis and also to assist in teaching the child. A sequenced curriculum emphasized Piagetian concepts appropriate to the child's level of intellectual and psychological development.

Gordon's original infant study (see Stallings & Stipek, 1986) was conducted in several small Florida communities between June, 1966 and September, 1967, employing a sample of 193 pairs of mothers and infants.[4] He obtained a large volume of data on the members of each mother/child pair, including the mother's self-esteem, attitudes, and expectations and several measures of the child's cognitive development. At age 1 the experimental children were superior in mental development to the control groups. Stallings and Stipek (1986) report that in 1972, when all children in the sample were at least age 4, those in the treatment group scored significantly higher on a variety of cognitive measures, and the effects were larger for those with longer participation in the program.

Ramey and Bryant (1982), as part of a larger study of four early intervention programs that all met high evaluation standards, conducted an independent evaluation of Gordon's Parent Education Program. They found that the program resulted in IQ gains that were significantly higher than those for the control group. Jester and Guinagh (1983) summarize the long-term outcomes of the Gordon program in a manner generally consistent with those of other reviewers:

> The cognitive and school performance data collected during the course of this project, such as IQ, achievement, and placement in special education classes, supported the hypothesis that those children in the program for two to three consecutive years performed better than control children for as long as 7 years after the active intervention had ended. However, the socioemotional and personality data relating to the mothers and their children, such as teacher ratings and inventories of personality variables, did not show such differences. Even though there were some small differences between treatment and control mothers early during the intervention, wherever these differences occurred they faded out shortly after the intervention ceased. [pp. 128–129]

Given the apparent success of Gordon's original Parent Education Program, the effort was subsequently expanded for use in Head Start preschool and Follow Through classrooms extending through Grade 3 and became known as the Parent Education Follow Through Program (PEFTP).

The second longitudinal analysis of a preschool program is Miller and Bissell's (1983) study. Conducted in the 1968–1969 school year, it compared the effects of four established programs for children who attended them for one year beginning at age 4. These programs were (1) Montessori; (2) Bereiter-Engelmann; (3) DARCEE (Demonstration and Research Center for Early Education), which was developed by Susan Gray and colleagues at Peabody College; and (4) a traditional nursery school program. Subjects ($N=214$) were randomly assigned to the programs, and a control group ($N=34$) was recruited from the same neighborhood where the experimental classes were held. Each of the four experimental groups attended a full-day program at age 4, followed by either a traditional or academic kindergarten at age 5. The children were extremely disadvantaged; for example, roughly 50% were in families receiving welfare, and more than 60% were in households without fathers present. The primary purpose of the study was to determine whether the four preschool models would have differential effects on students' academic and affective development at the end of 1 year of attendance and whether such effects would be sustained in later school years. The students were completing high school in 1982 and were still being followed up as adolescents.

Miller and Bissell (1983) describe the treatment as follows:

Two of the programs (Bereiter-Engelmann and DARCEE) were small-group programs that used didactic methods (direct instruction) to develop foundational skills necessary for school. The content was academic; for DARCEE, it involved association, classification, and sequencing in the processing of information along with the development of motivation to achieve, persistence in tasks, resistance to distraction, and delay of gratification. In B-E, the instructional materials were primarily visual and auditory. In DARCEE, there were also games and many materials to manipulate. Both the Montessori and traditional programs were oriented towards long-term development and did not involve group instruction. Montessori, however, was a more structured program in that prepared materials were designed to teach language and mathematical concepts whenever the child had progressed through exercises for daily living and sensorial materials. The traditional program had a much broader emphasis on social and emotional development, whereas Montessori was oriented towards cognitive skills and related attitudes. Traditional also enhanced fantasy and role-playing. Montessori did not. [pp. 179–180]

The program effects in the Miller and Bissell (1983) effort were complex, involving sex differences, sex-by-treatment interactions, and long-term trends. At the end of the preschool year the four experimental groups had higher IQs and had improved more on achievement and intellectual curiosity than did controls. In general, the effects were different across programs at the end of year 1 and consistent with program goals in that the two didactic programs (B-E and DARCEE) produced higher scores in academic areas such as IQ and arithmetic; DARCEE also significantly influenced achievement motivation and ambition. By the end of first grade, all experimental groups remained above national norms and higher than controls on achievement tests. By the end of Grade 2 these effects had faded, with Montessori males performing best. Over a 4-year period (i.e., through Grade 2), IQ had declined for all groups, but the decline was sharpest for B-E subjects and for females. At the end of Grade 8, essentially no significant differences remained between program and control subjects on either IQ or achievement, and there were no significant differences across treatment groups. Further, less than one-fifth of the students were achieving at national norms (Miller & Bissell, 1983). By the end of Grade 10, the only reliable program effects on IQ and standardized achievement were for boys enrolled in the Montessori curriculum, who had regained some lost ground and were scoring higher than controls. Stallings and Stipek (1986) speculate that the apparent lasting effects for Montessori boys may have been a consequence of a good match between their cognitive capacity and the "individually paced, self-correcting, cognitive materials of the Montessori program" (p. 735). They also point out that assessment of other long-term outcomes such as dropout rates, absenteeism, academic grades, and placement in special education classes might yield differences by sex, sex-by-program interactions, and long-term trends.

Consortium for Longitudinal Studies

In the middle 1970s there was sufficient evidence to indicate that several preschool programs such as High/Scope and Gordon's Parent Education had produced encouraging outcomes. Simultaneously, however, studies of the effectiveness of Head Start and Title I had convinced several critics that early compensatory education had, overall, been ineffective. These conflicting perspectives led officials of the federal Office of Child Development and a group of researchers at Cornell University to believe that a general assessment of the long-term effectiveness of preschool education across a variety of programs initiated in the 1960s was in order (Condry, 1983). The result was the formation at Cornell University, by Irving Lazar and colleagues, of the Consortium for Longitudinal Studies (Lazar et al., 1977; Consortium for Longitudinal Studies, 1983). The Consortium has produced perhaps the most well-known study of the long-term effects of local preschool compensatory education programs to date. A total of 12 research groups representing 14 longitudinal program analyses agreed to participate in the Consortium, including the Perry Preschool Program, which evolved into High/Scope; Miller and Bissell's study of four models in Louisville; and Gordon's Parent Education Program in Florida. The 14 programs were of three broad types: home-based parent programs, center-based preschool programs, and programs that contain both education and home visits.

Two primary types of data were collected and analyzed in the collaborative effort: (1) data collected independently at different times by each program and (2) common follow-up information collected in the 1976–1977 and 1979–1981 school years (when the participants were 9 to 18 years old) by the Consortium. The second type of data came from parent and child interviews, IQ and achievement scores, and information from school records on retention rates, participation in special education classes, and teenage pregnancy. The basic analytical approach for each dependent variable was to determine the difference between treatment and control groups within each program, convert such differences into standard scores, and then pool all standard scores. This procedure resulted in each program having equal weight and assured that each program group was compared to its own control group. The procedure also permitted testing for the presence of an overall "average effect" in the Consortium program (Royce, Darlington, & Murray, 1983, p. 421).

Some of the major findings of the collaborative evaluation are as follows:

1. Participation in the programs increased IQ scores for a period of 3 to 4 years after the preschool experience.
2. Arithmetic and reading scores were higher during most of the elementary years, for program participants.
3. Preschool participants were less likely to be placed in special education or remedial classes than were controls and more likely to be high school graduates.
4. Participants typically had higher self-esteem and valued achievement more than did controls.
5. For the most part, these program effects were present across the three types of programs and in programs that differed in intensity, duration, and age of participants.

Lazar (1983) thus asserts, "We can conclude that any well-designed, professionally supervised program to stimulate and socialize infants and young children from poor minority families will be efficacious" (p. 462). Lazar et al. (1977) argue that these pooled results provide sufficient rationale for increasing research funds for Head Start evaluations, with a larger proportion of such funds being available for field-initiated studies.

These conclusions concord with those of earlier evaluations from the late 1960s and early 1970s of successful preschool programs. Those programs showing the most success had attributes such as the following (McDill et al., 1972): (1) meticulous planning and lucidly stated objectives; (2) high ratio of instructional staff to students; (3) instructional objectives that are closely tied to program objectives; (4) high intensity of treatment; and (5) rigorous training of instructional personnel in the methods and content of the program.

SUMMARY AND CONCLUSIONS

In this chapter we first reviewed the literature on ameliorative efforts to promote the health care of disadvantaged mothers and their children, in an attempt to determine if the physical welfare of each has an influence on the intellectual and academic development of the children. The evidence is persuasive of a strong positive link between the physical health of mothers during pregnancy (especially teenage mothers) and that of their offspring during the perinatal period, infancy, and childhood years. Further, health problems of children have been shown unequivocally to affect adversely a variety of educational outcomes of children, such as IQ, school attendance, and academic performance. In addition, a more recent body of literature has begun to accumulate showing a meaningful positive relationship between (1) the health of mothers and the health care provided them during pregnancy and (2) the intellectual development of their children during the childhood years. Finally, a burgeoning literature indicates that the quality of child care provided by the mother during the perinatal period is directly tied to the physical and intellectual welfare of infants, especially those suffering from perinatal stress.

Long ago realizing the importance of providing adequate health care to poor women and their young children, the federal government established maternal and child health care programs in the 1930s. The decade between 1965 and 1975 brought a major expansion of programs such as the Maternal and Child Health Program, AFDC, Medicaid, and WIC (Davis, 1977). These interventions appear to have lowered infant mortality and morbidity and reduced developmental deficits such as low intelligence of low birthweight children. Further, the limited evidence from cost-effectiveness studies suggests that such efforts can be economically efficient. It also indicates, unfortunately, that federal programs such as Medicaid, WIC, and AFDC at the present typically are reaching fewer than 50% of eligible beneficiaries, a substantial decrease from those reached in the decade that ended in 1975.

Overall, convincing evidence is lacking concerning the effectiveness of state and local maternal and child health care programs because of a dearth of studies and because of methodological shortcomings in those that have been completed (U.S. GAO, 1987b).

Our second task in this chapter was to summarize and evaluate the effectiveness of Head Start, the "largest, broadest intervention program" (Zigler & Berman, 1983, p. 902) at the national level, established in 1965. Several national evaluations and hundreds of evaluations of local Head Start programs have been conducted over the past quarter of a century. The general conclusion is that the program as a whole has become effective in recent years in enhancing the "social competence" (p. 900) of students in coping with their present environment and later adaptation to school life, but that its significant effects on preschoolers' cognitive and affective development have been fairly shortlived, in that differences between treatment and control groups typically disappear or fade by the second grade.

Next, we critiqued four of the most widely acclaimed local preschool programs that originated in the 1960s and have remained credible, in original or modified form, to the present. The two we treated in the most depth and that arguably have remained the most prominent are the Bereiter-Engelmann Academic Preschool Program and the High/Scope Perry Preschool Program. Both have been characterized by attributes that evaluation research dating back to the late 1960s demonstrates are associated with successful outcomes of preschool intervention. Although each of these two programs has produced among the most impressive academic gains of those obtained by preschool programs, the differences between the treatment and control groups in both interventions typically disappeared in the early elementary years. Nevertheless, a series of follow-up studies of the High/Scope subjects into the adolescent and young adult years reveals that they were superior to those from the comparison group on a number of academic and social outcomes such as nonretention in grade, completion of high school, avoidance of going on welfare, and likelihood of having enrolled in postsecondary education.

We also reviewed the recent policy debate between the High/Scope program developers and those of the Bereiter-Engelmann effort, regarding the potential long-term effects on delinquency of the curricula of these two programs. After assessing the evidence in this heated disagreement, we concluded that the original claims made by the High/Scope proponents that the subjects participating in the B-E program engaged in significantly more delinquent acts than those immersed in the High/Scope program, and that direct-instruction programs such as B-E may fail to produce social conformity in adolescence, are not supported by the reasoning and data they have presented.

Finally, we briefly reviewed the results from the Consortium for Longitudinal Studies, which published a series of studies from 1977 through 1983 systematically addressing the issue of long-term effects of 14 of the most prominent local preschool programs on children from ages 9 through 18. The results of this effort indicate that most of these programs had significant long-term effects on affective outcomes such as self-esteem and achievement values, and measurable shorter-term influences on cognitive variables. These findings from the Consortium studies have been instrumental in enhancing public and governmental support for early compensatory programs, especially Head Start (Woodhead, 1988).

In reflecting on the results from a host of evaluations of both national and local preschool programs over the past quarter of a century, our most important conclusion is that the most carefully conceptualized and rigorously designed, implemented, and assessed of these efforts have decreased the educational deficiencies of disadvantaged children in the short term. However, the compensatory education movement has yet to document an appreciable cognitive impact that carries through well into the elementary years. One possible reason for this, as noted by Hartle and Bilson (1986), is that, "in the absence of a clearly agreed upon and articulated set of goals for either program [Head Start or Chapter I], it is hardly surprising that progress toward one rather general objective should be difficult" (p. 25).

This type of criticism seems to us relevant to the large-scale federal programs such as Head Start to which Hartle and Bilson directed it; however, it cannot be usefully applied to the more highly structured and cognitively focused efforts such as the Bereiter-Engelmann Program, whose hallmark was clearly defined cognitive objectives in a highly structured academic environment.

A second popular explanation for the fade-out phenomenon is that elementary schools are not organized to capitalize on the cognitive gains obtained during the preschool period. Stated simply, for many disadvantaged students, schools are essentially environments incompatible with other significant spheres of their lives (Comer, 1980). The effective-schools movement evolved in the 1970s out of this conviction, and it attempted to validate the belief by studying "effective" inner-city schools and abstracting a set of characteristics such as strong administrative leadership, a safe and orderly environment, and a strong academic climate (Edmonds, 1979; Phi Delta Kappa, 1980), which were believed to distinguish such institutions from those urban elementary schools that were plagued by low achievement, high absenteeism, and school vandalism and violence. In organizational terms, the "ineffective" school is viewed by such analysts as insensitive to the special academic and social needs of the concentrations of disadvantaged students they are obligated to serve. This extremely complex matter of organizing schools to create a close fit between the student and the environment is of sufficient importance that we devote all of Chapter 8 to it. There we present a conceptual framework for organizing schools and abstract from it a set of strategies for restructuring schools that could lead to more successful organizational and individual outcomes for their members.

A third popular line of reasoning for the fade-out phenomenon—which, in contrast to the previous two, has been articulated, implemented, and tested—involves the working hypothesis that the cognitive gains obtained in preschool programs have not been built upon or "followed through" in the elementary years. In contrast to the second line of argument, which encompasses a broad range of organizational features of schools, this attempt at explanation more narrowly focuses on how and what is taught in elementary schools, that is, on curricular, pedagogical, and testing matters. The "inadequate-follow-through" proposition was developed in the 1960s after it was found that Head Start failed to sustain the cognitive gains obtained in preschool programs through the early elementary grades. This realization led to the establishment in 1967 of the national program, Project Follow Through, which had the objective of providing educational continuity from kindergarten through Grade 3 in an attempt to sustain and build upon the academic gains attained by children in Head Start and other preschool programs. We review Project Follow Through in the next chapter, in the context of compensatory programs at the kindergarten and elementary levels that have been systematically evaluated over the past 25 years. This broader critique will permit us to address more systematically the assertion by preschool advocates that the disappearance of cognitive gains obtained in well-designed and carefully implemented programs during the early childhood years is attributable to a lack of systematic reinforcement and continuity in the elementary setting.

5

Elementary School Programs

The theoretical literature that provided the intellectual foundations for the rapid growth of compensatory education in the early 1960s emphasized the notion that the preschool years are a critical developmental period for cognitive and personal growth. Although a number of early childhood theorists adhered to this position, it was the publication of Benjamin Bloom's *Stability and Change in Human Characteristics* (1964) that had the major impact in popularizing the unsubstantiated proposition "that proportionately more development occurs during the early years" (Zigler & Berman, 1983, p. 897). However, the almost universal failure of preschool interventions to produce more than short-term effects on the academic development of poor and minority children led both the research community and policy makers to conclude that preschool programs are not adequate to enhance the educational success and life chances of such youngsters. Accordingly, by the early 1970s compensatory programs became "less concentrated on preschool-age children or narrowly focused upon disadvantaged children" (Stallings & Stipek, 1986, p. 741). Many of the most promising developments were directed at kindergarten and/or elementary students and involved either adaptations of existing preschool programs that were extended into the kindergarten and early elementary years (e.g., DISTAR) or innovative methods and techniques that have been used from Grade 2 through high school (e.g., peer tutoring).

In this chapter we deal with three programmatic areas that were significant parts of this expansion of compensatory education into the elementary years. First, we assess Title I/Chapter I, which expends a disproportionate amount of its resources and efforts on students in elementary settings. Next, we provide a brief overview of the explosive growth of kindergarten in the last 25 years and the debates regarding its organization, educational content, and academic effectiveness. Last, we critique a very limited number of local kindergarten and elementary compensatory programs and methods that have evolved since the late 1960s or early 1970s and show promise of enhancing the academic futures of disadvantaged youngsters.

TITLE I/CHAPTER I

The largest compensatory program funded by the federal government is Title I/Chapter I, which was originally authorized by Title I of the Elementary and Secondary Education Act of 1965. Title I was superseded by Chapter I with the enactment of the Education Consolidation and Improvement Act of 1981. We will use the term *Title I* for all information prior to that event and *Chapter I* since then. *Title I/Chapter I* will be employed when information is relevant to both programs.

The ultimate goal of this program is to overcome educational deprivation associated with poverty and race. Both Title I and Chapter I are based on the premise that poverty and academic achievement are substantially related. Consequently, economically disadvantaged students "are more likely to need extra help to compensate for the effects that an impoverished environment has had on their learning" (Kennedy, Jung, & Orland, 1986, p. 2). The complicated formula for allocating Title I/Chapter I funds has always been consonant with this premise, in that monies are distributed "primarily on the basis of the number of school-age students from low-income families who reside in school districts" (p. 2). Districts, in turn, are required to choose participating schools primarily on the basis of the low-income students they serve. Finally, eligible schools must select students on the "basis of their educational needs, rather than on the basis of their family's poverty" (p. 2). Thus, Title I/Chapter I funds are allocated according to both economic and educational needs.

In fiscal year (FY) 1966 the appropriation for Title I was $979 million (McDill et al., 1969); by FY 1985 Chapter I was being funded at more than $3.4 billion annually (serving more than 4.8 million students), constituting approximately 21% of the U.S. Department of Education's budget. Currently, its annual funding level is in excess of $4.3 billion. In the first 20 years of Title I/Chapter I's existence, the program had received more than $45 billion in federal funds (Kennedy, Jung, & Orland, 1986).

Title I/Chapter I funds have been expended at the preschool, elementary, and secondary levels, but they have been concentrated on preschool through Grade 8. School districts have used these funds to develop special curricula for enhancing cognitive skills, especially the subjects of reading, writing, and arithmetic. Districts also use funds to provide classroom aides and to recruit and train teachers who specialize in teaching disadvantaged students. Also, a small percentage of the funds have been spent on health and nutritional services.

From the inception of Title I, the federal government has required that local school districts collect program information for evaluation purposes. During the late 1960s and early 1970s the evaluations of Title I were generally plagued by serious inadequacies, such as the newness of the program, the diverse nature of instructional programs, the lack of cooperation between evaluation teams and local school systems, unreliable data, and flawed methodologies (House, 1979; McDill et al., 1969; McLaughlin, 1977). The few studies that yielded meaningful results did not find that the achievement gap between regular students and Title I participants was narrowed (Levin, 1977; Wargo, Tallmadge, Michaels, Lipe, & Morris, 1972). Further, evaluators often concluded (1) that the selection of schools and students did not assure that the most educationally and economically deprived or "needy" students were being served by the program (e.g., Glass, 1970) and (2) that noncompliance with federal regulations was a major reason Title I did not produce the expected outcomes. Thus, the federal government revamped its rules and guidelines in the 1970s in an attempt to direct funds to the most disadvantaged and deprived students, to implement programs more carefully, to monitor procedures for improved service delivery, and to focus efforts more on increasing the academic skills of students (Levin, 1977; Levine & Havighurst, 1984). Requirements for evaluations at the local, state, and national levels produced a spate of assessments in the early 1970s. The studies tended to indicate that by 1973 students in Title I and other compensatory programs were showing small gains in academic achievement (Lynn, 1973).

Critiques of state studies reported to the federal government, as well as national assessments in the middle 1970s, led some researchers to become more sanguine about the efficacy of Title I. For example, Hendrickson (1977), after reviewing the entire history of Title I evaluations, concluded, "Recent studies for the first time justify cautious optimism in the ability of Title I to raise the reading achievement of disadvantaged children within a given school year" (p. 12). However, Hendrickson's conclusion is not supported by McLaughlin (1977) who, in his contemporaneous review of Title I effectiveness, asserted that "no studies have been completed that provide an unequivocal answer to the question of how much effect Title I has had on achievement" (p. 53).

The Sustaining Effects Study (SES) of compensatory education, the "largest and most comprehensive evaluation of the effectiveness of Title I ever undertaken" (Carter, 1984, p. 6), was initiated in 1975 for the U.S. Office of Education by the Systems Development Corporation. In this multifaceted longitudinal effort, which was completed in 1982, data were collected on roughly 120,000 students in a representative sample of more than 300 elementary schools over 3 consecutive years. One of the major components of the study focused on the impact of Title I services on academic growth over the 3-year span. Four different cohorts of students enrolled in Grades 1 through 4 in 1975 were studied in this segment of the evaluation. The analysis revealed that Title I students achieved statistically significant gains in both math and reading during the first year of the study, and that the gains were greater in math than in reading. Separate analyses for math and reading by duration of treatment indicated that the least disadvantaged students improved their achievement appreciably in 1 year and were likely to be "promoted out" of the program, whereas the most disadvantaged or "needy" students were retained in the program for 3 years and failed to show achievement gains. Further, the study found no evidence of sustained or delayed effects into junior high school. The SES researchers concluded that "Title I was effective for students who were only moderately disadvantaged but it did not improve the relative achievement of the most disadvantaged part of the school population" (p. 7). Overall, "no demonstrated relationship was found between the costs of the instruction students receive and changes in academic achievement" (p. 5).

It is noteworthy that the SES researchers (Carter, 1984) may have overestimated the effects of Title I, in that they used fall achievement tests as the pretest measure and spring tests as the posttest measure. As noted by several evaluation researchers (Horst & Fagan, 1979; Mullin & Summers, 1983; Stonehill, 1985), measuring achievement gains from fall to spring overestimates gains because compensatory education students typically experience achievement losses during the summer months. Thus, a fall-to-fall measure of achievement gains in the SES most likely would have shown a smaller impact of Title I than the fall-to-spring measure they employed.

In a related study of "sustained effects" (Stonehill, 1985) the U.S. Department of Education (ED) examined how different patterns of participation in Chapter I were related to achievement trends over time. One segment of this effort was designed to address some of the same issues studied in the SES. The ED researchers relied exclusively on standardized achievement data obtained from existing school district or state data bases. Their sample consisted of 66,000 elementary school children in a nonrepresentative sample of school districts chosen according to availability of relevant data. Although the sample was purposively drawn, "the overall achievement levels and participation percentages in Chapter I for students in the sample appeared quite similar to overall national figures" (Stonehill, 1985, p. 2). Especially important, the ED staff used a design permitting a comparison between annual test-score gains and fall-to-spring gains and concluded that the former measure provided the more valid estimates of program effects. The most relevant finding from the assessment is consistent with results from the SES: The most disadvantaged students in Chapter I participated longer in the program, yet showed only very slight achievement gains in both math and reading.

Perhaps the second most comprehensive evaluation of Title I in the

1970s was completed by the National Institute of Education (NIE) in 1978. Congress, as part of the reauthorization of the Elementary and Secondary Education Act in 1974, instructed the NIE to conduct a systematic evaluation of compensatory education, especially Title I. The outcome was a seven-volume report (based on more than 35 contracted studies) focusing on funds allocation, service delivery, student development, and program administration (House, 1979). Unlike several prior evaluations by the federal government of the academic effects of Title I, the NIE rejected the notion of a national survey of student development, because the diverse nature of the program would result in "masking the effects" of local site variations (p. 406). Instead, they opted for a design that involved a year-long longitudinal study employing one standardized test of basic skills in 400 classrooms (not randomly chosen) in 14 school districts. Impressive gains in math and reading were reported for both first- and third-grade Title I classes. However, the authors themselves and other knowledgeable evaluation researchers (Glass and Smith, 1977) have questioned these results on a variety of methodological criteria, such as the lack of adequate control groups, the use of overly difficult cognitive tests (resulting in measurement error), and the use of the same tests at three times, which likely led to spurious gain scores attributable to "practice effects."

In a review of later evaluations of Title I in the late 1970s and early 1980s, Levine and Havighurst (1984) concluded that "national data clearly indicate that although Title I has had some positive impact, it has not substantially improved the achievement of disadvantaged students in big cities or otherwise contributed very successfully to the solution of academic problems at inner-city schools" (p. 239). This somewhat discouraging conclusion is consistent with a sophisticated meta-analysis of 47 compensatory education programs (both local and national) by Mullin and Summers (1983), which included roughly equal numbers of Title I and non–Title I program evaluations. Their primary findings are noteworthy because of the rigor of their review and the consistency of their results with the other few well-designed and executed syntheses of Title I/Chapter I evaluations:

1. The programs have a small positive effect on the academic achievement of poor and low-achieving students.
2. Most evaluations overstate the cognitive outcomes of compensatory programs because of faulty methodology that leads to upward biases in the estimation of effects.
3. The fade-out phenomenon is characteristic of the programs, in that cognitive gains are greater in early years, followed by a sharp decline or disappearance of program effects.

4. The programs are not cost effective, because no relationship exists between programmatic costs and achievement gains.
5. No particular model or characteristic of a given model is systematically related to effectiveness.

A more recent evaluation of Chapter I by the U.S. Department of Education (Carpenter & Hopper, 1985), relying on a compilation of annual evaluation reports by school districts receiving Chapter I funds, reached a conclusion similar to that of Mullin and Summers (1983); namely, that Chapter I programs appear to be having a modest positive effect on the academic development of disadvantaged students, especially in the early grades. It is doubtful, however, that the results are sustained into the junior and senior high school years. This assessment is reinforced by the most recent studies, both national and local, that we have been able to locate. Specifically, the national assessment by the Department of Education (Kennedy, Birman, & Demaline, 1986) concludes that:

1. Although Chapter I students experience larger increases in standardized test scores than do comparable nonparticipating students, these effects do little to close the achievement gap between them and advantaged students.
2. Chapter I appears to be more effective in enhancing mathematics achievement than reading achievement.
3. Chapter I is more effective at the early elementary grades than at later grade levels.

Slavin's (1987b) assessment at the local level yields a similar outcome. He contacted each of the 116 Chapter I programs labeled "exemplary" by the ED (Griswold, Cotton, & Hansen, 1986) and reports that all of them that provided multiyear data showed significant achievement gains on fall-to-spring testing. In almost every program, however, these effects had disappeared at the end of 1 year.

Much of the current debate regarding Chapter I's effectiveness revolves around the most appropriate design or structure for delivering its services to students. There are five different types of delivery modes, which are defined by the ED (Birman, Orland, Jung, Anson, & Garcia, 1987) as follows:

Pull-out programs, which remove eligible students from regular classes for special or remedial instruction.
Add-on programs, which provide instruction at times other than the regular school day or school year (e.g., summer school or before or after school).
In-class programs, which deliver services to students in their regular classrooms.

Replacement programs, which provide to eligible students all of the instruction they receive in a given subject. Typically, such instruction occurs in a separate classroom and includes only other compensatory education students.

Schoolwide programs, which provide services to all students in a school serving an attendance area where at least 75 percent of all students are from low-income families. [p. 61]

Carter (1984) noted that the pull-out mode is the most common arrangement for providing Title I/Chapter I services. (In this discussion of issues surrounding pull-out programs, we rely heavily on Slavin, Karweit, Madden, & Stevens, 1986.) There is perhaps no more controversial aspect of Title I/Chapter I than this "restricted" or isolated educational setting (Leinhardt & Pallay, 1982).

Pull-out programs have been criticized on a variety of grounds:

1. There often is a lack of coordination between instruction in the regular and pull-out classes, with teachers rarely and poorly communicating. The result is that poorly achieving students are burdened with having to reconcile different types of instruction.
2. Pull-out programs often "supplant" rather than "supplement" instructional time in basic skills, since the more compensatory programs in which a student is involved, the less instructional time she or he receives.
3. These programs lead to a diminution of the responsibility felt by regular classroom teachers for the academic welfare of disadvantaged students.
4. These programs stigmatize or "label" compensatory education students as inferior in the eyes of both teachers and student peers.

Slavin et al. (1986) emphasize that, despite the controversial nature of pull-out programs, there is little evidence to demonstrate the efficacy of alternative organizational practices (such as in-class instruction utilizing pairs of teachers) on the quality of instruction or student cognitive development. Nevertheless, several researchers have noted that in-class instructional arrangements have a potential advantage in that they permit the use of cooperative learning methods, in which students work in small groups and receive rewards contingent on all group members' individual performance. These have been effective in raising student achievement, improving race relations, and enhancing student perceptions of peer support (Slavin, 1983a, 1983b). Stevens, Madden, Slavin, and Farnish (1986, 1987) have recently developed and field-tested a cooperative learning method for teaching reading and writing to both regular and disadvantaged students in elementary school, which is being adapted as an in-class alternative to the Chapter I pull-out program. The method, Cooperative Integrated Reading and Composition (CIRC), involves low achievers in cooperative activities within academically heterogeneous learning teams, permitting all students an opportunity to contribute to team success. The predicted advantages of CIRC are as follows:

> While students would still receive instruction appropriate to their needs in their reading groups, they would remain in heterogeneous classes and teams at most times, rather than spending time in homogeneously low achieving classes or groups. This should help solve problems of stigmatizing low-achieving Chapter I students, of low expectations for these students, and of behavior problems arising from the presence of many poorly behaved classmates in homogeneously low achieving settings. Problems of coordination between regular and Chapter I teachers should be solved not only by having the two teachers present in the same class, but also by having a common program and objectives for both teachers. [Slavin et al., 1986, p. 127]

Of special importance, the academic effects of CIRC have been systematically compared to those of regular Chapter I programs using a true experimental design. Stevens et al. (1987) found significant effects in favor of CIRC students on a variety of standardized measures of reading and language performance, and on measures of writing and oral reading.

Carefully conceptualized, implemented, and evaluated cooperative learning models such as CIRC appear equipped to accept the challenge posed by Mullin and Summers (1983) in their penetrating critique of compensatory programs such as Title I/Chapter I: "The burden is on the monitors. Rigorous evaluation of compensatory education programs, involving appraisal of achievement and cost-effectiveness, is essential — as is the implementation of the full range of policy recommendations that flow from the evaluation" (p. 342).

THE NATIONWIDE GROWTH OF KINDERGARTEN

Kindergarten attendance has become a common occurrence in education in the United States. For example, at the turn of the century only about 5% of children were enrolled; by the late 1950s slightly more than 50% attended, and by the early 1980s more than 92% of all 5-year-olds in this country attended educational programs, primarily kindergarten (Spodek, 1985). Currently it is estimated that about 93% of all 5-year-olds are enrolled in some form of schooling, mostly in kindergarten (Karweit, 1987b, 1989; Slavin, 1986a).

In recent years the orientation of kindergarten educators has shifted from a focus on the socioemotional development of children to a concern for enhancing their cognitive skills (Karweit, 1987b; Spodek, 1985). This development has been criticized by some childhood education theorists, who argue that formal academic instruction for young children is harmful to them, both in the short and long term. For example, Elkind (1986) asserts that the short-term risks derive from stress placed on young children and that long-term risks are motivational, intellectual, and social in nature. Engelmann and Engelmann (1981) offer a diametrically opposite position.

The growth of kindergarten and its shift from an affective focus to a more structured academic approach in the past 25 years has been accompanied by a trend toward full-day rather than the traditional half-day sessions. It is estimated that in 1961 roughly 90% of all programs were half-day in length. The current estimate is that approximately one-third of public school kindergarten programs involve full-day sessions (Karweit, 1987b). Variation in the scheduling of kindergarten (e.g., half-day sessions every day, compared with full-day sessions every other day) has also been introduced in recent years, apparently with no systematic effects on students (Nurss & Hodges, 1982).

Several studies of the effects on students of the length of the kindergarten day have been conducted in the past two decades. Karweit (1987b) has recently conducted a best-evidence synthesis of this literature, covering the period 1965 through 1985. She evaluated the studies in terms of methodological rigor, quantitatively synthesizing the evidence from the 18 publications that met minimum scientific standards. She further grouped studies by design (random assignment versus nonmatched), population served (regular versus disadvantaged), and timing of assessment (end of kindergarten versus longer term). The only category of study that showed consistent effects of full-day kindergarten on academic growth was that which served disadvantaged students, and such effects were short term (i.e., they existed at the end of the kindergarten experience or shortly thereafter). Karweit (1987b) concludes, however, that extending the kindergarten day is likely to be an effective strategy in promoting academic readiness for first grade, especially for disadvantaged students. Further, she argues that the limited available evidence does not permit firm conclusions concerning which types of kindergarten programs are effective in promoting such development, but that highly structured, language-based curricula are likely to be more effective for students from low socioeconomic backgrounds. She views these tentative conclusions as being consistent with the substantial body of evidence on academic learning time and effective teaching practices, which indicates that the proper utilization of teaching time is more important than the amount of time available for instructional purposes (Karweit, 1987a).

As is evident from Karweit's (1987b) synthesis of kindergarten effects, the volume of systematic research on the issue has not kept pace with the rapid expansion of this level of schooling in American society. Entwisle, Alexander, Cadigan, and Pallas (1987) concur with this position. Those evaluation studies that are available have assessed the effects of kindergarten attendance on IQ; academic readiness for the first grade; and reading, math, and spelling achievement in the early elementary grades. Nurss and Hodges (1982), in reviewing this literature, conclude that kindergarten enrollment has positive effects on such outcomes, but that such benefits usually fade by the end of the third grade. Several of the studies they cite, however, suffer from methodological flaws such as uncontrolled selection factors which raise doubts about the validity of the conclusions (Entwisle et al., 1987).

In attempting to correct such weaknesses, Entwisle et al. (1987) conducted a longitudinal study of a large representative sample of Baltimore first-grade students, to measure the effects of the amount of kindergarten (ranging from no exposure to full-day, full-year participation) on their academic and socioemotional development. They employed an elaborate multivariate model to assess kindergarten effects on a variety of first-grade outcomes. Measures included the California Achievement Test (CAT) in math and language at the beginning and end of Grade 1, report card grades early in Grade 1 and at the end of the year, the students' personal maturity as judged by the teacher, the students' marks in deportment at the beginning and end of the year, student expectations for academic performance early and late in the year, and popularity with peers. They found that more kindergarten leads to early positive effects on selected academic variables (fall CAT scores and first marks in reading and math), which were more pronounced for black students than for whites. This appears to be an instance of the "differential sensitivity" phenomenon originally noted by Coleman et al. (1966), wherein black children are more influenced by school organizational and environmental characteristics than are white students. Further, kindergarten experience had essentially no effects on the socioemotional growth of students. The authors conclude that the amount of kindergarten improves the cognitive status of children on a short-term basis only and does not socialize them for first grade.

Entwisle et al. (1987) draw two related conclusions from this study, which they view as being consistent with prior work on kindergarten effects and relevant to the education of disadvantaged students. First, the short-lived nature of kindergarten effects on academic development is a rather pervasive phenomenon in the study of compensatory education. Nevertheless, this modest first-grade cognitive impact can be compounded over time into larger effects (Entwisle et al., 1987). Quoting Saks (1984), we made the same point in our earlier discussion of preschool programs. Second, the ephemeral nature of kindergarten effects, which are stronger for disadvantaged children, argues for extending compensatory or supplementary education for such children into the elementary grades, in an effort to sustain the temporary benefits of kindergarten attendance.

Recently, Karweit (1989) has conducted a best-evidence synthesis of the content and structure of kindergarten programs for at-risk students, using two primary sources of information—programs approved by the U.S. Department of Education's Joint Dissemination Review Panel (JDRP) and those included in the Office of Educational Research and Improvement's *Effective Education Sourcebook* (Griswold, Cotton, & Hansen, 1986). Like Entwisle et al. (1987), Karweit (1989) concludes that there are few convincing examples of the effectiveness of kindergarten programs in increasing the basic cognitive skills of enrollees. Common weaknesses revealed by such program evaluations include (1) lack of specificity of programmatic goals and reliable measures of them; (2) lack of a close correspondence between goals and measures of outcome; (3) lack of integration of the academic skills proposed in the program and the linguistic and numerical background of students required to acquire such skills; and (4) lack of common goals in programs for treatment and comparison groups, which leads to misleading positive outcomes regarding program effectiveness. Further, the JDRP evaluations generally failed to address the important problem of the relative effectiveness of various kindergarten programs for at-risk populations. Nevertheless, Karweit was able to uncover limited instances of programs that appear to be effective, at least in the short term, in producing positive results. Such examples notwithstanding, she concludes that data are lacking to determine the relative effectiveness of these various promising strategies. In the next section we review some of these examples.

LOCAL KINDERGARTEN AND ELEMENTARY SCHOOL COMPENSATORY PROGRAMS

Many of the promising local elementary programs that have evolved since the 1960s have included a kindergarten component; thus we include such instances in our review, along with those that focus solely on the kindergarten year. The examples of successful programs, briefly reviewed here, have all been evaluated and approved by the JDRP, which signifies that panel members have examined evidence on the program's effectiveness and "are convinced that the program met its stated objectives at the original development or demonstration site. In addition, the program developer has proved that the program will meet the educational needs of others in similar locations" (National Diffusion Network, 1986, p. v). The examples of such programs we present here have also been carefully reviewed by either Karweit

(1989), Madden and Slavin (1989), or Slavin and Madden (1989), who have independently evaluated the evidence for each program submitted by the program developers to JDRP and have concluded that there is credible evidence of program effectiveness, based on a comparison of treatment and control groups. We employ Madden and Slavin's (1989) and Slavin and Madden's (1989) classification scheme and provide a brief critique of one or more programs under each of the following headings: continuous progress programs, cooperative learning/continuous progress programs, individualized instruction programs, tutoring programs, diagnostic/prescriptive programs, and computer-assisted instruction programs.

Continuous Progress Programs

Students in continuous progress programs are taught in small academically homogeneous groups and evaluated on the mastery of specific skills or objectives in a specified time period. Students are frequently regrouped, often across class or grade lines, in an attempt to insure that each of them is working at the appropriate point in the curriculum. An outstanding example of this type of program is the Utah System Approach to Individualized Learning (U-SAIL), which is described by the National Diffusion Network (1986) as "an effective, economic, and exportable system for individualization and improvement of instruction" (p. B4) for use in kindergarten through Grade 9. U-SAIL specifies appropriate tasks for each learner, based on assessment of individual needs. Teaching, monitoring, providing appropriate practice and application of skills acquired, giving students immediate feedback, and accurate record keeping are fundamental attributes of the program.

We have chosen a second very prominent continuous progress program, DISTAR, for brief description and appraisal. It is one of the most widely recognized and frequently assessed efforts of the past 20 years (Becker & Carnine, 1980). As noted earlier, it evolved from the Bereiter-Engelmann (B-E) preschool program. The DISTAR program evolved for two reasons. First, evaluation research in the late 1960s indicated that cognitive gains of B-E students tended to fade fairly early in the elementary grades (Beller, 1973). Second, DISTAR was viewed as one of the most innovative and promising programs in existence and thus was included as part of the Follow Through experiment initiated by the Johnson Administration to determine which compensatory models were able to maintain achievement gains produced by preschool programs through the elementary school years (Stebbins, St. Pierre, Proper, Anderson, & Cerva, 1977). Follow Through was organized on a "planned variation" basis, involving the implementation and evaluation of a substantial number of compensatory models in kindergarten through Grade 3, in a variety of local sites around the country. Thus DISTAR, developed by Wesley Becker and Siegfried Engelmann at the University of Oregon, became one of the fundamental approaches tested in this large and expensive educational experiment.

The basic premise of DISTAR is that virtually all children can learn math, reading, and language if three conditions are met: (1) lessons are designed in such manner that students can grasp the material being presented, (2) significant practice with corrective feedback is provided, and (3) progress through the curriculum is assessed on a regular and systematic basis (Gersten & Carnine, 1984). Students engage in daily programmed learning tasks that require immediate oral responses and must be mastered before moving on to materials of higher levels of difficulty. Students often work in small teaching groups, with teachers and aides engaging in highly structured activities and adhering to scripts and a standard set of instructions. Continuous monitoring of the program is often provided by observation, videotaping of classroom performance, and continuous evaluation, both of student progress and of teacher performance (Gersten & Carnine, 1984).

A large number of evaluations of DISTAR by both its developers and outsiders offers consistent evidence that the program is effective in teaching basic skills in subjects such as math and reading. For example, in the original nationwide evaluation of Follow Through conducted by Abt Associates (Bock, Stebbins, and Proper, 1977), DISTAR was by far the most successful program in lessening the academic deficits of disadvantaged students. However, in a trenchant critique of this evaluation, House, Glass, McLean, and Walker (1978) concluded that the Abt study was sufficiently flawed in terms of design, measurement, data analysis, and interpretation that one could not make an informed judgment of which Follow Through models were effective or ineffective. Further, in their own limited reanalysis of a portion of the Abt data House et al. found no evidence of statistically significant differential effectiveness among the various Follow Through models or between them and other programs.

A number of other observers acknowledge several shortcomings of the Abt evaluation (e.g., Becker, 1978; Bereiter & Kurland, 1981–1982a; Kennedy, 1978; Levine & Havighurst, 1984; McDaniels, 1975). These weaknesses include (1) lack of adequacy of outcome measures, especially their limited range in relation to the breadth of objectives promised by Follow Through sponsors; (2) high attrition rates of students, teachers, and sites; (3) methodological problems in comparing gain scores at different levels of performance; and (4) difficulty in determining whether a particular model at a specific site was properly implemented, in order to provide an adequate test of its effectiveness. Despite these shortcomings several knowledgeable par-

ticipants in the Follow Through program, as well as researchers independently conducting their own analyses of the Follow Through data, either
explicitly or implicitly reject the categorically negative conclusions of House
et al. (1978) that the program evaluation yielded essentially no results of
scientific or educational policy value regarding compensatory education
(Anderson, St. Pierre, Proper, & Stebbins, 1978; Wisler, Burns, & Iwamoto,
1978).

One systematic reanalysis effort of Follow Through was conducted by
Bereiter and Kurland (1981–1982a). Rather than comparing various Follow
Through models with non-Follow Through programs, as had both Abt
(Bock, Stebbins, & Proper, 1977) and House et al. (1978), Bereiter and
Kurland (1981–1982a) used site means for various achievement measures to
compare the relative effectiveness of different Follow Through models. The
major outcome of this analysis, which directly contradicts the conclusions
of House et al. (1978), is that on every subtest of the Metropolitan Achievement Test (MAT) Bereiter and Kurland (1981–1982a) found significant differences among the Follow Through models, with the results favoring two
"structured" or "behavioral" approaches (direct instruction and behavior
analysis) that "give a priority to the three R's" (p. 17). Further, their results
indicated that the two lowest-scoring models were "child-centered," which
they concluded have *"evolved sophisticated ways of managing informal
educational activities but . . . have remained at a primitive level in the design of means to achieve learning objectives"* (p. 20, italics in original).

Given the weaknesses of the original Follow Through study, some of
which we have just adumbrated, one should be cautious in drawing conclusions from any reanalysis of the data, however sophisticated. However, there
is a high degree of "consensual validation" for the findings of Bereiter and
Kurland (1981–1982a) concerning direct-instruction models for disadvantaged elementary school students. For example, Stallings' (1975) research on
Follow Through models revealed that first- and third-grade students in the
Oregon Direct Instruction model performed higher in math and reading
than those in six other models in the Follow Through experiment. Further,
Becker (1978) showed that for 6 cohorts of students in 13 sites in the Follow
Through program, from kindergarten through Grade 3, disadvantaged students in DISTAR scored at or above the national norms on every subtest
except one of the MAT and the Wide Range Achievement Test (WRAT).

The results from more long-term evaluations of DISTAR are also encouraging. For example, Becker and Gersten (1982) assessed the later effects
of the model, in five diverse Follow Through sites, on fifth- and sixth-grade
students from low socioeconomic backgrounds who had spent 3 years in the
program. They employed a quasi-experimental design involving comparison
groups of students with similar sociodemographic characteristics. Their

analysis revealed that, in most cognitive domains covered by the MAT and WRAT, the DISTAR students scored significantly higher than the controls who had not attended the program. On the negative side, Becker and Gersten (1982) found that, when measured against national norms, the students "lose ground in the three years after they leave Follow Through" (p. 89). They conclude that, for gains in the early elementary grades to be sustained into the adolescent and adult years, high-quality structured compensatory education is necessary.

A second long-term evaluation of DISTAR's effectiveness is reported by Meyer (1984), who followed into high school a sample of students from an extremely disadvantaged neighborhood school in Brooklyn, New York, who were enrolled in the program from kindergarten through third grade. The control group consisted of students from an elementary school in the same district with similar patterns of achievement and comparable ethnic and socioeconomic backgrounds, but who had not participated in the program. In the ninth-grade comparisons the DISTAR students scored significantly higher in math and reading than the control group. Further, they were more likely to graduate from high school and more likely to apply for and be accepted into college than were the comparison students.

Unfortunately, there are almost no evaluations of DISTAR for the kindergarten year *per se,* in contrast to a large number for the combined years of kindergarten through third grade. An exception is reported by Gersten, Darch, and Gleason (1988), who analyzed data from East St. Louis, Illinois, one of the original Follow Through sites. They compare performance in reading, math and language for a kindergarten and a first grade cohort of disadvantaged students, each of whom received the direct-instruction curriculum through Grade 3. A "demographically similar quasi-experimental comparison group" (p. 231) which received the school district's traditional curriculum was employed for each cohort, and achievement data were available for all four groups for Grades 3 and 9. Consistent with results from earlier studies, students receiving DISTAR generally scored significantly higher in the three academic areas in Grade 3 than did those enrolled in the traditional academic program. In addition, those students enrolled in DISTAR in kindergarten scored significantly higher in all three areas than those enrolled in the program in the first grade, with the strongest effects appearing in reading.

Comparisons of the various groups by treatments at Grade 9 revealed the following results: (1) with only one exception, DISTAR students outperformed their comparison groups in all three academic areas, and (2) students enrolled in the academic program in kindergarten achieved at a higher level in reading, language, and math than did their peers who enrolled in the first grade. As noted by Carnine, Carnine, Karp, & Weisberg (1988), the results from this study "suggest an enduring effect from the extra year of intensive instruction provided by a direct instruction kindergarten" (p. 85). Gersten et al. (1988) are cautious in drawing generalizations from this single investigation because a true experimental design was not employed, making it impossible to rule out selection biases as the valid explanation for the observed effects of both the kindergarten experience and the DISTAR curriculum. Nevertheless, these suggestive findings are consistent with a substantial body of literature (Stallings & Stipek, 1986), some of which we cited earlier, indicating that, with few exceptions, DISTAR has been an effective curriculum model for teaching basic academic skills to educationally disadvantaged students in the pre-primary and primary years.

Cooperative Learning/Continuous Progress Programs

Slavin (1986a), one of the major contributors to the literature on cooperative learning, defines it as any of several practical classroom methods of group learning in which students work in small, mixed-ability learning teams, with the instruction delivered to homogeneous groups drawn from the teams. Activities within the teams can be individualized, paired, or whole-team, with teams being evaluated and/or rewarded on the basis of how much each team member improves. The basic rationale underlying cooperative learning methods is that, since each student's performance enhances the success of the entire group, individual team members are motivated to work toward a common academic goal. A variety of cooperative learning methods have been developed and systematically evaluated in the past two decades (Slavin, 1983a, 1983b). The results imply that this approach can be effective in increasing student achievement, especially that of disadvantaged students (Johnson, Maruyama, Johnson, & Nelson, 1981), improving interracial cooperation (Slavin & Oickle, 1981), and enhancing student self-esteem and confidence (Slavin, 1983a).

Two of the most prominent cooperative learning methods developed for elementary school students are Team-Assisted Individualization (TAI) and Cooperative Integrated Reading and Composition (CIRC), which were produced by Robert Slavin and colleagues at the Johns Hopkins University Center for the Social Organization of Schools. We earlier discussed CIRC in our review of in-class alternatives to Chapter I pull-out programs; thus we will confine ourselves here to a brief overview of TAI. This program was developed in an attempt to overcome some of the problems associated with programmed instruction such as low quality of instruction, poor student motivation, and loss of instructional time. Our description of TAI here is paraphrased from Slavin (1986a, pp. 324–327).

TAI (Slavin, Leavey, & Madden, 1984) combines cooperative learning and individually programmed instruction approaches in the teaching of mathematics for Grades 2 through 8. As in programmed instruction models, students in TAI work on individualized self-instruction materials at their own levels and paces. However, the individualized work is carried out in multi-ability learning teams consisting of four members. Since the teams are rewarded (with certificates and recognition) on the accuracy and number of assignments completed by all team members, members provide assistance to each other, use answer sheets to check each other's work for accuracy, and encourage each other to work accurately and rapidly. The mutual assistance provided by team members frees the teacher to teach groups of students drawn from the various teams who are performing at the same level in the individualized programs, a form of within-class ability grouping. Dividing students into these teaching groups is designed to solve the problem of quality of instruction by having instruction come from the teachers rather than solely from written materials. Also, utilizing a team reward and a student checking system motivates students, individually and collectively, to work accurately and rapidly and encourages greater time on task. Slavin (1986a) argues that TAI, in contrast to earlier programmed instruction approaches, is effective in enhancing mathematics performance, and he cites several studies to buttress his claim. For example, Slavin (1985) reports on six studies involving students in Grades 3 through 6 which show that TAI students gained, on average, twice as many grade equivalents in math computation as did students taught in traditional classes (Slavin & Karweit, 1985; Slavin et al., 1984).

Although TAI and related cooperative learning methods require more long-term and varied replications, the evidence to date indicates that they show considerable promise in providing individual students with instruction at their own level while utilizing the peer group to address the managerial and motivational problems inherent in individualized instruction (Slavin et al., 1984).

Individualized Instruction Programs

Individualized instruction programs are designed to accommodate the needs of each learner by tailoring instruction precisely to his or her aptitudes. Students progress through a well-defined sequence of objectives, without constant supervision, and are frequently assessed. Teachers work closely with individual students. Perhaps the best-known example of this approach is the Behavior Analysis model developed at the University of Kansas by Donald Bushel and colleagues (Becker, 1978; National Diffusion Network, 1986). The program focuses on basic skills in reading, arithmetic, handwriting, and spelling for kindergarten through Grade 3. It makes systematic use of positive reinforcement to achieve clearly stated instructional objectives. A classroom staff consisting of a certified teacher, a teacher's aide, and a parent educator allow for small-group and individualized instruction. Programmed instructional materials are used extensively to permit individual learners to proceed at their own rate. Social praise, tokens that can be traded for desired activities, and a contract system are employed by all members of the teaching team. The staff utilize curricular materials that accommodate a continuous progress monitoring system. They make systematic efforts to involve parents in many phases of the learning process, as instructional personnel and as active participants in policy-making bodies. As educators, parents are provided training in the relevant phases of the program.

In analyses of the data from the nationwide evaluation of Follow Through conducted by Abt Associates (Stebbins et al., 1977), two highly structured, direct-instruction models, DISTAR and Behavior Analysis, were the most successful in raising the mathematics and reading achievement of disadvantaged students (Stallings & Kaskowitz, 1974). Further, these results were corroborated by Bereiter and Kurland (1981–1982a) in their more recent reanalysis of the Follow Through data, which we discussed earlier. Finally, Ramp and Rhine (1981) present a variety of data from the national evaluation of the Behavior Analysis model as part of Project Follow Through and reach conclusions consistent with those of the original evaluation team (Stebbins et al., 1977) and Bereiter and Kurland (1981–1982a).

A local Follow Through site which has systematically evaluated the Behavior Analysis model is in Trenton, New Jersey. There, the Behavior Analysis approach is used to teach reading, arithmetic, and language arts to disadvantaged students in kindergarten through Grade 3 (Barber, 1977). The program was assessed by the site team in conjunction with the University of Kansas sponsor. In the evaluation of reading performance it was shown that seven cohorts of students (K–3) continuously enrolled in the program from 1969 (the end of the first program year) through the spring of 1975 scored at or above grade level in 16 of the 22 data points on the Wide Range Achievement Test (WRAT). The second evaluation of reading performance, unlike the first, involved a comparison group. Students in all four grades (K–3) who had been continuously enrolled in the program for the 1974–1975 school year were compared with all students from a control school who never enrolled in the program but were comparable on several relevant sociodemographic characteristics. For all grades, the average scores on the WRAT were above grade level for the treatment group but below grade level for the control group. Third-grade students in the program were, on the average, 2 months above grade level, while the comparison group was 6 months below. In another component of the 1974–1975 evaluation, the WRAT results on reading, arithmetic, and spelling for students continuously enrolled in the program (K–3) were compared with those for control students. Across all subject areas statistically significant differences favoring the treatment group were found in 10 of 12 instances. By third grade the treatment group was, on the average, 9 months above the control group in reading, 5 months ahead in spelling, and 4 months in front in arithmetic.

The local implementers of the program and the University of Kansas sponsors (reported in Barber, 1977) interpret the following results as additional strong evidence that the Behavior Analysis program is of educational significance. First, the relative stability of mean scores on the WRAT for each grade level from year to year indicates the successful replication of program effects with seven successive cohorts of students. Second, students in the program rather consistently scored at or above the expected grade-level norms in reading. Slavin and Madden (1989), however, note the extreme cross-site variability in the effects associated with the Behavior Analysis program. Given the overall effectiveness of the program, such intersite discrepancies appear more likely to be a consequence of variation in the fidelity of local implementation rather than inadequacies in the design and development of the program by its originators.

Tutoring Programs

In tutoring programs, where the instruction is on a one-to-one basis (Ellson, 1976), low-achieving students are provided instruction either by an adult paraprofessional or volunteer or by a peer (either same-age or cross-age) on a frequent basis. Adult tutoring by professionals has long been recognized as an effective means of increasing the academic performance of the tutee; however, its chief drawback has been its high cost (Slavin, 1986a). One approach to this problem has been to use adult volunteers such as parents or senior citizens to provide the one-on-one instruction. School systems now use large numbers of adult paraprofessionals as tutors, making widely available an instructional strategy that once was considered a luxury for elite segments of society (Cohen, Kulik, & Kulik, 1982).

In the past two decades several narrative reviews of studies on the effects of peer tutoring in the late 1960s, 1970s, and 1980s indicated that tutoring programs can, depending on their attributes and conditions, contribute to the achievement of both tutors and tutees (e.g., Devin-Sheehan, Feldman, & Allen, 1976; Ehly & Larsen, 1980; Ellson, 1976; Fitz-Gibbon, 1977; Rosenshine & Furst, 1969). More recently, Bloom (1984) has noted that students in effective peer tutoring programs achieve at higher levels than those in conventional or mastery-learning situations.

Of special importance to success are highly structured programs that employ a programmed approach (Slavin, 1986a) in which tutors are given explicit, cognitively oriented instructions that they follow precisely. A more recent, comprehensive, and rigorous evaluation of peer tutoring effectiveness has been provided by Cohen et al. (1982), who conducted a meta-analysis of 65 studies that met minimum methodological standards such as employing both treatment and control groups. Their statistical analysis revealed a set of results generally consistent with the earlier reviews, in that peer tutoring was shown to have "modest" positive effects on the achievement of the tutored students. By "modest," Cohen et al. (1982) meant that "the average child in the tutored group scored at the 66th percentile of the students in the untutored or control group" (p. 241). The tutees also expressed more positive attitudes toward the subjects being taught, but showed no change in self-concept. Effects on student tutors were also encouraging, in that, on average, they performed higher on exams in the subjects they were teaching and their attitudes toward those subjects improved moderately. However, no meaningful effects on tutors' self-esteem were discovered. Of special significance, Cohen et al. found that structured programs produced stronger achievement results for both tutors and tutees than the less-structured ones.

Levin and colleagues (Levin, Glass, & Meister, 1984; Levin & Meister, 1986) have recently extended the knowledge base on tutoring effects by conducting a cost-effectiveness analysis of both peer and adult tutoring in comparison with three other types of interventions—reduced class size, computer-assisted instruction (CAI), and a longer school day. Their results show unequivocally that peer tutoring is the most cost-effective of the four interventions, for both reading and math achievement. Niemiec, Blackwell, and Walberg (1986), however, challenged the validity of these conclusions and asserted that CAI is more cost-effective than peer tutoring. In a rejoinder to Niemiec et al. (1986), Levin, Glass, and Meister (1986) staunchly defended their findings and argued persuasively that their original conclusions were valid. These reviews of the literature on peer tutoring indicate that this form of individualized instruction produces moderate positive benefits, both cognitive and affective, for both tutor and tutee.

Two JDRP-approved tutoring programs in the greater Miami, Florida area exemplify the attributes of successful tutoring approaches identified in the literature just reviewed. One of them, the School Volunteer Development Project (National Diffusion Network, 1986), provides a delivery system of adult school volunteer services that focuses on student learner needs for math and science in Grades 2 through 6. The program includes a comprehensive plan, the accompanying support materials, recruitment procedures, training for volunteers, and a systematic evaluation system for all phases of the effort.

A second tutoring program in the Dade County, Florida public schools,

Training for Turnabout Volunteers (TTV), is a cross-age tutor-training program that prepares students in Grades 7 through 9 to serve as reading or math tutors for low-achieving students in Grades 1 through 6 (National Diffusion Network, 1986). The program includes a multimedia training program and an extensive delivery system for the tutors, who participate in a large number of training sessions that provide them with teaching skills and strategies applicable to the tutee's curriculum. The preservice training program is divided into minicourses, each of which has videotaped lessons for concept development, workbooks with practice and extension activities for the tutor, and reinforcement activities for use with tutees. Tutors then attend in-service training in a math or reading course and engage in tutoring of elementary students. The delivery system includes strategies and procedures for close monitoring and evaluation of the program.

Evidence on the effectiveness of TTV in its home site and its likely replicability in other settings is found in the submission forms to the JDRP from the program coordinator (Bullock, 1981). The program was approved by the JDRP in June 1981. The evaluation results were derived from an analysis of covariance of data on reading and math performance from the MAT, using a nonequivalent control group design. It revealed that tutees taught by the trained tutors performed significantly higher on both reading and math than did those students taught by the untrained tutors. The mean differences between the two groups on math and reading (.92 and .51 standard deviation units, respectively) were described as educationally significant (Bullock, 1981). Regarding effects on tutors, it was shown that those trained in the program scored significantly higher (approximately one-half of a standard deviation) on mathematics than did the untrained tutors, but no differences existed between the two groups on reading achievement. The program staff attribute this lack of difference in reading performance to the greater difficulty in teaching reading than teaching mathematics (Bullock, 1981). The developers of the program and the JDRP view these results as indicating that cross-age peer tutoring has educational benefits for both tutors and tutees. The training of the former enhances their cognitive skills, which they, in turn, are able to employ successfully in raising the reading and math skills of the latter.

Diagnostic/Prescriptive Programs

Diagnostic/prescriptive programs are defined typically as Title I/Chapter I pull-out programs involving careful diagnosis of student needs followed by prescriptions based on such diagnosis. Special instruction is presented either to individuals or small groups, usually within a small pull-out class ranging in size from three to eight (Madden & Slavin, 1989). Our choice of an example of this type is called Make Every Child Capable of Achieving

(MECCA), a kindergarten program that originated in Meriden, Connecticut. It is described as follows by the National Diffusion Network (1979):

> In the MECCA program, a learning disabilities teacher, with the help of the classroom teacher and a classroom aide, provides daily intervention and observation within the regular kindergarten classroom for children with potential learning problems. (The MECCA programs provide daily observation, profiling, and intervention of such services.) The program utilizes a team made up of a special education teacher, a classroom teacher, and an aide, who together analyze the activities of the curriculum into the tasks that a child must accomplish in order to be successful in the activity. The purposes of this task analysis process are to think carefully about what is asked of the child and to observe where the child is successful and where he/she needs help. The intervention aspect of the MECCA program is based on the principle of beginning at the level where the child achieves success and proceeding sequentially through the difficult steps to new successes. After the initial training period, the classroom teacher and the special education teacher train each other to combine teaching strategies and curricula for individualized instruction. [p. 5-29]

During the period 1973 to 1979, the project was frequently evaluated by an outside agency, which found "significant differences on standardized measures of readiness compared with children in both alternate treatment and control groups. On standardized measures, 70% of the MECCA children evidence average or above-average performance in readiness skills at the end of kindergarten" (National Diffusion Network, 1979, p. 5-29).

Karweit (1989) provides more recent and detailed evaluation information on the program, and it reinforces these earlier positive results. Karweit's findings are based on an experimental design involving random assignment of students to experimental and control groups using the Jansky Predictive Screening Index, which is composed of five predicting tests: letter naming, picture naming, Gates Word Matching, Bender Motor Gestalt, and the Binet Sentence Memory. She reports large differences in posttest effect sizes, ranging from .57 to .96 on various tests, and concludes that "the curriculum, materials, and approach are important factors in MECCA's effectiveness. Screening, diagnosis, and task analysis of learning activities target the time and resources within the school in a productive way, especially for students very much at risk of future failure" (p. 135).

Computer-Assisted Instruction

Computer-assisted instruction (CAI) is part of the broader concept of computer-based interactive instruction (Hall, 1982). CAI, or tutorial instruction, assumes that the learner is approaching the content to be learned for the first time. Therefore, new content is presented in an expository style followed by (1) a question to which the learner will respond, (2) a computer analysis of the learner's responses, (3) appropriate feedback, and (4) presentation of new material (or questions) to fit the demonstrated need of the learner. [p. 354]

Research on the effectiveness of using computers as an instructional device dates back to the middle 1960s (Hall, 1982), with a series of research syntheses and meta-analyses of these earlier studies being conducted between 1980 and 1985 (Becker, 1986). In reviewing these syntheses and meta-analyses, Becker states that the CAI programs conducted in the 1960s and 1970s "were generally more effective in raising students' scores on standardized tests than alternative approaches" (p. 84). Nevertheless, he challenges the relevance of these earlier studies to the current usage of computers in schools because the individual studies on which they were based utilized obsolete hardware and software and used computers in the classroom differently than they typically are used today. In addition, at least two authors (Becker, 1986; Clark, 1985) point out methodological weaknesses in both the individual evaluation studies and the research syntheses and meta-analyses that utilized the individual studies.

Becker (1986) focuses his best-evidence synthesis on more recent studies of CAI effectiveness in schools that use microcomputers and their software, observing that more than 95% of the computers now in use in schools are microcomputers. Using a set of stringent criteria for selecting studies that have been completed since 1984 and included academic effects, he uncovered only 17 that provided reliable and valid results. Two of his conclusions are especially relevant to our interest here. First, most recently completed studies of CAI are inadequate on one or more of the following standards: research design, reporting detail, size, score, and time frame. Second, available evidence of CAI effectiveness is "scanty" (p. 81) and the evaluation studies overall provide only limited guidance for how schools should employ microcomputer hardware and software in the teaching/learning process. Nevertheless, Becker did locate a very limited number of sophisticated studies that provide unequivocal evidence of both statistical and educationally significant effects on cognitive skills such as math, reading, and logic.

We use here one of the local programs reviewed positively by Becker (1986) as our example of a successful microcomputer CAI program. Called Basic Literacy Through Microcomputers, it has been systematically implemented and evaluated in Salt Lake City, Utah. Recently it has been designated as a JDRP-approved program (National Diffusion Network, 1987). The program, designed for Grades 1 and 3 and also tested in Grades 2 through 8, focuses on reading achievement and computer keyboard skills. It employs a phonetic approach to reading, with a microcomputer or electric typewriter as an integral part of instruction. The instructional process stresses typing skills, oral activities with computer programs directed by the teacher, and rapid recognition of words flashed on the computer screen. The teacher and class work together in the school's computer laboratory. The student typically spends 30 minutes per day using the various programs.

The program developers report summary information indicating positive effects of the program on reading comprehension, speed-and-accuracy scores, typewriting, and computer usage skills (National Diffusion Network, 1987). Becker (1986), utilizing more detailed information supplied by the developer, corroborates claims of the program staff concerning treatment effects. He reports on data covering Grades 1 through 6, split among two elementary schools which were compared with control classes from the same schools. Becker concludes that the program has huge effects on reading and math scores from the MAT; namely, an average effect size of 1.0 in favor of the treatment group across six grade levels. An effect of this magnitude indicates a quadrupling of achievement gains of the treatment group over the comparison group during the 4-month period of evaluation.

SUMMARY AND CONCLUSIONS

Our review of compensatory programs at the kindergarten and elementary levels provides mixed results. The evaluations of Title I/Chapter I over the past 20 years indicate that some progress has been made in this largest of all federal initiatives. In both the late 1960s and early 1970s one could fairly label the program as a qualified failure in that there were very few rigorous evaluations of Title I, and those that did meet minimal scientific standards produced either null or ambiguous results concerning the achievement of participating students.

Critiques of the local and national studies of Title I in the middle and late 1970s led researchers to more optimistic overviews of the program, despite disagreements about the validity of the research base. Research in the decade between 1975 and 1985 led to the justifiable conclusion that, although Chapter I students attained short-term academic benefits, the program has not yielded positive results on a long-term basis. These findings are reinforced by the most recent local and national studies (Kennedy, Birman, & Demaline, 1986; Slavin, 1989; Stein, Leinhardt, & Bickel, 1989), which correspond to the recent conclusion of Levine and Havighurst (1989) that "Chapter I students appear to make small gains in reading and math but . . . these gains do relatively little to offset their large learning deficits" (p. 293).

In short, our view is that Chapter I now, relative to its status 20 years ago, can be labeled as a highly qualified success in two related respects. First, we now have a limited number of fairly rigorous (not ideal, but careful) assessments of the program. Second, there is a substantial degree of consistency across these studies to the effect that Chapter I has produced short-term effects on the academic growth of at-risk pupils.

Our overview of kindergarten as a component of the American educational system serving disadvantaged students leads to four straightforward conclusions. First, it is rapidly becoming an integral part of our educational system, with fewer than 8% of all 5-year-olds not currently enrolled. Second, it is shifting away from an emphasis on students' socioemotional growth and toward a focus on their cognitive development, with a concern for mastery of reading or reading readiness, number concepts, and language acquisition (Wynn & Wynn, 1988). This shift from an affective focus to a more structured academic approach is linked to a trend toward full-day rather than half-day program activities. Third, participation in kindergarten "appears to be beneficial for disadvantaged students" (Karweit, 1987b, p. 33). Fourth, there is rather convincing evidence of the effectiveness of a limited number of programs in accelerating the academic development, on a short-term basis, of kindergarten enrollees. However, these evaluations do not provide evidence on the various programs' effectiveness for at-risk students, in that data typically are not available on the race, sex, academic aptitude, and socioeconomic background of students. As pointed out by Karweit (1989), however, it is likely that kindergarten programs whose effectiveness has been replicated across sites are effective for most students, since aptitude-by-treatment interactions in compensatory programs for elementary school students have been detected only infrequently.

Perhaps the most obvious shortcoming of this body of literature is a lack of evidence on the relative effectiveness of the various programs and on their cost effectiveness. Thus, it is important that a systematic program of research be launched using randomized field experiments to test various initiatives.

Given the approaching universality of kindergarten in our society, however, school systems need to make informed programmatic decisions now about the nature of the kindergarten experience. A sufficient knowledge base appears to exist to offer the following two suggestions (McDill, Karweit, Natriello, & Pallas, 1989). First, school districts should specify and articulate their priorities regarding the kindergarten year and select one or more validated programs that correspond to those priorities. Second, districts should be prepared to experiment with programmatic alternatives, to determine the conditions under which various strategies are more or less effective in the differing local settings. We hope such an approach will provide a basis in the foreseeable future for making informed decisions about how kindergarten can provide the most effective mediating link between preschool and first grade for disadvantaged children.

In conducting a critique of elementary school and kindergarten/ elementary compensatory programs, we have employed a typology that subsumes the following categories: continuous progress programs, cooperative learning/continuous programs, individualized instruction programs, tutoring programs, diagnostic/prescriptive programs, and computer-assisted instruction programs. Under each of these headings we located one or more examples of a local initiative that provided systematic evidence of differences between treatment and comparison groups, favoring the former. Such programs tend to be flexible in that they are sensitive to adjusting instruction to the individual needs of students while maximizing academically focused, teacher-directed activities involving sequenced and structured approaches. In these programs students are taught a hierarchy of skills and are frequently evaluated on the acquisition of such skills (Rosenshine, 1979; Slavin & Madden, 1989). Programs such as DISTAR and cooperative learning exemplify these important characteristics.

Although the results of the limited number of rigorous evaluations of both national and local elementary programs reviewed in this chapter are somewhat encouraging, in that they provide evidence indicating that the programs are having a short-term cognitive impact on students, these results are far from adequate in two respects. First, as a number of spokespersons have emphasized (e.g., Committee for Economic Development, 1987; Grant Foundation Commission, 1988; Levin, 1985), the severity of the learning deficits of disadvantaged students is such that their participation in the typical Chapter I program, for example, does no more than raise their performance to the top of the bottom quartile on tests in critical skills areas. The long-term consequences of such modest effects is that by the 10th grade one of two of these students will be a dropout and/or functionally illiterate (Levin, 1985).

The current outcome is inadequate in a second respect; namely, the magnitude of the problem in terms of the disadvantaged population is already daunting, and it will grow rapidly for the next 30 years, as we have shown in Chapters 2 and 3. What are the implications of these sociodemographic changes for the future role of compensatory education, especially the large federal efforts such as Head Start and Chapter I? One needs to make a tenable assumption to confront this critical issue. Both Head Start and Chapter I are politically alive and well, in that they have significant political support in Congress and thus are likely to have modest budgeting increases in the near future, just as they have received in the recent past. Given the overwhelming federal deficit problems, however, funding for educational amelioration initiatives is not likely to grow in concert with the severity and magnitude of our educational deficit problems. This means that federal, state, and local initiatives in compensatory education will have to be more efficient and effective in closing the academic gap between disadvantaged and advantaged students.

Unfortunately, carefully planned, executed, and evaluated programs of the types we have critiqued in this chapter are typically not used in kindergarten and elementary schools, especially those sponsored by Chapter I. In fact, as Slavin (1987b) has recently noted, historically such promising programs have not been implemented in most schools under Chapter I, because they would be serving non–Chapter I students, in violation of Chapter I regulations. Because of such restrictions, most school districts have relied on pull-out programs to insure that only students eligible for Chapter I receive those services. Slavin and Madden (1989) have offered a list of steps which need to be established by federal authority to increase the effectiveness of the massive Chapter I program:

> One approach to identifying effective, transportable instructional models for students at risk would be learning from the mistakes of the Planned Variation Follow Through evaluation but trying again to accomplish its objectives. A very small proportion of the enormous Chapter I budget, for example, could fund development of promising models, evaluation and component analyses of such models, and ultimately evaluation of the models in new sites with multiple measures (not only standardized tests), with random assignment of programs to schools. . . . In this way, we could finally achieve the ambitious goals of Chapter 1 to make a meaningful difference in the lives of disadvantaged students. [p. 47]

We would add that there is an urgent need for providing the financial and human resources to insure that such scientifically verified models are adequately disseminated to educational practitioners and also communicated to the public in a clear and concise manner, in order to build a political constituency that will guarantee the secure future of the compensatory education enterprise.

6

Secondary School Programs

Programs to assist disadvantaged students at the secondary level have been many and varied. Despite the fact that most federal funds for compensatory education have supported programs at the elementary level, efforts at the local, state, and federal levels have combined to provide a wide range of offerings in secondary schools. Although, for the most part, only the federally supported programs have been carefully evaluated, there are many interesting and seemingly effective programs at the secondary level that deserve serious consideration by those interested in enhancing the educational achievement and attainment of disadvantaged youngsters.

We consider these programs under four broad categories suggested by the major reasons that students perform poorly in and withdraw from school at the secondary level. Two of these categories focus on different dimensions of a student's experience in school. Students are motivated to attend to the demands placed upon them by schools when they have opportunities for academic success and for positive social relationships in school. When either of these kinds of opportunities is lacking students may perform poorly and eventually withdraw from school. Some secondary school programs primarily attempt to provide for academic success and others seek to provide positive social relationships for disadvantaged youth.

Two additional categories of programs focus on conditions outside of school that affect the performance and attendance of disadvantaged students. Students are motivated to attend and perform well in schools when they perceive the activities of the school program to be relevant to their future lives outside of school and when factors in their lives outside of school, such as personal, family, and community conditions, are conducive to participation in school. When either of these conditions is absent, students are likely to perform less well and/or to drop out of school. Some school programs seek to enhance the perceived relevance of school to students' future lives, while others seek to mitigate any negative effects of outside interferences.

In this chapter we discuss each of these four reasons for poor school performance and early school leaving among disadvantaged youth, in each case reviewing general programmatic approaches to improving the performance and attainment of these students. We also provide several major examples to illustrate each approach. The programs included as examples have not all been carefully evaluated, but where they have been, we examine the results. Programs with evaluations that did not show them to be effective and those without careful evaluations are included as illustrations of the various approaches only when no programs with documented positive effects could be identified. This is necessary because most programs have not been carefully evaluated. This strategy is appropriate when null effects are the result of improper implementation rather than a poor theory of action.

ACADEMIC SUCCESS IN SCHOOL

One of the strongest correlates of dropping out found in research on students is the lack of academic success in school (Ekstrom, Goertz, Pollack, & Rock, 1987; McDill, Natriello, & Pallas, 1985; 1986; Wagenaar, 1987). Students who obtain low grades, fail subjects, and are retained in grade have a much higher probability of performing poorly and subsequently leaving school before high school graduation. Simply put, many students who have trouble meeting the academic demands of school will leave rather than persist in the face of the frustration they often experience trying to pass their courses. Even among those disadvantaged students who remain in school physically, many often withdraw in other ways. Student difficulties with schoolwork can derive from different aspects of the academic criteria set by the school, the students' own current abilities in each subject area, and their willingness to direct efforts toward learning and performance on academic tasks. Moreover, studies of the sequence of events relating to dropping out indicate that the mismatch between school demands and student behaviors can grow over time; thus opportunities for success become more remote and motivation to remain in school becomes weaker (Grant Foundation Commission, 1988; Natriello, 1982). It is useful to examine the different aspects of the match between school demands and student behavior in considering the points for possible programmatic intervention.

One of the reasons most often cited for the high dropout rate in American schools is the lack of an appropriate match between the academic program of the school and the skills and interests of students (Fine, 1987; Wehlage and Rutter, 1987). Accounts of problems with the academic program specify three dimensions connected with dropping out. First, for many students the academic program is too difficult and overwhelming. Second, for other students it is not sufficiently challenging and engaging. Third, for substantial numbers of students the academic program is simply not an important part of their lives; that is, it is not salient in their thinking about their priorities. Each of these failures to engage students with the school program can be instrumental in causing them to exert less effort and subsequently to leave school.

For many disadvantaged students the problem with the academic program is that the curriculum presented is too difficult for them to achieve respectable grades. In the nationally representative sample of students in the High School and Beyond study, 30% of the ones who dropped out of high school between the 10th and 12th grades reported that poor grades were a reason for leaving (Ekstrom et al., 1987). These students failed to achieve success with the school program presented to them.

Students whose every effort fails to elicit a positive response from the school come to view its organization as nonresponsive to them and beyond their control. It is interesting to note that students who drop out do not seem to fare any worse in the development of self-esteem or internal locus of control than those who remain in school, and there is some evidence that dropouts' self-esteem and sense of control improve after leaving school (Wehlage & Rutter, 1987).

While many students leave school because they find the academic program too difficult or overwhelming, others leave because they find it insufficiently challenging. Sometimes students encounter teachers whose expectations for them are too low. For example, Natriello and Dornbusch (1984), in a study of the standards for student academic performance in classrooms, report that students are less likely to attend in those classrooms where teachers' standards for student performance are lower than in classrooms where the standards are high. They conclude that students are less likely to attend classes with low standards because they know that they will miss relatively less academic content.

Finally, schools may fail to engage students because the curriculum seems irrelevant. Some students see the school curriculum as not useful for their current and future endeavors. Others, particularly those who are not members of the white middle class, see the school curriculum as alien to the culture in which they are growing up (Fine, 1987; Grant Foundation Commission, 1988). For example, for some black students, to participate actively in the school curriculum means renouncing their black community and "acting white" (Fordham & Ogbu, 1986).

In light of these reasons that students become disengaged from the school's academic program, we posit three basic strategies that can be used to counteract the lack of match between the school program and the needs of students. First, it is possible to modify the academic standards of the school curriculum to accommodate students more effectively. Second, students' skills and abilities might be strengthened to permit them to meet the expectations inherent in the school curriculum. Finally, the school's academic program can be made more salient to the lives of students. Each of these basic strategies might strengthen the connection of students to the school program, and each of these has led to different forms of action in attempts to retain disadvantaged youth in secondary school through graduation.

Adjusting Academic Standards to Fit Students

If students become disengaged from school because they find the standards too difficult or too easy, then one strategy to minimize disengagement is to develop standards that meet the needs of students; that is, standards that are challenging but attainable.

A number of methods have been suggested and implemented for meeting the needs of students. Perhaps the most widely discussed and used is that of individualizing the curriculum and instruction so that they are tailored to each student's ability. This strategy is designed to present each student with attainable standards for academic performance (Hahn and Danzberger, 1987; McDill et al., 1986). In so doing, students might experience both academic success, with its attendant benefits to their self-esteem, and a more responsive school environment in reaction to their efforts.

Of course, matching the difficulty of the school curriculum, whether individualized or not, to the ability levels of students requires improved diagnostic strategies on the part of schools. In the absence of adequate diagnostic information it is impossible to tailor the curriculum to the students' abilities. At the very least, such diagnostic techniques should be used to determine when students are ready to move on to a new grade level. Such a program is in operation in Minneapolis where criterion-referenced tests are administered each year to students in kindergarten through the ninth grade, to follow the academic progress of students and determine whether they have mastered the knowledge required for the next grade (OERI Urban Superintendents Network, 1987).

One key strategy for addressing the lack of school responsiveness to academic performance for students with records of consistently poor performance is an alteration in the process for evaluating student work. Natriello and McPartland (1987) show that teachers make use of four evaluation or grading strategies in their classrooms: predetermined external standards, relative performance of the class, student effort, and growth or change in student performance level. Only the last two strategies provide low-performing students with an opportunity to obtain positive evaluations, suggesting that these are the most likely to be effective for disadvantaged students.

Another approach to providing opportunities for success for students who would otherwise experience consistent failure in the classroom involves a restructuring of the tasks of the classroom so that they draw on a wider range of ability dimensions. Such multiple-ability classrooms (Cohen, 1986;

Rosenholtz, 1977) attempt to move beyond the narrow range of academic tasks, all of which rely upon reading skills, so that every student can experience some success. In the multiple-ability classroom, the intention is for all students to find some task at which they can experience a sense of competence.

Finally, to combat the low standards that lead to students not being sufficiently challenged in school, there are strategies that seek to raise standards in a demonstrable way. Whether it is the "high standards" of the effective schools movement (Edmonds, 1979), the high aspirations of Operation PUSH (Murray, Murray, Gragg, & Kumi, 1982), the accelerated schooling model of Levin (1987), or the Johns Hopkins "Success for All" project (Slavin, Madden, & Karweit, 1989), these programs are explicit about having high standards that are worth achieving.

Enhancing Student Abilities and Skills

Adjusting the standards of the school program may go only a limited distance in closing the gap between the demands of the curriculum and the abilities and skills of students. A second basic strategy to improve the match between students and schools involves techniques for strengthening the skills and abilities of students so that they are better able to meet the demands of the school program. Various programmatic approaches to enhancing student abilities and skills have been developed. Remedial instruction in one form or another has often been used in an attempt to raise student skills to the level demanded by the school curriculum. Such remedial services take a variety of forms, from special classes to programs that involve a total alteration of the entire school curriculum, with the provision of additional resources throughout the program (Birman et al., 1987).

Remediation also occurs in special programs added onto the regular school program. For example, the Comprehensive Competency Program (CCP) is a self-paced, individualized, competency-based program that packages the best available educational technologies developed in Job Corps and other basic and vocational skills programs and makes them available to public schools and other institutions. Students in CCP attend learning centers where they work at their own pace on academic skills, life-skill competencies such as reading the newspaper and calculating overtime pay, and pre-employment skills such as job seeking (Hahn & Danzberger, 1987).

The provision of opportunities for learning during the summer months is another remediation strategy. For example, the Summer Training and Education Program (STEP), developed by Public/Private Ventures of Philadelphia with support from the Ford Foundation, is designed to respond to a number of problems that lead low-income youth to drop out of school before graduation by "sandwiching" two intensive summers around the academic year.

A particularly interesting approach to providing students with additional assistance when instructional resources are limited is the use of peer tutors to help students experiencing difficulty with the school curriculum. Both the tutors and the students being tutored have reported improved attitudes toward school as a result of participation in peer tutoring programs (Ashley, Jones, Zahniser, & Inks, 1986). This reinforces for secondary programs a point we made for elementary programs in Chapter 5.

Increasing the Salience of the School Curriculum

Whether or not students have sufficient skills to meet the standards of the school program may be unimportant if they are not initially motivated to try to perform in school. Many students simply do not perceive the curriculum to be sufficiently important or salient to motivate them to devote the required effort to succeed. A variety of approaches have been used to make schools more salient to students.

Some programs have made use of a multi-ethnic curriculum to appeal to minority students who view the dominant white culture as foreign. Such curricular approaches attempt to relate the subject matter of the school to the lives of the students and their communities and cultures. For example, the Indian Heritage Middle/High School in Seattle enrolls Native American students. In addition to the basic skills, the school program includes work in Native American culture and ethnic background (OERI Urban Superintendents Network, 1987).

Other programs have incorporated some form of career education designed to communicate explicitly how the school curriculum can be connected to future careers for those who are successful. A contemporary example is the New York City Job and Career Center. Using facilities and counselors provided by the New York State Department of Labor, the Center sponsors field trips, exhibits, visual displays, and discussions from the city's major employers. The services of the Center are available to students in public and private schools, to dropouts, and to unemployed adults (Grant Foundation Commission, 1988).

Another approach to making the program of the school more meaningful to students is to attach some type of incentive to school performance. The Cleveland Public Schools have adopted a program that relies on cash as an incentive. With funding from corporations and local foundations, the Cleveland program pays students in Grades 7 to 12 $40 for each A grade, $20 for each B, and $10 for each C. This money is usable for postsecondary education (Grant Foundation Commission, 1988).

Summer Training and Education Program (STEP)

Many programs have attempted to overcome the lack of fit between the needs and abilities of students and the academic demands of the school. We have selected the Summer Training and Education Program (STEP) for special examination because it has several promising features that could make it very successful.

STEP was developed by Public/Private Ventures with support from the Ford Foundation, and is designed to respond to a number of problems that lead low-income youth to drop out of school before graduation. In their report on the program, Sipe, Grossman, and Milliner (1987) state, "The STEP model aims to increase basic skills and lower dropout and teen pregnancy rates by providing poor and underperforming youth with remediation, life skills, and work experience during two consecutive and intensive summer programs, with ongoing support and personal contact during the intervening school year" (p. i). The program requires only moderate additional resources because it builds on existing public school programs and the work experience provided by the federal Summer Youth Employment and Training Program (SYETP).

During each summer session, participants earn minimum wage for a full day, 5 days a week for 6 to 8 weeks. They engage in three core activities during this time. First, they receive 90 hours of group and individually paced instruction in basic reading and math skills. Twenty percent of the time is spent on computer-assisted instruction, and 20 minutes a day are spent on silent reading.

Second, participants receive 18 hours of instruction on responsible social and sexual attitudes and behavior. Lectures, discussions, films, role-playing, field trips and outside speakers are used to stress the need to set goals, plan for the future, and take responsibility for decisions about sexual activity.

Third, participants spend at least 80 hours in part-time work provided by the federally funded SYETP. During the school year following the initial summer session, students participate in group activities and meet regularly with mentor/counselors who refer them to needed services, monitor their attendance and progress, and encourage them to return for the second summer session (Sipe et al., 1987).

To be eligible for participation in STEP, students must (1) be 14 or 15 years old, (2) be from low-income families, and (3) be performing below grade level in reading or math. The program is being conducted in five demonstration cities: Boston, Fresno, Portland, San Diego, and Seattle.

One of the strengths of the design of STEP is the inclusion of a rigorous evaluation. The demonstration project includes random assignment of youth to treatment and control groups, with members of the control groups working full time on SYETP jobs. Students in both the control and treatment groups are tested at the beginning and end of the summer, using the Metropolitan Achievement Test. Data on attendance, standardized test scores, credits earned, grade advancement, and dropout status are collected from each school district. Pre- and postprogram questionnaires assess attitudes, knowledge and behavior regarding sexual and social issues, and career awareness. The 4,500 students are about equally divided between the treatment and control groups (Sipe et al., 1987).

STEP has served or is continuing to serve three cohorts of youths. The first participated in the program in the summers of 1985 and 1986, the second in the summers of 1986 and 1987, and the third in the summers of 1987 and 1988. Data on the impact of STEP are available for the first cohort for the summers of 1985 and 1986 and for postprogram experiences in the summer and fall of 1987. For the second cohort, data are available for the summers of 1986 and 1987; for the third, data are available for their first summer experience in 1987.

During the summer of 1985, STEP was able to reduce by half the learning losses that would have occurred over the summer without the program. Cohort 1 program participants outscored those in the control group in both reading and math by about one-quarter of a grade equivalent. However, both program participants and those in the control group had lower test scores at the end of the summer than they had at the beginning; control group losses were significantly larger than those experienced by students in the program. The school-year performance of students in this first cohort was also examined. Attendance, test scores, credits earned, grade promotion, and dropout behavior were examined. The only program effect detected was for grade promotion: Treatment youth were 22% less likely to be retained in grade than controls.

The net impact of the program on students in the first STEP cohort during the summer of 1986 was assessed at one site, San Diego, where participants in the control group were given a second summer of work experience in exchange for being tested. The control group youth lost significantly more over the summer than treatment youth in both reading and math. Participants in STEP showed significant losses in reading and little change in math. When student performance over the entire 15-month period of the program is considered, however, students in the STEP program experienced a small nonsignificant loss in reading and a substantial gain in math.

During the 1986–1987 school year, following their second summer in STEP, students in cohort 1 who participated in the program had higher math scores and were more likely to be promoted than students in the control group, but there were no significant differences on reading scores, attendance and suspension rates, credits earned, and levels of schooling achieved. There were also no significant differences in employment rates and wage levels during the summer of 1987. However, interviews in the fall of 1987 revealed that STEP participation significantly reduced the dropout rates among Hispanic youths 14 to 17 months after participation in the program (Sipe, Grossman, & Milliner, 1988).

Based on the first year's experience with the first cohort, the program was strengthened for the second cohort, in the summer of 1986. Participants in the control group of the second cohort experienced summer losses ranging from about three-quarters of a grade to a full grade equivalent in reading and about one-half of a grade equivalent in math. The impact of the program on reducing these losses for the second cohort in the summer of 1986 was more than double what it had been for the first cohort in the summer of 1985. Most of the learning loss in reading was eliminated, with STEP youth scoring six-tenths of a grade equivalent higher than control youth. Learning loss in math was eliminated; in fact, a gain was produced. At the end of the summer, cohort 2 students participating in STEP scored slightly higher than they had at the beginning of the summer and eight-tenths of a grade equivalent higher than those in the control group (Sipe et al., 1987).

During the school year following their first summer in the program, cohort 2 students in the program did not differ significantly from control students in terms of attendance, reading and math test scores, credits earned, grade promotion and dropout behavior. However, those who had the most contact with the school-year support activities earned more credits and were more likely to be promoted than the control group students. Hispanic students in the program had better attendance than Hispanic students in the control group.

During the summer of 1987, cohort 2 students participating in STEP experienced no significant changes in either math or reading scores, but students in the control group experienced substantial losses, so that the net impact of that summer's participation in STEP at the two sites for which data are available (Seattle and San Diego) was 0.7 of a grade equivalent in reading and 0.8 of a grade equivalent in math. The net impact of 15 months of STEP for cohort 2 students was 0.9 of a grade equivalent in reading and 0.7 of a grade equivalent in math (Sipe et al., 1988).

Cohort 3 entered STEP in the summer of 1987. Students in this cohort achieved significant gains in both reading (0.3 of a grade equivalent) and math (0.2 of a grade equivalent) in their first summer of the program. Students in the control group once again suffered learning losses, so that the net effect of STEP participation was even greater than that suggested by the gains of the participants. Students in the program scored 0.5 of a grade equivalent higher in reading and 0.6 of a grade equivalent higher in math than students in the control group.

Based on these results, STEP appears to offer a modestly successful model for improving the academic performance of at-risk youngsters. It represents one strategy for offering extended basic educational programming and practical knowledge to potential dropouts, and linking such opportunities to valued economic incentives.

The program appears to be replicable, as shown by a feasibility test involving 11 new sites implementing the program during the summer of 1988. In the wake of a congressional mandate to make remediation available to youth in the federal summer jobs program, STEP expanded into 50 new sites in the summer of 1989. Together with the 5 research and demonstration sites and the 11 feasibility sites, this brings to 66 the number of settings in which this promising approach is currently operating.

Upward Bound

The national Upward Bound program began as a pilot program under the auspices of the Office of Economic Opportunity in the summer of 1965. It was authorized as a national program in 1966 under Title II.A of the Economic Opportunity Act and transferred to the U.S. Office of Education (USOE) in 1969.

Upward Bound (UB) was established for economically deprived, underachieving students who showed the potential for completing a postsecondary education (PSE) program but who, because of lack of motivation and/or academic preparation, failed to meet standard criteria for admission to PSE institutions (Burkheimer, Riccobono, & Wisenbaker, 1979). Colleges and universities or secondary schools with residential facilities operate UB projects through cooperative arrangements with high schools and community action programs. Local UB projects typically recruit students during their sophomore and junior years of high school and attempt to retain them through the summer following graduation from high school. Various intervention strategies such as remedial instruction, immersion in new curricula, tutoring, cultural enrichment practices, and counseling are used to develop in students the academic competencies and motivation needed to complete a PSE program. In summer sessions UB enrollees typically reside on a PSE campus and undergo intensive training for a period of 6 weeks or longer. These PSE sponsoring institutions attempt to establish academic and social relationships with the enrollees, and the staff are committed to helping students gain admission to a PSE institution and locate appropriate financial aid. Follow-up tutoring sessions during the regular high school year are sometimes used to reinforce any summer gains.

During 1966, the first full year of Upward Bound operation, approximately 20,000 secondary school students and 218 educational institutions were involved in the program. By 1971 these numbers had increased to 24,000 and 300, with a cost to the federal government of $28.5 million and an average expenditure of less than $1,200 per student (McDill et al., 1972). In fiscal year 1985, more than 32,000 students were served with a federal budget allocation of $73.6 million and an average federal cost per participant of approximately $2,265 (U.S. Department of Education, 1985). In FY 1988, its allocation increased to $80.4 million (U.S. Department of Education, 1988).

Over the more than 20 years of Upward Bound's existence, numerous national evaluations have been sponsored by the U.S. Office of Education and the U.S. Department of Education; further, individual projects at local sites have been privately evaluated (Davis & Kenyon, 1976). These range in quality from "rhetoric" (McDill et al., 1972, p. 146) for a number of early studies, to sophisticated and rigorous for some of the more ambitious of the past dozen years. An excellent example of this latter type of assessment is Burkheimer et al. (1979).

In reviewing the early portion of this evaluation literature Levin (1977) concluded that "The evidence of . . . programs [such as UB] suggests that they had little or no impact on increasing the educational attainments of disadvantaged youngsters, and those programs that appeared to be successful, such as Upward Bound, tended to concentrate on the least disadvantaged of the poverty groups" (p. 164).

The most extensive literature review of the educational effects of UB during the 1970s was prepared by Davis and Kenyon (1976), who systematically critiqued both the published and unpublished sources for the decade 1965–1974. They reached the following conclusions regarding types of impact:

1. High school performance, as measured by grade point average and standardized test scores, was not affected by participation in UB.
2. UB participation substantially increased college enrollment rates.
3. No conclusive evidence existed at the national level regarding academic performance in college.
4. No conclusive evidence existed regarding graduation rates from college, but information indicated high persistence rates through five or six semesters of college.
5. No data were available regarding occupational attainments.
6. Only a very limited number of cost/benefit studies was available.

The most sophisticated of the cost/benefit analyses was by Garms (1971, 1973), who concluded that, from an economic perspective, UB was at best only marginally effective. Garms's conclusion has been challenged on the grounds that some of his assumptions concerning the proper rate for discounting social benefits were inappropriate (Christoffel & Celio, 1973). However, Davis and Kenyon (1976) and Levin (1977) have concluded that his assumptions were tenable and his results valid.

Without doubt, the most extensive and sophisticated evaluation in the 1970s of the effects of Upward Bound on student participants was conducted by the Research Triangle Institute (RTI) under contract with the U.S. Office of Education. This multiphased longitudinal project was initiated in 1973 and completed in 1979. The base-year study, which covered the program as it existed in the 1973–1974 school year, examined its effects on short-term educational outcomes and attempted to determine the relative effectiveness of different types of UB projects on these outcomes (Burkheimer, Levinsohn, Koo, & French, 1976). The first follow-up study, conducted in 1976–1977, measured educational progress in relation to the extent of prior participation in UB and assessed students' educational plans and the problems experienced by participants between the 1973–1974 and 1976–1977 school years (Burkheimer, French, Levinsohn, & Riccobono, 1977). The second follow-up study, covering the 1978–1979 program year, focused on long-term educational outcomes such as PSE persistence, progress, and performance, as well as receipt of financial aid and use of support services (Burkheimer et al., 1979).

Using a sophisticated sampling design, the RTI evaluators selected from 54 local sites a nationally representative sample of 3,700 UB participants in the 1973–1974 school year. These students were matched on several relevant sociodemographic attributes with a comparison group of nonparticipants from high schools that provided UB students. Data were obtained from several sources on the students at three times between 1973 and 1977. No systematic differences were found between the UB students and the comparison group in terms of high school achievement and graduation rates, but the UB students had appreciably higher educational expectations and aspirations. The RTI researchers also found that the UB experience had a sizable impact on the educational aspirations and expectations, and the PSE progress and persistence of its participants at all times.

The greater progress in PSE for Upward Bound participants was primarily a function of the greater rates at which they entered PSE institutions and their tendency to enroll in 4-year institutions. It should be noted, however, that neither group had normal PSE progress. For example, among the 12th-grade cohort in 1973–1974 who completed high school, only 20% of

UB participants had completed a 4-year program 4.5 years later. The comparable figure for controls was 5%. Upward Bound students were also appreciably more likely to attend institutions with predominantly ethnic minority student bodies, more academically selective institutions, and institutions that hosted UB programs.

The RTI staff also found that UB participants were more likely than controls to make use of tutoring services in PSE settings, but no differences existed with respect to use of remedial services. UB students also received more financial aid than did nonparticipants, which was a consequence of their receiving larger grants and scholarships.

Among those enrolling in PSE settings, the two groups did not differ on measures of persistence, when the type of institution in which they enrolled was controlled. Further, no notable differences existed between the two groups on measures of academic achievement such as academic probation or dismissal, and they were comparable in terms of educational progress as measured by graduation rates, number of PSE credits earned, and rate of earning credits. Surprisingly, the UB participants achieved a slightly lower grade-point average at both 4-year and vocational/technical schools. The RTI staff speculated that this difference could be attributable to selection bias among the nonparticipant group. That is, despite the two groups being statistically comparable in terms of several personal and social background factors, one cannot rule out with certainty that any group differences in educational outcomes were not a consequence of unmeasured input differences. This reasoning is appealing when one considers that non-UB students epitomize the label "educational survivors." As would be expected, the progress of both groups was much slower than average—only about 60% of what would be expected under regular academic progression.

Finally, with respect to the employment status of Upward Bound participants, the RTI researchers found that, among those not currently enrolled in PSE, former UB enrollees were significantly more likely to be unemployed than nonparticipants; among those currently enrolled in PSE, essentially no differences in employment rates were observed.

The overarching conclusion of the RTI staff (Burkheimer et al., 1979) is encouraging:

> The UB program is effectively meeting its mandated objective to provide participants with the skills and motivation necessary for entry and success in education beyond high school. Program impact is greatest on short-term outcomes, and evidence UB is providing the skills, motivation, and assistance necessary for entry into PSE is substantial. While it is less clear that the program also provides the skills and motivation necessary for success in PSE, there are some results to support the contention of an overall positive impact of UB participation on PSE success. [p. 133]

The RTI study of Upward Bound remained the definitive assessment into the 1980s. For example, the *Annual Evaluation Reports* of federally funded education programs (U.S. Department of Education, 1981) continued to cite the RTI reports as their primary sources of evaluation data into the 1980s.

A search of ERIC Document Service files for the period between 1981 and 1987, on the impact of Upward Bound on educational attainment and academic achievement, produced a short list of unpublished reports, government documents, and published journal articles. These materials typically report results of studies of single local projects (e.g., Exum & Young, 1981; Young & Exum, 1982) or a very limited number of projects (e.g., Mims, 1985).

These studies are also less rigorous than the RTI evaluation. For example, the studies by Exum and Young (1981) and Young and Exum (1982), although longitudinal in design, measured the short-term impact of an 8-week UB project on a postsecondary campus for a nonrepresentative sample of only 56 high school students. No control group was employed, and the sample was slightly above the national average on American College Testing Program (ACT) scores, which represents an instance of "creaming" of the disadvantaged population of high school students. Results for this atypical sample reinforce Levin's (1977) earlier conclusion that the Upward Bound program was selective in recruiting students who were the "best" among the disadvantaged. Thus, because of the nonrepresentative nature of the sample and the methodological flaws in this study one should treat very cautiously Young and Exum's (1982) conclusion that the UB experience produced significant gains in quantitative and language arts skills.

A more recent evaluation of UB, which has national implications, was conducted by Steel and Schubert (1983), who studied all students in the nationwide High School and Beyond survey (Sebring et al., 1987) of the sophomore and senior high school classes of 1980 who reported they had participated in a UB project. These students were compared with a matched sample of nonparticipants. Although this study has a number of methodological weaknesses, the authors are cognizant of them and thus cautious in their conclusions. Further, their results are based on a nationally representative sample of high school students and are generally consistent with those of the RTI survey. For example, they found that UB students were more likely to be enrolled in college preparatory courses in high school and more likely to plan on college attendance and completion. However, the two groups did not differ on academic performance in high school or academic motivation. Steel and Schubert conclude that Upward Bound appears to increase the likelihood that participants will enter a PSE program.

Jung (1984), analyzing data from the High School and Beyond survey, reports results consistent with those of Steel and Schubert (1983): (1) Upward Bound enrollees were more likely than comparable nonenrollees to apply to college, receive financial aid, enroll in college, and remain therein for 1 year; (2) UB students earned significantly more college credits than did nonparticipants during their first three semesters of college; and (3) college retention rates for UB students were not significantly higher 21 months after high school than those of the control group.

In our view, the evaluations of Upward Bound in the 1970s and 1980s reinforce the early conclusion of McDill et al. (1972) that "Upward Bound seems quite successful in getting students to remain in high school and to enroll in college; yet it appears to have far less impact on developing the basic academic skills necessary to attain the college degree" (p. 148).

The RTI researchers (Burkheimer et al., 1979), in our view, pinpoint the reasons for this: Local UB projects devote very little time to academic instruction; further, the projects are not provided any clearly articulated strategies for intervention once a UB student enters a postsecondary institution. Unless these long-standing deficiencies in program planning, execution, and oversight are corrected by federal officials, PSE outcomes for UB participants are not likely to change.

POSITIVE RELATIONSHIPS IN SCHOOL

A second major cause of poor school performance and early school leaving is the lack of positive relationships in school. Although quantitative scientific evidence is scarce, several qualitative studies of disadvantaged students who dropped out strongly suggest that many of them feel that no one at school pays attention to them or cares about their progress (Fine, 1987). Even beyond feeling ignored or unimportant at school, many disadvantaged students seem to have a sense that the goal of school officials is to rate and sort them, rather than to find ways to help them be successful. Students who have a weak attachment to the school are likely to drift away and eventually drop out. Students who maintain a strong bond with the school are likely to continue to attend school regularly, and hence are more likely to graduate (G. Gottfredson, 1987).

There are several ways in which young people interact with their school environments. Students maintain relationships with peers, teachers, and the school itself. Schools have developed strategies to strengthen these attachments, both separately and in combination. We have identified three ways in which schools can attempt to strengthen students' bonds to school. These involve influencing (1) their associations with adults in the schools, (2) their associations with their school peers, and (3) their attachment to the school as an institution.

Strengthening Students' Connections to Adults in the School

The first strategy involves creating a mentor relationship linking students to adults in the school. Most secondary schools are large, relatively impersonal institutions. High schools are designed and organized to process large batches of students. They also are highly differentiated, in the sense that a student may have a different teacher for every period of the school day. Conversely, a given student may be one of 150 or more taught by a particular math or English teacher. The end result is that students rarely have sustained and in-depth social contact with their teachers.

The quality and quantity of contact that students have with other school staff also typically are inadequate. Although a student usually is assigned to a single guidance counselor, student/counselor ratios are frequently as high as 500 to 1. Although some students demand less attention than others, it still is highly unlikely that at-risk students can gain sufficient access to their counselors to forge strong social bonds. Under these circumstances, students may well come to the conclusion that no one at the school cares about their welfare. To counteract this trend and its likely consequences, the school must reorganize the daily schedule to allow students to have more close contact with adults in the school and to insure that this contact has a positive valence.

Strengthening Students' Connections to Peers in the School

The second strategy for strengthening students' attachment to school operates through students' relations with their peers. Both surveys of students and ethnographic studies of schools have long suggested that adolescents are not opposed to the *idea* of school; and many of them like school (Epstein, 1981; Epstein & McPartland, 1976). The school plays a central role in the adolescent social structure. Adolescents spend more than 40% of their waking hours in school during the school year. It is not surprising, then, that the school becomes a locus of social activity for youth.

As some youth drop out of school, however, the balance of in-school social contact to out-of-school contact begins to shift. Adolescents want to spend time with their friends. If most of a student's friends are no longer attending school, the student may withdraw in order to keep contact with them. After all, most secondary schools are not organized to facilitate social interaction among students. Students rarely spend much of their school day with their friends, and classroom instruction typically constrains peer contact.

For school personnel to hold such students in schools, they must develop ways to promote peer networks that provide support and attachment. The major vehicle for this is a program of extracurricular activities that allows students to interact with their peers in the school setting. These before- and after-school activities include sports, recreation, and school clubs, some of which double as academic enrichment programs. Although these activities may be intrinsically interesting to adolescents, they mainly serve to allow teens to socialize in a setting officially sanctioned by the school.

Another way to strengthen peer attachments in the school context is to socialize entering students into the life of the high school. This strategy uses orientation programs as an in-service socialization mechanism. In some settings, students new to the school are paired with students who have been in the school for some time. The more experienced student can then act as a mentor to the new student, providing information about the school and lending social support (Grant Foundation Commission, 1988). Students are thus guaranteed to know someone in the high school, thereby reducing its impersonal and alienating character and helping to forge a social bond between the new students and those already in the school.

Mentoring programs like this can have positive consequences for the mentor as well. Acting as a mentor provides a student a sense of responsibility and of being needed. The mentors are aware that the school is depending on them to perform a valuable function and that new students are relying on the help of their mentors. This sense of being needed may be related to better attendance among at-risk youth who serve as mentors. This strategy also has been used for purposes other than school orientation, such as academic instruction. There are several examples of cross-age remedial peer tutoring, for instance, which show positive academic effects (Larrivee, 1989).

Strengthening Students' Connections to the School As an Institution

The third strategy for strengthening attachment to schools is based on linking the student to the school as an institution. The goal here is to foster student interest in the school. We have already noted that the size of most secondary schools renders them impersonal, and many students can pass through a high school with the sense that the school has had little effect on them and they have had little impact on the school. Schools must take active steps to integrate the student into the school environment.

The recognition of poor integration into the school is fundamental to the well-known effective schools model (Edmonds, 1979). This model is predicated on the premise that students confronting clear and consistent goals in a safe, orderly environment will succeed in school. In addition, Newmann (1981), writing on student alienation in high schools, has hypothesized that student participation in school policy and management may help prevent disengagement. More recent analysts (Bryk & Thum, 1989; Cusick, 1983; Oakes, 1985) have reasoned that the psychological alienation with which many disadvantaged students enter high school is likely to be magnified by the high degree of organizational or structural differentiation of the typical large comprehensive high school, through devices such as curriculum tracking and a plethora of low-level, nonchallenging course offerings.

One possible way to promote linkages is to convince students that they will receive fair and equitable treatment in school. This involves making the school rules explicit so that all students know them; making them appear fair; and applying them consistently to students (Coleman, 1981; Fullam, Miles, & Taylor, 1980). Gottfredson and Gottfredson (1985) found that schools whose students reported that the rules were fair and clear experienced less disruption than schools where students reported inconsistent and unfair applications of rules. They did not conclude, though, that student participation in rule-making was related to levels of school disruption.

It is plausible that students will be more attached to settings where they can exercise some control over their environment. This might take the form of student control over which school to attend (Perpich, 1988), which course to select, and which school-related extracurricular activity to choose. Among at-risk middle school students in New York City, for example, those reporting greater control over planning their programs tend to like school more than those reporting less control, though there is no evidence of a net effect on attendance rates (Grannis, Riehl, Pallas, Lerer, & Randolph, 1988).

Another way of linking students to the school involves anticipatory socialization, that is, providing junior high school students with opportunities to learn what the high school is like and what is to be expected of them, so that when they do go on to high school the setting is not mysterious or foreboding. In New York City, this strategy is implemented under the rubric of linkage programs, involving collaborative efforts between junior high schools and high schools. Large numbers of at-risk middle school students report listening to students or adults from a high school describe high school life, but far fewer students report having gone to a high school for a special event or after-school activity, or with a class. Moreover, there is little evidence of sustained efforts at linking middle school students to high schools; most attempts are one-shot efforts. This may account for why linkage activities seem so ineffective in promoting positive student outcomes in New York City (Grannis, Riehl, Pallas, Lerer, & Randolph, 1988).

The Alternative School

The school program that best ties together the three strategies just reviewed is the alternative school. Programs in this category are considered "alternative" because they are typically designed as nontraditional educational programs marked by considerably more flexibility in educational activities than is found in traditional school settings. Alternative schools usually are smaller than traditional schools, with lower student/teacher and student/counselor ratios.

A structural feature that is common to many alternative schools, delinquency prevention programs, and dropout prevention programs is their small size. Among traditional schools, small size is associated with lower levels of school violence (Diprete, 1982; Garbarino, 1978; Gottfredson & Gottfredson, 1985; McPartland & McDill, 1977) and higher rates of student participation in extracurricular activities (Barker & Gump, 1964; Morgan & Alwin, 1980). Garbarino (1980) also speculates that smaller schools promote higher levels of social interaction among students.

In small schools with higher ratios of adults to students, students have more direct social contact with both school staff and other students. Smaller school environments are thought to be less anonymous than larger schools. The greater amount of social interaction may promote an attachment to the school by making the student feel valued and wanted. As Gottfredson and Gottfredson (1985) put it, "School size is very likely related to the availability of opportunities for students to engage in a variety of roles that provide a stake in conformity" (p. 171).

The most sophisticated empirical analysis we have encountered regarding the effects of school size on the behavior of disadvantaged students has been recently completed by Bryk and Thum (1989). Using a multivariate analytical technique, they investigated the effects of a variety of organizational, structural, and compositional characteristics of high schools on the probability of dropping out for a large subsample (160 schools and 4,450 students) from the High School and Beyond data base (Sebring et al., 1987), which contains results from the questionnaire and standardized achievement tests administered to a nationally representative sample of approximately 30,000 sophomores in 1,100 schools in the spring of 1980. Both those students remaining in school and those who dropped out were resurveyed 2 years later. The views we have just articulated are compatible with Bryk and Thum's (1989) conclusion regarding the effects of school size on dropping out:

Our analyses suggest that school size may be an important moderating variable. Organizational correlates of school size . . . indicate that larger schools are more problematic social environments for both students and teachers. Although such schools have greater faculty resources in terms of teachers with more experience, with more advanced degrees and where starting salaries are higher, principals are also more likely to report a greater incidence of staff absenteeism and lack of interest. Student discipline problems are greater in such schools and there is greater internal academic differentiation through tracking. The correlations reported . . . are among the largest we encountered in examining bivariate relationships among school-level variables. This suggests that the effects of school size are in fact substantial, but mostly indirect acting to either facilitate (in small schools) or inhibit (in larger schools) the development and maintenance of a social environment conducive to student and faculty engagement with the school. [pp. 25–26]

Dropout prevention programs, like other alternative programs, typically are small, particularly those that have adopted a case-management approach, where a battery of services are targeted to specific youngsters thought to be at risk of dropping out of school. Some programs operate as a component within a larger environment — a school within a school. Others are physically segregated from the traditional school environment. Physical separation tends to highlight the distinctive features of the dropout prevention program, and students may be more disposed toward an educational setting that does not remind them of their regular school, often a site of failure and frustration. On the other hand, if the goal is to reintegrate the student into the original school environment, physical segregation may be disruptive. Physical separation also may serve to label the at-risk students, making it harder to "mainstream" them at some later date. In many alternative school programs, however, there is no intention to lure these students back to the traditional school environments in which they floundered earlier.

Gold and Mann (1984), in their study of effective alternative schools, point to the schools' flexibility as key to the academic prospects of at-risk youth. In their view, a flexible school does not impose conventional rules governing teacher/student interactions and is responsive to variations in students' needs and moods in the planning of daily activities. Important to achieving this flexibility is the location of the school in a building separate from the high school that students would normally attend. Such separation allows for the casual coming and going of students, the sometimes higher noise level, and other deliberate informalities. Gold and Mann also note that the stigmatization often thought to accompany programs that separate groups of students did not manifest itself in the schools they studied.

Middle College High School

An example of an alternative high school that is widely cited as exemplary is Middle College High School (MCHS) in Long Island City, New York. MCHS is a selective alternative high school located on the campus of LaGuardia Community College. The description we give here is adapted from Eisman (1986).

The classes at Middle College High School are small, and there are more guidance counselors than in other schools. The school is divided into small "houses," each with its own students and staff. Teachers and students know each other personally, and the environment is safe and friendly. There are no bells to signal the beginning or end of classes as in other schools. Applicants to MCHS are interviewed by students already in the school as part of the selection process, and the school's student council plays a role in resolving discipline disputes. The school has an extensive array of extracurricular activities and emphasizes the use of the cafeteria for student socializing. Students are encouraged to exercise choice in scheduling their classes.

MCHS has tutoring available for every course before or after school. Technically, no one fails a course because a course is repeated until it is passed, and no grade is assigned for failure. Also, MCHS students spend one-third of their school year working at unpaid internships in various settings outside of the school.

Middle College High School is widely regarded as a highly successful alternative school program, and the model is currently being considered for replication at several sites. Between the 1982–1983 and 1987–1988 school years the rate of dropping out from MCHS was below the dropout rate for all New York City high schools, every year but one, and throughout that period was well below the average for the 16 alternative high schools in the New York City system. In addition, the attendance rates of students at MCHS have hovered around 75% to 80% in recent years, substantially above the attendance rates of students targeted in New York's Dropout Prevention Initiative, who may have comparable academic histories. Because of the selectivity of the program, though, it is difficult to say what the actual effects of attending MCHS are. There are no careful evaluations providing evidence on how the kinds of students enrolling at this school would have fared had they been in some other educational setting.

RELEVANCE OF SCHOOL TO THE STUDENT'S FUTURE

A third major cause of poor school performance and early school leaving lies in students' perceptions that the program of the school is not relevant to their future endeavors. A 25 year tradition of informed speculation and empirical research in the educational and social science literature supports the idea that much of the psychological alienation and rebellious behavior experienced by working- and lower-class adolescents is partly explained by their perceptions that social conformity and academic achievement in school are not clearly linked to their future status in society. This is often referred to as the "articulation" hypothesis, which was specified and tested in 1964 by Stinchcombe in his widely cited study of a working-class high school in California.[1]

The articulation hypothesis, as applied to the problems of disadvantaged youth, holds that significant numbers of students fail to devote effort to schoolwork, and even leave school, because they fail to see any connection between remaining in school and improving their job prospects. Such a perception seems widespread in many urban settings which have high rates of youth unemployment, reinforcing the perceptions that a high school diploma is no guarantee of a job (Natriello, Pallas, & McDill, 1986a). Although the empirical status of the proposition is a subject of debate (e.g., Wheeler, 1967), it has remained popular in the ensuing years, especially among sociologists and anthropologists of education (Fine, 1987; Ogbu, 1974; Willis, 1977).

In fact, the Grant Foundation Commission (1988) avowedly subscribes to the articulation hypothesis, stating,

> When they [young people] observe a direct relationship between what they do in school, their work experience, and accessible future careers, they are more willing to make present sacrifices in hope of future gains. When they believe their futures will be dim regardless of their own effort, they have less incentive to behave in personally and socially responsible ways. [p. 28]

The Grant Foundation Commission (1988) report is merely the latest in a series of documents issued by blue-ribbon panels in the past 15 years to address the broad problems of the link between secondary schools and youth socialization. For example, five such reports were issued in the United States in the 1970s by prestigious panels, "all beginning from the premise that the larger society's principal institution of socialization, the school, was not functioning properly" (Coleman & Husen, 1985, p. 20). The best known of these, *Youth: Transition to Adulthood* (Coleman et al., 1974), produced by the President's Science Advisory Committee (PSAC), strongly advocated a lessening of the school's isolation from other institutional spheres of society through diversification of schools, more experiential learning, and closer linkages between school and the world of work. Coleman and Husen (1985) have recently updated the PSAC report for the Organization for Economic Cooperation and Development (OECD). They attempt to account for the current linkages and changes among the institutions of work, the family, and school as they influence the transitions from youth to adulthood and to specify institutional innovations that can smooth this transition.

Given the continued currency of the articulation hypothesis in attempting to account for the unsteady transition from school to work for a sizeable segment of youth, it is important to evaluate the effectiveness of different programmatic responses (strategies, methods, and techniques) that have been proposed and implemented in recent years to convince disadvantaged students of the value to their adult status of performing adequately in school and remaining until graduation.

In the past decade a variety of approaches for "bridging the gap from school to work" (Grant Foundation Commission, 1988) have evolved or have been developed. All of these efforts attempt to demonstrate to adolescents a meaningful link between school learning and success in the labor market, and to provide clearly defined incentives for students to remain in school and to perform to the maximum of their abilities.

Efforts of this type include updated vocational education programs involving a blend of transferable vocational skills and basic skills training, school/business partnerships, and part-time employment that is dependent upon satisfactory school attendance and performance. These incentive programs often involve partnerships between schools and the private sector (Committee for Economic Development, 1985). Three of the most visible of the programs designed to increase the articulation between school and future adult status are the Job Corps, the Boston Compact, and the "I Have a Dream" program. We consider each of these.

The Job Corps

One explicit education and training strategy employed in the War on Poverty in the 1960s was to develop the specific job skills of disadvantaged youth. Thus, vocational education programs such as the Manpower Development Training Act (MDTA), the Neighborhood Youth Corps, and the Job Corps were either expanded or established, in the attempt to narrow the gap in work skills between the poor and nonpoor segments of society (Haveman, 1977).

The Job Corps was originally established under the Economic Opportunity Act of 1964 and was incorporated into the Comprehensive Employment and Training Act of 1973 under the authority of the Department of Labor (DOL), which combined work and training programs such as the Neighborhood Youth Corps and MDTA. Since 1982 the Job Corps has been authorized under the Job Training Partnership Act (JTPA) and is administered by the Office of the Job Corps, a component of the DOL's Employment and Training Administration (U.S. General Accounting Office, 1986a).

The specific objective of the program since its inception has been to provide both remedial basic skills education and vocational skills training for youth aged 16 to 21 (mainly school dropouts) who are "severely educationally or economically disadvantaged" (U.S. GAO, 1986a, p. 6). Training has been provided primarily in residential settings at Job Corps centers throughout the United States, the District of Columbia, and Puerto Rico. Enrollees are provided housing, food, clothing, and medical and dental care.

Training is provided in both Civilian Conservation Centers (CCCs) operated by the federal government and those run "by local government entities and private for-profit and non-profit contractors" (U.S. GAO, 1986a, p. 6). The CCCs, located on public lands primarily in rural settings, provide programs of work experience for the conservation, development, and management of public natural resources or recreational areas or the development of community projects in the public interest. They tend to provide trade skills training such as construction, bricklaying, and heavy equipment operation. The contract centers, in contrast, tend to be located in urban settings and concentrate their vocational training in service occupations such as food servers, retail store clerks, file clerks, and clerk typists (U.S. GAO, 1986a).

Appropriations for the Job Corps increased from $175 million in fiscal year 1966 to roughly $300 million in FY 1967, but by FY 1970 funding had declined to $169 million because many of the centers were dismantled and the remaining ones were taken over by the DOL (Levin, 1977).

In the summer of 1977 the Youth Employment and Demonstration Projects Act (YEDPA) was passed by Congress and signed into law by President Carter. Congress wrote the legislation in response to the high levels of unemployment and employment-related problems of American youth (Betsey, Hollister, & Papageorgiou, 1985). YEDPA was terminated in 1981 and replaced by the Job Training Partnership Act (JTPA) of 1982 by the Reagan administration. YEDPA substantially increased funding for the Job Corps. For example, federal outlays for the program increased from $280 million in FY 1978 to $465 million in FY 1981 (Elmore, 1985). In FY 1986 the funding level was $640 million for the operation of 106 centers, which have a capacity of 40,500 trainees. Approximately 60,000 youth receive training in these centers each year, with an average length of stay of approximately 8 months (U.S. GAO, 1986a).

Despite the increase in funding between 1981 and 1986, lack of adequate and predictable financing has been a major problem over the years, as noted by Levitan and Gallo (1988):

The major source of program instability has been widely fluctuating funding support and attempts by Presidents Nixon and Reagan to abolish the corps, resulting in capacity enrollment ranging from 25,000 to 40,000. In inflation-adjusted 1986 dollars, Job Corps funding reached over $1 billion in 1966, but dropped to $300 million in the mid-1970s. . . . Financing rose initially following President Carter's inauguration but declined again, subsequently increasing when the administration made reducing youth unemployment a major domestic priority. Since 1981, constant dollar funding for the Job Corps has ranged from $600 to $680 million. Center enrollment capacity has closely followed the available funding. [pp. 125–126]

The Job Corps was mired in controversy during the early years of its existence (e.g., Levitan, 1969). One of the most strident criticisms was of the high costs of operating the program. In FY 1968 the total annual cost per trainee was more than $8,000 (Levitan, 1969); in FY 1986 the average annual cost per trainee was approximately $14,000 (U.S. GAO, 1986a). Other problems included the ethnic mix (the large proportion of black enrollees allegedly led to racial tensions); an undesirable age mix (too many 16- and 17-year-olds who dropped out disproportionately); the great distance that trainees had to travel from their homes to center locations; high dropout rates (Levin, 1977); discipline problems with trainees in the centers; and strained relations with surrounding communities concerning trainees' deportment.

Not surprisingly, given the operational and management problems encountered by Job Corps administrators in the early years of the program, evaluation researchers who assessed the program's effectiveness during this period reached one of two conclusions. For some, the results were "discouraging" (Levine & Havighurst, 1984), in that the program costs were high and graduates typically were no more successful in the labor market than nonparticipants. For others, the results were conflicting, suggesting that the program had a short-term impact on outcomes such as earnings, which "decayed" or faded quickly (Betsey et al., 1985). However, Betsey et al. emphasize that most of the evaluations prior to 1982 were based on the experience of trainees who were enrolled in the middle 1960s, and the program has undergone major modifications since then. In their comprehensive review, these authors refer to the program as unique in that

1. It serves an extremely disadvantaged population (with 90% of trainees coming from households below the poverty line).
2. It provides comprehensive services to its clientele in a residential setting.
3. The program is stable, having been in continuous existence for almost 25 years.
4. There is now a high quality evaluation of the program's effectiveness.

The evaluation effort to which they refer is the widely cited study by Mallar,

Kerachsky, Thornton, and Long (1982), which is viewed as an exemplar of a rigorous nonexperimental assessment of a social program and "the most extensive and sophisticated of the studies of the Job Corps undertaken over the years" (Betsey et al., 1985, p. 111).

Since Mallar et al. (1982) were unable to employ a true experimental design in their assessment of the Job Corps, because the Department of Labor had "ruled out" (Betsey et al., 1985, p. 114) such a methodology at the outset, one cannot be certain that observed program effects were not attributable to selection biases in comparisons of participants and nonparticipants. Nevertheless, the study has a number of strengths that provide considerable confidence in its findings and are unusual in the literature on the evaluation of manpower training programs (Betsey et al., 1985). These characteristics included (1) a large sample of Job Corps participants (2,800) and nonparticipants (1,000) who were statistically comparable on a number of relevant sociodemographic and personal attributes; (2) a longitudinal design that extended 42 to 54 months after the program period; (3) relatively low rates of attrition (30%) for both the participant and control groups; and (4) measurement of a variety of outcome variables, including educational attainment, the value of economic production by participants, receipt of welfare payments, extent of criminality, employment and unemployment rates, wage rates, and hours worked.

The Mallar et al. (1982) study indicates that the Job Corps is effective. Specifically, the following positive results were detected:

1. Participants were employed about 13% more per year (3.5 years after the experience) than were nonparticipants, and their earnings gains were estimated at 28% higher than they would have been without the training.
2. The amount of time Job Corps enrollees received cash, welfare, or unemployment compensation benefits was significantly less than for controls.
3. The training had a substantial impact on the educational attainment of participants; that is, the probability was almost 25% that they would receive a high school diploma or GED diploma within 6 months of completion of the program, which was five times the rate for nonparticipants.
4. Job Corps participants reported fewer health problems in the years immediately following the program than did their counterparts.
5. During the program the participants had lower arrest rates than nonparticipants, and during the follow-up period they reported fewer arrests for serious crimes.
6. During the initial 6-month follow-up period, enrollees had *lower*

employment rates and earnings than the control group; however, this effect quickly reversed, and the enrollees maintained an advantage in both earnings and employment rates throughout the 4-year follow-up period.

7. A duration effect was detected in the evaluation: Enrollees who completed the program benefited the most from the Job Corps experience; partial completers benefited an intermediate amount; and early dropouts experienced little or no gain on the various outcomes. Of course, this difference could be an artifact of more competent enrollees being more likely to complete the program.

8. A sophisticated cost/benefit analysis revealed that the net social benefits exceeded costs by $2,300 per enrollee, and the net personal benefit per trainee was $2,400. These financial benefits were primarily a function of decreased criminal behavior and increased economic output among the trainees.

These apparent substantial benefits from the Job Corps program led the evaluators of the YEDPA to conclude that occupational skills training programs can be an effective tool in combating the structural unemployment problems of out-of-school disadvantaged youth, and also to recommend to the DOL that opportunities to enroll in the Job Corps for such youth be continued (Betsey et al., 1985). The Grant Foundation Commission (1988), relying essentially on the same sources we have cited, is more positive in its recommendations: "The Job Corps, a program of proven effectiveness in improving the employment and life prospects of high-risk youth, should be expanded" (p. 62).

Levitan and Gallo (1988), who have conducted the most recent in-depth critique of the Job Corps, also relied primarily on the Mallar et al. (1982) evaluation of the postprogram experiences of trainees. Their conclusion is relevant to our concern here: "Although the evaluation of the Job Corps reviewed the experiences of enrollees who entered the program a decade ago, there is no reason to believe the corps is less effective today. In fact, the current program is probably more effective because the proportion of early dropouts has declined and average training duration has increased" (Levitan & Gallo, 1988, p. 158).

A more recent study of the Job Corps by the U.S. GAO (1986a) in response to a request from the U.S. Senate reinforces some of the results of the YEDPA critique (Betsey et al., 1985), even though its objectives were different. The U.S. GAO (1986a) study was designed "to compare and contrast the costs, placements, starting wages and public service activities" (p. 7) of Civilian Conservation Centers with contract centers. Currently there are 30 CCCs operated by the Departments of Agriculture and Interior, under interagency agreement with the DOL. The remaining centers, mostly in urban areas, are run by local government agencies and private for-profit contractors. In February 1986, the Reagan administration proposed rescinding almost one-third of the FY 1986 appropriation ($196 million) for the Job Corps. In supporting this proposal, DOL officials argued that efficiency could be achieved by closing the most expensive CCCs, which are operated solely by the federal government. Congress rejected this proposal for rescission, thereby permitting the Job Corps to spend all of its 1986 appropriation (U.S. GAO, 1986a).

The GAO conducted its study by analyzing information from 29 of the 30 CCCs and 13 comparably-sized contract centers. A number of revealing findings emerged from this effort (U.S. GAO, 1986a).

1. CCCs are more costly to operate than are comparably sized contract centers. This difference in costs of about 40% is primarily attributable to the more extensive and expensive vocational training and residential living costs of the CCCs.
2. CCCs have a higher job placement rate than do contract centers, whereas the percentage of "not placed" (i.e., in a job, the military, or an educational program) is higher among students leaving the contract centers. Staff from the Departments of Labor, Agriculture, and Interior saw the higher job placement of CCC trainees as a result of more effective trade skills training which made them more marketable. Further, a duration effect was observed in that those students who completed either type of program were more likely to be placed in a job, educational institution, or the military than those who did not complete the same program. However, the length of time enrolled did not influence the placement advantage of participants in the CCCs when compared with those in the contract centers.
3. The starting wages for youth trained at the CCCs were approximately 14% higher than those trained at contract centers. Federal officials knowledgeable about the different types of Job Corps programs also attributed this advantage to the trade-skills training received at the CCCs, which resulted in job placement with a higher starting wage than the service occupations training offered in the contract centers.
4. CCCs have greater involvement in public service projects such as conservation and community improvement than do contract centers, and the appraised value of public service projects performed at CCCs is approximately 11 times greater on an annual basis than those conducted at contract centers.

In conclusion, the U.S. GAO (1986a) evaluation of the Job Corps, although not appraising the social and personal benefits and costs of participation in the program *per se,* is useful in that it shows results consistent with the statutory objectives of the program in terms of type and duration of training. Further, this evaluation suggests that certain types of labor market training are more effective in preparing out-of-school disadvantaged youth for their future work lives than are others. Of course, these results must be labeled tentative, because the GAO study had no systematic control of any personal characteristics of enrollees in the two types of Job Corps programs being contrasted. Thus, measured outcome differences between the two types of training could be a consequence partly or wholly of selection bias. Only random assignment of persons to types of programs would rule out such factors completely.

A search of the literature for more recent evaluations of the Job Corps (i.e., through 1986–1989) yielded no additional assessments of its effectiveness. A disproportionate amount of the available information consists of documents printed by the U.S. Government Printing Office which typically are records of oversight hearings conducted by relevant committees of the U.S. Congress. In addition, a very limited number of articles in social science journals are available. These publications do not, however, address the critical issue of the degree of efficacy of the program. Instead, they typically involve studies of local Job Corps sites on issues such as (1) a teacher's college training program providing field experiences for interns working with Job Corps trainees (Ramsey, 1986) or (2) isolation of biographical and sociodemographic characteristics of Job Corps enrollees that distinguish those who complete the training program from those who drop out (Gallegos & Kahn, 1986).

Because the most important national study of the Job Corps (Mallar et al., 1982) is now quite dated, a new national evaluation addressing both its efficacy as a job training and basic educational skills program and its cost effectiveness needs to be conducted.

The Boston Compact

The Boston Compact is a formal written agreement among leaders of the Boston City government, the public schools, labor unions, and the business community "which established a system of priority hiring for students graduating from the public schools in return for the school system's assurance that it would take steps to improve the education and qualifications of its graduates" (Schwartz & Hargroves, 1986–1987, p. 14). The program has become so popular that local adaptations of it have been established in at least 30 other communities around the country (Grant Foundation Commission, 1988).

The Boston school system, in its participation in the Compact, has established firm goals such as increased attendance, lower dropout rates, and mastery of basic skills for all of its students. After 1986, each school in the system was required to submit and implement a plan for mastery of basic skills in reading and math, as measured by a minimum competency test (MCT) (Schwartz & Hargroves, 1986–1987). The business sector and higher education community conduct a variety of collaborative efforts with the school system, including partnerships with individual schools, collective guarantees for summer jobs, part- time work during the school year, jobs for high school graduates, cooperative educational programs, financial support for career counseling in all high schools, and financial assistance for prospective college students (Spring, 1987).

Evaluations of the Boston Compact's success in achieving its goals are described as "promising" (Spring, 1987, p. 12), with an increase each year between 1983 and 1986 in the number of graduates who obtained jobs or attended postsecondary education, and reasonably high wages for Compact jobs for high school graduates in areas typically outside the fast food sector. For the class of 1987, the most recent year for which data are available, over 1,000 graduates were hired through the Compact with an average wage of $6.18 per hour (Boston Compact Evaluation Subcommittee, 1988). During the 1986–1987 school year 1,200 students were placed in part-time after school jobs, and in the summer of 1987 over 3,000 students were placed in summer jobs.

The school system's efforts, however, appear less encouraging. For example, despite the fact that MCT results increased for all racial/ethnic groups in all grades between 1983 and 1985, during the 1985–1986 school year, average scores dropped and in some grades "dramatically decreased" (Hargroves, 1986, p. 21). Hargroves attributes part of this decline to a renorming of the results from the Metropolitan Achievement Test (MAT); however, she also notes that, for most grades Boston students are below national norms in reading and math achievement. For the class of 1988, 45% of the seniors scored at the 40th percentile or lower on the reading scale of the MAT. Results concerning the goal of reducing the percentage of dropouts are even less encouraging. For each graduating cohort of students between 1982 and 1986, the percentage of dropouts increased modestly to the point that in 1986 46% of the cohort left school (Boston Compact Evaluation Subcommittee, 1988).

These two sets of negative results, especially the consistent increase in dropout rates, suggest an inherent weakness in the design and implementation of the Boston Compact, in dealing with the most at-risk segment of the school population. The program appears to suffer from the age-old "creaming" phenomenon (Grant Foundation Commission, 1988; McDill et al., 1972) whereby social or educational programs frequently select the least disadvantaged subjects for treatment, leaving the most at-risk segment of the population unaffected. Gottfredson (1988), in an elaboration of his designation of the Boston Compact as a flawed example of a school/business partnership to ease the transition from school to work, provides a compelling criticism of the program:

> This (increase in dropout rates in Boston) parallels other results implying that promising jobs to students or dropouts so that they continue in school does not reduce dropout (Hahn & Lerman, 1985). Why not? First, no single remedy or approach would be expected to be of much help in solving such a "multiply nested problem" (Mann, 1987). Equally important, however, the incentive structure of the Boston Compact (and similar programs elsewhere) may be wrong. It is the best students—the graduates—who are rewarded by the program; the employment incentives are clearest for them. It is the students with the poorest attendance, who are failing in school, who have already been retained in grade one or more times who are most likely to drop out of school and have the most difficulty finding well-paid and stable work because they have not demonstrated a record of behavior, attitudes, and scholastic performance that employers demand. It is this group of youths at which a program's incentives must be directed if it is to be effective in reducing dropout. . . . Finally, the Boston Compact's incentives are in the future, not "now." The future time perspective of students most at risk of dropout and adolescent problem behavior may often be somewhat limited, implying that to be effective incentives must be realized in the short-term. [pp. 1–2]

The negative results from the Boston Compact concerning dropout rates are not unlike those from national assessments of the labor-market preparation programs that were developed as a component of the 1977 Youth Employment and Demonstration Projects Act. YEDPA programs for in-school youth typically involve some combination of three basic elements that are similar to those of the Boston Compact: career exploration training, basic skills training, and direct work experience. In fact, to a considerable degree the Compact is an outgrowth of a large labor market preparation project sponsored by YEDPA (Spring, 1987). Results of the evaluations of these YEDPA initiatives are typically not positive (Betsey et al., 1985), in that one of two conclusions was the norm: Either the methodological weaknesses of the evaluations did not permit reliable conclusions to be drawn or the treatments produced only marginally positive effects, which decayed rather quickly.

The dropout rate and the most recent basic skills training results from the Boston Compact, in conjunction with those for the YEDPA efforts, underscore the importance of Gottfredson's (1988) recommendation: "What is needed is a program for incentives for those persons who are doing worst to do better than they are. The incentives must be realized in the form of rewards or recognition as progress is made, not later, if they are to be effective" (p. 2). He concluded that no school system appears to have implemented such a task and reward system. We would add that when such a school-to-work incentive system is implemented, it should be conducted as a true experiment (involving random assignment of subjects to treatments), in order to rule out the types of selectivity bias that plague the Boston Compact and make it difficult to draw secure conclusions about programmatic effects.

The Boston Compact has not enjoyed the success envisioned by its original framers. It has, however, led to continuing interaction among the leaders of government, labor, business, higher education, and the school system to address the educational problems of the city's young people. This is illustrated by the development of Compact II, a second agreement by the relevant parties. Compact II is based on five shared goals that include (1) school-based management, (2) parental involvement, (3) comprehensive follow-up services for up to 4 years after high school graduation for students who enter the workforce and for those who enter postsecondary education, (4) a reduction by 50% of the number of dropouts and a doubling of the number of alternative education opportunities available to dropouts, and (5) assurance that Boston students have the academic skills needed to achieve their potential (Boston Compact Measurement Committee, 1989). These goals reflect a maturing of the relationships among the parties involved. They are more focused on processes and less decisive in proclaiming certain end states that must be reached. They are also more realistic, in view of the earlier performance of the Compact.

I Have a Dream

Another widely publicized example of an incentive program to encourage students to remain in school and to establish realistic postsecondary plans is Eugene Lang's "I Have a Dream" Foundation which in 1981 guaranteed financial support for college attendance to each member of the sixth grade in the New York City elementary school of which Lang was an alumnus. The award was contingent on the student's completing high school with acceptable academic performance and avoiding a criminal record that would interfere with college admission (Grant Foundation Commission, 1988; Hahn & Danzberger, 1987).

Mentoring, tutoring, and other intensive support services, as well as follow-up of students for Lang's initiative have been provided by the Harlem Youth Action Corps (Hahn & Danzberger, 1987). The effort has been emulated in varying degrees in a number of other urban centers. Of the original sixth-grade cohort of students in the program, 70% (i.e., 43 of 61) are reported to have graduated from high school, or received an equivalency degree, and approximately 56% of this cohort were enrolled in college at least part-time in 1989 (Berger, 1989).

Although this program has been justifiably praised as a noble philanthropic initiative, its educational effectiveness has not been systematically demonstrated for a variety of methodological reasons. For example, there is an inherent self-selectivity bias in the design, in that those students predisposed to attend college (and thus advantaged in a variety of ways) are most likely to select themselves into the program. Further, this predisposition is likely reinforced by Hawthorne effects; that is, students in the program may be more likely to graduate from high school and more likely to attend college solely because of the public attention they receive as a member of a select group, independent of the incentive structure of the program (Grant Foundation Commission, 1988).

These methodological weaknesses can be completely eliminated only by a true experimental design with random assignment of subjects to at least three groups: an experimental group who receive the full benefits of the Lang treatment; a second group who receive some form of favorable recognition but none of the incentives provided in the Lang program; and a control group who receive neither type of treatment. Further, even if such an experiment produced outcomes favoring the first treatment group, there is the matter of cost effectiveness of this program. Could an alternative approach provide the same level of benefits at a lower cost per student?

Even ignoring the aforementioned methodological flaws and accepting the limited evidence of positive results for some students as valid, there is doubt about the Lang program's effectiveness. Of the 61 self-selected subjects in the original sixth-grade cohort referred to earlier, only 10 (about one-sixth) completed their sophomore year of college "on schedule" (Berger, 1989). This is not an impressive percentage for a self-selected group of students who committed themselves 6 years earlier to attending college.

SUPPORTIVE CONDITIONS OUTSIDE OF SCHOOL

In this section we direct our attention to the current school-related (but often out-of-school) liabilities of the most disadvantaged youth, which are widely believed to contribute both to dropping out and a variety of earlier within-school deviant behaviors such as truancy, delinquency, and poor academic performance. These liabilities include a host of personal, familial, and community problems such as teenage pregnancy, alcohol and drug abuse, delinquent gang membership, single-parent families, family violence including child abuse, and family financial need. They also include socially disorganized communities characterized by poor social control, which is linked to a variety of forms of social deviance such as delinquent gangs, high rates of personal and property crime, and widespread distribution and consumption of drugs (Empey, 1978; Gottfredson & Gottfredson, 1985).

In attempting to deal with these most socially "estranged" youth (Hahn & Danzberger, 1987, p. 51), schools have come to recognize that the reasons for such students' disaffection are multiple and interrelated, that they often manifest a variety of nonconforming behaviors (McDill et al., 1986; Neill, 1979; Quay & Allen, 1982), and that such behaviors are persistent over time from early in their school careers to well into adulthood (G. Gottfredson, 1987). Given the versatility and perseverance of nonconforming behavior of the most disadvantaged segment of the at-risk population of youth, schools have come to realize that traditional structures and staffing are incapable of systematically addressing these problems. Thus they are beginning multi-faceted and coordinated approaches to treating these manifold problems in collaboration with the public and private sectors (Bloch, n.d.). The Grant Foundation Commission (1988) states precisely the premise underlying this newer approach: "Programs should offer multiple options and comprehensive services. Problems of high risk youth have many causes. Therefore, piecemeal approaches won't work" (p. 95).

Strategies to improve the external conditions of disadvantaged youth or to ameliorate their most negative effects on student participation and performance in school take a variety of forms. Some efforts focus on single problems such as pregnancy prevention or parent education and day care for adolescent mothers. Others are deliberately more comprehensive, attempting to meet a variety of needs of disadvantaged youth. Some programs are based totally in the schools, while others use the school as a location for coordination and delivery of services provided by other agencies, and still others are based in the community. The latter two types require careful and continuing cooperation among the various agencies providing services to youth.

A prominent feature of recent comprehensive community-based programs has been an emphasis on involving youth in the development and operation of such efforts. Arguing for the importance of youth participation in a variety of community development efforts, the Grant Foundation Commission (1988) asserts that

> youth can help build the kind of communities we all want and need. If trusted and respected, young people readily learn to evaluate situations, make decisions,

and solve problems — skills that people need in everyday life and employers look for in their workers. Youth then develop not only a sense of belonging and a strong ethic of responsibility, but also an understanding that they are accountable to themselves, their families, and their communities. [p. 51]

This emphasis on youth involvement and participation is consistent with what Fuller (1981) labels the "self-determined community development model," which recognizes the key role of indigenous sources of development within minority comunities.[2]

Chicago Area Project

Without question, the prototype of the self-determined community development model is the Chicago Area Project, organized in 1934 by Clifford B. Shaw of the University of Chicago. It is a delinquency prevention project based on three premises: (1) high rates of delinquency in poverty-stricken areas are a product of the social experiences in the family; (2) effective treatment and prevention can be attained only by constructive changes in the community life of the delinquency-prone individual; and (3) local residents must assume responsibility, both individually and collectively, for defining objectives, formulating and implementing policies, providing financial support, and exercising administrative control over funding, staffing, and programs (Korn & McCorkle, 1965).

The main programmatic activity of the Chicago Area Project has been the establishment of youth welfare organizations among community residents and direct work with predelinquents, delinquent gangs, and adult offenders. Although there is no conclusive evidence about the effectiveness of the program in reducing delinquency rates in the areas served (Kobrin, 1959), it remains the model community program in delinquency prevention and treatment.

KidsPlace Seattle

KidsPlace Seattle is a community development project aimed at making Seattle a better place for children and adolescents. The project has had the participation of youth throughout its history. In 1984 6,000 youths between the ages of 13 and 18 answered a survey about how they viewed Seattle. The results of the survey were reported back to the young people themselves before being presented to others (Grant Foundation Commission, 1988).

The organization's governance committee, KidsBoard, is an advocacy group of 13- to 18-year-olds, including those who are not leaders in their schools and many who would be classified as being at risk. The KidsBoard fosters youth involvement, and its policy committee advises the mayor on youth issues.

In 1986 KidsPlace developed an Action Agenda that included goals to be reached by 1990 in the areas of leadership, health services, safety, schooling, cultural activities, and transportation. Young people are involved in identifying and planning ways to address these issues (Grant Foundation Commission, 1988).

New York City's Dropout Prevention Initiative

Currently schools' participation in cooperative efforts with community agencies to mitigate the effects of out-of-school liabilities ranges from minimal involvement (which is probably the norm) to participation as a full community partner, working in concert with a variety of human service agencies to provide such services as recreation, drug abuse counseling, health, sex education, and counseling to at-risk students. An example of minimal participation is the school functioning merely as a referral agency by directing teenage parents to an alternative school that permits them to continue their schooling while it provides on-site child care (Cahill, White, Lowe, & Jacobs, 1987).

An example of intermediate participation of the school is New York City's Dropout Prevention Initiative (DPI), in which 13 high schools with large concentrations of highly at-risk students, and their 29 "feeder" middle schools, have been assigned to one of several program models. The models vary along two dimensions—the type of services delivered and who delivers those services. The delivery method is either systemic, in which services are directed toward changing the entire school environment; or via case management, where services are directed toward specific young people. In addition, services are provided either by community-based organizations (CBOs) under contract with the Board of Education, or by school personnel. Although this originally resulted in there being four program models, defined by variations along these dimensions, this format was quickly abandoned. During the first few years of the program, all of the DPI schools ended up contracting with at least one CBO (Grannis, Riehl, Pallas, Lerer, Randolph, & Jewell, 1988).

The DPI high schools deliver, in conjunction with the CBOs, a range of services to students, including guidance and counseling, attendance monitoring and outreach, health services, school-level linkages, alternative educational programs, and program facilitation. Funds were also used to improve the security of the schools. Of these strategies, only alternative educational programs deal directly with the curriculum and instruction to which at-risk students are exposed. The guiding premise of the DPI is that students will be able to succeed in school if schools can help students with those problems both inside and outside of school that block their normal progress (Grannis, Riehl, Pallas, Lerer, Randolph, & Jewell, 1988).

Most students have received individual guidance and attendance monitoring services, but much smaller proportions have been exposed to the other program services. Relatively few of the DPI schools have restructured or reorganized schooling for at-risk students. When they have, the most common strategies have involved the clustering of students into programs. Some schools have had block programs for at-risk students; some have formed minischools or "houses," while others have offered transitional classes for long-term absentees returning to school. Several of these organizational forms have also involved curricular innovations. But not all students have been exposed to these special programs. The evidence is quite clear that, while some students have been placed in special academic programs and others have had special components added to their regular academic programs, a great many students, targeted and nontargeted alike, have received no special attention whatsoever, experiencing few of the services the program was designed to deliver to all of the at-risk youth targeted for help.

In light of the sporadic services that many students have received, it is not surprising that the DPI has not been highly successful in shoring up the performance of the low-achieving students it purports to serve. Throughout its first 3 years, the attendance of targeted students fell approximately 8% during the time these students were in the program. This is approximately the same dropoff observed among comparable groups of students who were not enrolled in the DPI. Moreover, the targeted students passed a lower proportion of the courses they took during the program than they did prior to the program. Again, while these downward trajectories are common among at-risk high school students, there is little evidence that these students passed more of their courses than they would have in the absence of the program.

The most telling finding, though, is that the vast majority of targeted students in the DPI have not been accumulating academic credits at a pace that would allow them to graduate from high school in a reasonable amount of time. The result emphasizes that merely retaining students in school is not sufficient to produce competent high school graduates (Pallas, 1989). In this regard, the failure of the DPI to incorporate academic instructional concerns explicitly into its design may be a serious drawback.

SUMMARY AND CONCLUSIONS

In this chapter programs to enhance the educational achievement and attainment of disadvantaged youngsters in secondary school were considered under four broad categories: (1) those that provide disadvantaged students with opportunities for academic success, (2) those that provide them with positive social relationships, (3) those that enhance the perceived relevance of school to the future lives of disadvantaged youth, and (4) those that mitigate the negative effects of outside interferences on school performance and attendance.

In view of the fact that the lack of academic success in school is one of the strongest predictors of early school leaving, programs designed to provide disadvantaged youth with opportunities to achieve such success are a key element in any attempt to address the educational needs of disadvantaged students. We reviewed three basic approaches to providing opportunities to achieve such success: (1) adjusting academic standards to fit students through practices such as individualizing the curriculum, improving diagnostic techniques, evaluating students on the basis of effort and progress, structuring classroom tasks to draw on multiple abilities, and presenting students with challenging standards; (2) enhancing the skills and abilities of students to allow them to meet the standards of the school more readily through practices such as remedial classes, summer learning opportunities, and the use of peer tutors; and (3) increasing the salience of the school curriculum to improve student motivation through practices such as multiethnic curricula, career education, and monetary incentives.

The Summer Training and Employment Program (STEP) and Upward Bound are examples of efforts to provide students with opportunities for academic success. STEP attempts to enhance student abilities and skills and lower the dropout and teenage pregnancy rates by providing students with work experience, academic remediation, and life skills training during two consecutive summers in high school, and by providing support during the intervening school year. Students are guaranteed a job and earn the minimum wage for hours spent in classes and in work. One of the strengths of the design of STEP is its careful evaluation. Based on experience with three cohorts of students, STEP appears to be successful in reducing or eliminating the summer learning losses typically experienced by disadvantaged students. However, the program seems to have little effect on attendance and the level of schooling attained. Nevertheless, the program seems worthy of continued study and refinement at this time.

Upward Bound was the second program that we considered in detail that provides opportunities for academic success. Students in UB participate in remedial instruction, immersion in new curricula, tutoring, cultural en-richment, and counseling to enhance their competence and motivation to succeed in postsecondary education. UB has been subjected to a series of evaluations, some of which were quite carefully done. The program seems effective at holding students in high school through graduation, and in encouraging them to enroll in postsecondary education. It is far less success-ful, however, in developing in students the academic skills required to attain a college degree. These deficiencies appear to be the result of the fact that local UB projects spend relatively little time on academic instruction and the fact that projects are not provided with a clearly articulated strategy for intervention after a program student enters a postsecondary institution.

A second major category of programs for disadvantaged youngsters at the secondary level includes programs designed to provide students with positive social relationships in school. Because many disadvantaged youth feel ignored or unimportant in school—as if no one at school cares about them—programs utilizing this approach seem reasonable. Such efforts rely upon three broad strategies: (1) strategies to link students to adults in the school, including mentor programs and efforts to reorganize school sched-ules to promote closer contact between teachers and students; (2) strategies to link students to other students in the school, including extracurricular activities and orientation programs; and (3) strategies to link students to the school as an institution, including fair and equitable policies and greater student choice over their school programs.

We discussed alternative schools in general and Middle College High School in particular as examples of programs that provide students with positive social relationships in school. Alternative schools are smaller, have lower student/teacher and student/counselor ratios and greater flexibility, and allow students to have extended direct contact with both school staff and other students.

A third major category of programs for disadvantaged youth includes those that aim to enhance the relevance of school to the students' future. If it is true that working- and lower-class adolescents believe that the social conformity and academic achievement demanded in school are not clearly linked to their future status in society, then efforts to establish this linkage in the minds of students should be successful in promoting academic achieve-ment and educational attainment.

The Job Corps, the Boston Compact, and the "I Have a Dream" Pro-gram are examples of programs that attempt to make clear to students the link between current school performance and future adult status. The Job Corps achieves this by providing basic skills education and vocational skills training linked to future employment. The Boston Compact links school completion to employment by guaranteeing jobs to graduates of Boston City high schools. The "I Have a Dream" Program links school completion to financial support for college attendance. Each program strengthens the connection between school participation and future opportunities to motivate disadvantaged students.

The fourth broad category of programs includes those that deal with the out-of-school problems of disadvantaged youth. Such programs respond to problems such as teenage pregnancy, alcohol and drug abuse, delinquent gang membership, single parent families, child abuse, financial need, and communities that are socially disorganized and exhibit poor social control. These problems interfere with school attendance and performance for large numbers of disadvantaged youth.

Several comprehensive efforts to deal with such out-of-school problems were considered. The Chicago Area Project, the prototype of the self-determined community development model, aims to ameliorate problems such as adolescent delinquency and dropping out of school by mobilizing the community to provide services to troubled youth. Services take the form of the establishment of youth welfare organizations by community residents and direct work with youth. KidsPlace in Seattle is a more contemporary version of the community development approach to reducing the barriers to education for large numbers of disadvantaged youth. Youth are involved in identifying problems and developing solutions. The New York City Dropout Prevention Initiative provides a good example of a school system working with community based organizations to offer services to students designed to help them overcome out-of-school barriers to attendance and performance. The severe implementation problems experienced by the high schools in this program illustrate the difficulty of forming new working relationships to respond to problems that emanate from forces outside the school.

As we have moved from preschool programs to elementary programs to secondary programs, the research base on the effectiveness of programs has become increasingly weaker. This is particularly apparent at the secondary level, where most programs have not been systematically evaluated. Nevertheless, the practices assembled into specific programs offer a wealth of ideas about the ways to respond to the needs of disadvantaged youth. We can take from our review of programmatic approaches some understanding of the information needed to develop solutions to the educational problems of disadvantaged youth and insights to guide the development of a comprehensive strategy for more effectively meeting the challenge they present to schools.

Part III

NEW DIRECTIONS FOR ADDRESSING THE NEEDS OF DISADVANTAGED YOUTH

In Part III we move beyond the examination of the current and emerging conditions presented by disadvantaged students and beyond the programmatic responses to those problems to develop proposals in three areas with the potential to affect the education of disadvantaged youth over the next generation. First, in Chapter 7 we develop proposals for improving the capacity of schools and school systems to gather data on the school experiences of disadvantaged youth. Until we have a better understanding of the problems of these youth, we may never be in a position to develop and implement, in a timely fashion, the most appropriate programs for meeting their needs. Second, in Chapter 8 we present our proposals for restructuring schools to meet the needs of disadvantaged youth. Our proposals differ from others currently being discussed in that they focus on developing schools that are more responsive to students in general and disadvantaged students in particular. Finally, in Chapter 9 we develop the broader policy implications of our understanding of the current and future conditions of disadvantaged students in U.S. schools. Taken together, the three chapters in this part constitute an agenda for action to address the problems likely to confront U.S. schools over the next generation.

7

Developing New Information to Address the Problems of Disadvantaged Students

In Part I we showed that a great deal of information is available about the population of disadvantaged youngsters in our schools. In Part II we presented some of the most helpful information that is known about programs to educate the disadvantaged. Sometimes it seems that so much is known about the educational problems of disadvantaged students that addressing their problems is a matter of will rather than a matter of better data. Despite this seeming abundance of data and knowledge, there are serious gaps in information available to educators and policy makers attempting to address these problems. In this chapter we identify some critical data needs that, if satisfied, would enable us to respond more appropriately.

Whether at the national, state, district, school, or even classroom level, we need three kinds of data to be in a better position to deal with the educational problems presented by disadvantaged students. First, we must develop mechanisms for collecting better and more complete data on disadvantaged students themselves. Such data should not be limited to summary statistics of the background characteristics of large aggregations of disadvantaged youth. Data on the students should include a broad array of background, school experience, and performance indicators that would permit educators to develop an accurate understanding of disadvantaged students' needs for educational services. The data should be collected and prepared to allow for school-level analyses of the distributions of disadvantaged youth.

Collecting data on disadvantaged youth carries certain risks. Such youth may be labeled as disadvantaged and be forever classified as such in the minds of school staff. Moreover, schools serving large proportions of disadvantaged youth may be similarly labeled. If these labels lead communities and individuals to expect less of the disadvantaged, then these students will be ill-served. However, refusing to collect data on the disadvantaged makes it nearly impossible to plan educational services to meet their needs.

The second kind of data needed is more thorough and more systematic information about the characteristics of programs designed to help disadvantaged students. Currently, data on the educational programs for disadvantaged students are not collected and assembled carefully enough to allow students to be matched to educational experiences. There are accounts of educational programs with minimal descriptive data on the students served by the programs and almost no data collected on disadvantaged students that can be linked to educational experiences for evaluation purposes.

Third, there is a need to develop a broader array of evidence on the performance of all students, including disadvantaged students ("Schools urged," 1988), since all students may require specialized services at some point in their school careers. Systematic information on student performance is generally limited to a narrow band of information provided by standardized tests.

The identification of the needs for these three types of additional data must occur at each level at which decisions regarding educational policies and practices are made. Accordingly, in this chapter we identify the kinds of data that would be helpful to policy makers and educators at the federal, state, local district, school, and classroom levels. There have recently been extensive discussions in the literature on the problems with educational statistics in general (e.g., Cooke, Ginsburg, & Smith, 1985; Oakes, 1986; Silverman & Taeuber, 1985). Much of this discussion has been spurred by a project sponsored by the National Center for Education Statistics (NCES) to invite widespread participation by members of the research community in the redesign of its major data collection programs. Silverman and Taeuber (1985) provide an account of this process. In this discussion we limit ourselves to consideration of the data most needed to begin to improve the plight of disadvantaged students. In many cases, however, the strategies we suggest, if implemented, could result in improved information and eventually improved educational services for all students.

DATA NEEDS AT THE NATIONAL LEVEL

Data at the national level should be useful to national policy makers and educational leaders attempting to identify current problems and long-term trends that federal policy might ameliorate. Over the years, the data-collection and research efforts sponsored by the federal government, despite their shortcomings, have been exposed to the widest range of comment and criticism and are likely to be so in the future (e.g., Center for Statistics, 1986; Flax, 1987; Hertling, 1986; Mirga, 1986; Mirga & Nienhuis, 1986; Pavuk, 1987). This makes it more likely that federal data-collection efforts will be more consistent with the latest professional standards than those sponsored by state and local agencies. Thus, in addition to collecting data useful to national policy makers, the federal government has a role in promoting data-collection activities of a high quality for more general use.

There has been considerable controversy about the overall federal role in education. For example, it was viewed as quite limited by the Reagan administration, as evidenced by the plans developed during President Reagan's 1980 campaign to dismantle the Department of Education. There seems little disagreement, however, that the federal government has an important role to play specifically in the collection and dissemination of information on educational activities throughout the country (Cooke et al., 1985).

There are a number of areas in which increased federal attention could result in better information on the plight of disadvantaged students and the potential of social and educational policies to address their needs. The following six areas are the ones we think are most salient.

1. There is a need for better data on the Hispanic population. As we have earlier documented, the Hispanic population is the fastest growing group in U.S. society. While the federal government has developed the capacity to collect useful data on the black population, due largely to the civil rights movement, mechanisms for collecting data on the Hispanic population are still less sophisticated than they should be. In the past 20 years, the Census Bureau has changed the way it identifies Hispanics several times, making it difficult to follow changes in the condition of the Hispanic population over time.

While the attempts by the federal Office of Management and Budget, which oversees all federal data collections, to standardize racial/ethnic reporting categories are a step in the right direction, there is little consensus about the appropriateness of their categories, or about the best way to collect information on the Hispanic population. Spencer (1986) provides useful comments on the quality of Hispanic data collected by the Census Bureau.

Other factors complicate the task of collecting data on the Hispanic population. For example, the U.S. Census Bureau identifies only individuals of Hispanic ethnic status who participate in the census, while the Immigration and Naturalization Service provides estimates of millions of additional Hispanic aliens (Anson, 1980). The development of a standard method for identifying Hispanics (both black and white) that enjoys widespread acceptance should be a top priority, if we are to be able to understand the rapidly changing nature of the Hispanic population.

The need to collect more and better data on the Hispanic population is only a special example of the more general need to collect data in ways that are sensitive to heterogeneous minority populations (Portes & Truelove, 1987). Both blacks and Asians are often treated as single groups in government data-gathering efforts, but of course there are important differences among the subgroups of both the black and Asian populations in the United States.

2. There is a need for systematic data on the distribution of students with various types of disadvantages throughout the nation. While data are available on the current poverty rates in school districts, similar information on other indicators of disadvantaged status (as discussed in Chapter 2) would be useful in planning the distribution of appropriate levels of federal resources. Since the disadvantaged population is concentrated in certain states and central cities, the demands for resources in these areas are likely to exceed the capacities of states and localities. Only federal resources can lighten the heavy burden placed on schools in the different states by such concentrations of disadvantaged students. To understand more fully the responsibility that must be met requires better data on the number of disadvantaged students as well as data on the severity of the disadvantaging characteristics.

3. There is a need to develop better indicators of educational problems facing the nation. Although efforts have been mounted by the federal government (Olson, 1987) and the Council of Chief State School Officers (Sirkin, 1985, 1986), much work remains to be done to develop a comprehensive set of indicators of educational problems, particularly as those problems are visited upon the disadvantaged. It is not enough to understand the overall rates of various phenomena; it is also necessary to understand the distributions of such phenomena among different segments of the U.S. population.

4. There is a need for high-quality evaluations of educational programs, particularly those programs targeted at the disadvantaged population. Our earlier review of programs designed to correct the problems of disadvantaged students (McDill et al., 1986) illustrates the importance of carefully designed evaluations of programs. We found few evaluations of programs that provided convincing evidence of program effectiveness. Only when all programs are subject to rigorous evaluations will we be able to determine their effectiveness individually and in relation to other programmatic approaches. Insightful discussions of strategies for strengthening program evaluation efforts in the context of program development are provided by Boruch (1985), Gottfredson (1984), and Gottfredson, Rickert, Gottfredson, and Advani (1984). An example of how program evaluation has been used as part of program development in urban schools is provided by Gottfredson (1986), who outlines the process as practiced in the Charleston County, South Carolina School District.

Several elements are key to strengthened efforts at program evaluation. We note only two of the most important here. First, as Betsey et al. (1985) and Boruch (1985) point out, much evaluation research does not make sufficient use of random assignment of subjects in defining participant and control groups, even though random assignment yields estimates of program effects that are far less biased than results based on any other methods. Second, Gottfredson (1984) discusses the importance of clarifying the theoretical rationales of programs to be evaluated, in order that such assessments can also serve as tests of theories. Both strategies would do much to increase the value of program evaluations.

5. There is a need for coordination of data-gathering activities among the various departments and agencies of the federal government. As we noted in developing our definition of the educationally disadvantaged, the sources of educational opportunities extend well beyond the schools. The problems of the disadvantaged are not only school-related in nature; they also stem from conditions in the family, community, and larger society. Data collected on schooling and its effects on disadvantaged populations must be understood in the context of information on experiences outside schools (Natriello, 1985). Coordination of data collection plans among departments and agencies of the federal government with different mandates should insure that data collected by one agency can be utilized in conjunction with data collected by another. For example, data from a national survey of children should be compatible with data from a national survey of students. Likewise, data on educational problems such as dropping out collected by the Census Bureau should be usable in conjunction with data collected through national studies of secondary schools by the Department of Education (Pallas, 1987, 1989).

6. There is a need for national leadership to develop models for state-level data-gathering activities. A recent study by the Council of Chief State School Officers (Olson, 1986) revealed that the methods used by the states to collect information about schools varies so widely that it is impossible to make comparisons across states or to assemble accurate national data on ostensibly straightforward aspects such as the number of public schools or the numbers of graduates and dropouts. Natriello (1985) has recommended a two-stage process for the educational statistics arm of the federal government to use in working with states to develop model data systems that might later be adopted nationwide. In the first stage, federal officials would identify several states interested in developing a state-level data base relevant to state policy making and work with state education agencies in these states to develop the data-gathering procedures. In the second stage, federal officials might select the most successful data base design and use it as the model for a national data base assembled from data collected by individual states.

There are several advantages to such an approach. State-level data bases would insure that the data gathered are at the appropriate level of aggregation for federal and state policy making. Also, federal officials could provide a leadership role in helping state departments of education to develop the capacity for collecting and interpreting educational data. In addition, national data sets could be developed with some assurance that the actual data collection was useful to the state education agencies and that the states collected the data properly.

7. There is a need to link the basic and periodic data-gathering activities of the federal government in a systematic way to the progress of basic research on education. As new insights are developed about the educational problems of disadvantaged students and the interventions that address those problems, there should be a mechanism for incorporating such insights into the larger federal data collection process. For example, if researchers determine in small scale studies that greater time on task is beneficial for disadvantaged students, federal data collection might incorporate such variables in national studies of student attendance and school processes.

8. There is a need for more broadly based information on the competencies that disadvantaged students may lack or possess. Most traditional outcome measures focus on a narrow range of cognitive abilities, yet a variety of both cognitive and noncognitive traits may be important for adult social and occupational success (Inkeles, 1966; Jencks et al., 1979). While middle class students may have little difficulty in acquiring these important traits, disadvantaged students may not be exposed to the socialization experiences that instill them. As a result, disadvantaged students may have hidden deficiencies that prevent them from participating fully in mainstream society.

DATA NEEDS AT THE STATE LEVEL

States need additional data on both the basic operation of the system of schooling and on the impact of specific programs and reforms. Such data-gathering activities could take several forms.

First, while state departments of education currently collect a wide array of information, frequently there is no coherent approach to the management of this information. Different offices within the state education departments collect different information that is seldom brought together and considered in a coherent way. Earlier federal efforts to enhance the capacity of state education agencies in this regard have met with mixed success (Murphy, 1973), but renewed efforts in a climate of greater interest in the performance of educational systems might be more successful. Thus, there may be much to be gained by organizing and analyzing data that are currently collected for other purposes, to obtain a greater understanding of the educational progress and needs of disadvantaged students.

Second, in addition to improvements in regular information-gathering activities, state education agencies should be encouraged to redouble their efforts to monitor and evaluate special programs and reforms as they are put into operation. Careful evaluations of programs and policies could lead to better services for all students, most particularly disadvantaged ones. In view of the large number of reform activities currently under way in states across the nation, surprisingly little attention and few resources have been devoted to evaluations of the effectiveness of such efforts. This is particularly disturbing when we consider the plight of disadvantaged students, for, as we have noted elsewhere (McDill, Natriello, & Pallas, 1985, 1986; Natriello, McDill, & Pallas, 1985), the most recent wave of reforms may have both positive and negative effects on disadvantaged students.

Third, over the last decade, state education agencies have greatly enhanced their capacities to collect data on student outcomes through statewide testing programs. Few states, however, have developed the capacity to link data on student outcomes to data on educational resources and programs, and to data on student characteristics. States are thus not in a good position to determine which levels of particular kinds of resources are effective with particular groups of students. Some states have begun to collect data on students and school programs in conjunction with testing data (California State Department of Education, 1984; Pennsylvania Department of Education, 1984). These efforts should be encouraged and others initiated.

California provides an example of a state that has developed a broader set of performance indicators and used them to report on the performance of individual local schools (California State Department of Education, 1984; Kirst, 1985). The California system is part of an accountability program that includes statewide targets for performance, performance reports on each school, and recognition of those schools that exhibit exemplary achievement and/or growth.

The California State Department of Education established sets of performance indicators for high schools, intermediate or junior high schools, and elementary schools. The process of developing the indicators permitted review and comment by teachers, administrators, local school board members, and various professional organizations. The indicators touch on a range of performance dimensions. For example, the high school indicators cover five categories: (1) enrollments in academic courses, (2) test scores, (3) performance of college-bound students, (4) dropout and attendance rates, and (5) participation in extracurricular activities and homework and writing assignments completed (California State Department of Education, 1984). Each school receives a report that displays its performance in comparison to its previous performance, to statewide targets, to all other schools statewide, and to other schools with similar students.

In addition to statewide indicators, each school selects additional indicators of educational quality based on evidence available locally. Local indicators can provide a more detailed description of the schools and might include dimensions such as descriptions of the school's curriculum, the number and types of books read by students, and the support the school received from parents and the community in general (California State Department of Education, 1984). Although the California system may be too simplistic (Kirst, 1985), it has initiated the process of integrating data from various sources to provide a more comprehensive set of indicators of school performance.

Pennsylvania has also mounted a state-level data-gathering effort. The Educational Quality Assessment (EQA), conducted on a continuing basis from 1970 to 1988 by the Division of Educational Testing, Pennsylvania Department of Education, has operated under a 1963 legislative mandate that required the State Board of Education to develop an evaluation procedure that would measure the adequacy and efficiency of the educational program offered by the state's public schools (Pennsylvania Department of Education, 1985). The EQA, as a school profiling instrument, provides an assessment at the school level of 14 goal areas that are linked to Pennsylvania's adopted goals of quality education. These 14 areas include both cognitive and noncognitive domains. Examples of the former are reading, writing, and mathematics, while examples of the latter are self-esteem, societal responsibility (citizenship), and health and safety practices. The EQA also includes 33 "condition" variables (Blust, Coldiron, & Cica, 1985), which measure teacher and student perceptions of various dimensions of school climate, organizational characteristics, and student sociodemographic characteristics.

The EQA program has provided two types of school-level scores on the 14 school outcome variables. One is a school percentile rank based on state norms. The other, a predicted school score range, has been obtained by employing the condition variables in a multiple-regression analysis in which they are treated as input variables and the 14 goal areas are treated as output variables. The analytic procedure adjusts these school level outcomes for differences across schools in the various conditions.

The EQA data have provided statewide information to the Pennsylvania Department of Education for evaluations on the effectiveness of the public education system at the state level, as well as for interdistrict comparisons. Further, at the state level the EQA provides diagnostic reports on various indicators of school effectiveness, as well as baseline information for between-school comparisons of educational programs.

DATA NEEDS AT THE LOCAL DISTRICT LEVEL

In local districts, where educators have more control over the deployment of educational resources, it may be even more useful to have reliable and valid information on the distribution of educational resources and its subsequent effects on student progress. Yet, aside from a few oft-noted exceptions (Hammack, 1987), the available evidence suggests that most local districts lack the capacity to collect and process data on the performance of the school system and its students. Indeed, there is even some resistance to such data-gathering and analysis as a basis for decision making. Local districts could take several steps to improve their capacity to serve disadvantaged students through better data collection and analysis efforts.

First, local districts should be encouraged to invest in data systems that allow them to track individual students and groups of students over time. Too many districts treat each school year as a separate entity for data-collection purposes, making it impossible to follow students from grade to grade or school to school within the district. Since many of the positive and negative effects of educational programs may be long term and cumulative, local districts are seldom in a position to understand the effects of their educational efforts. For example, districts lacking the ability to track students over time cannot understand the patterns of school experiences, beginning in the elementary grades, that lead to dropping out at the secondary level. Even when districts do invest in longitudinal data systems, disadvantaged students are often lost because of their less consistent attendance and greater residential mobility. Special efforts will be required to collect data on disadvantaged students.

Second, local districts almost always collect data on student background and outcomes, sometimes collect data on the quality of instruction, and only occasionally collect data on educational programs. Further, they almost never have the capacity to link data on educational programs and instructional quality to student outcomes (Hammack, 1987). Local districts need to develop systems that link programs and students. For example, if a student participated in a special mathematics program in fifth grade, that experience should be recorded in a system that is later used to understand performance in mathematics in secondary school. Such a system will also enable the leaders of local districts to understand which subgroups of students have access to various types of educational resources throughout the district. This will lead to analyses specifying which educational programs have the most favorable impacts on different groups of students.

The work of Cooley (1983) and Bickel and Cooley (1985) provides a good example of improvements in the use of data at the local district level. Since 1978 these authors, on staff at the Learning Research and Development Center at the University of Pittsburgh, have been working with the Pittsburgh Public Schools to improve the use of educational research within the district by conducting district-level evaluations in conjunction with school district personnel. Their work began with a districtwide needs assessment to determine the extent to which the schools were meeting the needs of their children and to suggest priorities for improvement. The initial assessment consisted of a survey of stakeholders regarding their perceptions of current conditions in the district and an examination of available data on student performance (Cooley, 1983). It was followed by a series of other evaluation activities for the district.

Cooley (1983) describes these experiences in the Pittsburgh Public Schools as being consistent with the cybernetic paradigm, which involves developing and monitoring a variety of performance indicators and then taking corrective action—which he refers to as "tailoring"—whenever an indicator moves into an unacceptable range. Moreover, he notes that one important function of district indicators is their contribution to districtwide priority setting. As Cooley (1983) states, "Since the objective is to improve the performance of the system, district-level aggregates are important for a dialogue about what aspects are in greatest need of improvement and, over time, for indicating whether progress is being made" (p. 8).

Cooley (1983) also discusses the distribution of district-level performance indicators, which is particularly relevant to the education of disadvantaged students. Identifying unusually low performance can guide action to correct the deficiency. As an example, he notes that the original districtwide needs assessment in Pittsburgh identified reading achievement in the primary grades as a major problem. Further analyses at the classroom level "revealed some second- and third-grade classrooms in which little or no reading growth was occurring in the course of the year" (p. 8). Cooley explains that, in order for analyses of this type to lead to improvements, there must be a process for confirming the indication (e.g., an instructional supervisor visiting the identified classrooms to confirm that reading instruction is not going well) and, if the problem is confirmed, a process of corrective action (e.g., intensive clinical supervision to improve reading instruction). The Pittsburgh case provides a useful illustration of the potential of district-level data gathering to improve educational experiences for all students, but perhaps particularly for disadvantaged students.

DATA NEEDS AT THE SCHOOL LEVEL

It is within individual schools that many educational decisions are made, and it is there that many of the most serious inequalities in access to educational services and differences in educational performance develop.

However, it is within these same schools that the least information is systematically gathered, recorded, and made available to school professionals. Teachers, counselors, and administrators all have occasion to collect and use information on students and educational programs, but such information is seldom made available and shared in ways designed to assist students who are having difficulty with school. A number of steps can be taken to improve this situation.

First, schools should be encouraged to collect useful information on the home and community conditions of students. Without systematic information on the backgrounds of their students, schools may not be in a position to design and target educational programs in the most appropriate way. If schools are to succeed with disadvantaged students, they must learn more about the conditions under which students live and learn when they are not in school.

Second, schools need to make the available information accessible to classroom teachers. Some teachers pride themselves in not inquiring about the backgrounds of their students, in an attempt to remain unbiased (Natriello & Dornbusch, 1984). However, professional educators should not have to resort to studied ignorance to maintain a fair stance toward their students. If doctors attempted to treat their patients without being cognizant of their medical histories, they would be accused of malpractice. The same should be true for teachers. Particularly in the case of disadvantaged students, educators should be aware of the home and community conditions that are likely to influence school performance.

Third, schools should employ personnel who have the experience to use aggregated data on programs and students. Most educators are trained to approach students as individuals. While this is important in providing direct educational services, it is not a useful approach for making decisions about the deployment of resources to aggregates of students, decisions that affect the course of school activities and programs. Placing personnel with experience in social, community, and institutional analyses in schools would enhance the capacity of schools to use data in appropriate ways to improve the educational process.

An example of one type of data collection and management system that might be employed at the school level is the Behavior Tracking System (BTS) in use in the Charleston County School District in Charleston, South Carolina. Developed by researchers from the Johns Hopkins Center for Research on Elementary and Middle Schools, the BTS is part of Project 2001, a school-system improvement program that systematically collects, maintains, and retrieves data at the student, classroom, school, and system levels, for purposes not only of school improvement but also of educational research and development. It is a physically secure and confidential computer system used to monitor the behavior of individual students (Karweit,

Gottfredson, & Gottfredson, 1988). It can generate three different types of materials:

1. Summary information on the behavioral incidents (both positive and negative) recorded in a school, broken down by categories such as grade, sex, race, teacher, date, and type of action taken (which must be consistent with the school's clearly specified disciplinary policy)
2. Routine letters and related documents such as detention slips, and suspension letters to students and parents, as an integrated part of the recording of a behavioral incident
3. Special-purpose letters, which are not linked to any particular action but require information stored in the BTS data base for execution

In addition to providing the school with useful information about students and classes for educational policy purposes, the BTS also facilitates frequent communication between the school and students' homes, which is important to involving parents in providing consequences in the home for student behavior in the school and thus reducing undesirable school behavior (Atkeson & Forehand, 1979). Further, the BTS promotes effective classroom organization and management by monitoring student behavior and providing the student with clear and specific information about rules and feedback on the social consequences of breaking such rules (Emmer, Evertson, Sanford, Clements, & Worsham, 1984). Finally, the system provides useful information on the school disciplinary policy, and the students' degree of conformity to it, to a school-based management team that utilizes it in developing plans for school improvement.

DATA NEEDS AT THE CLASSROOM LEVEL

At the classroom level, where teachers actually interact with and instruct disadvantaged students, teachers collect data in several ways. Herman and Dorr-Bremme (1984), in a national survey, note that teachers collect information on student performance through routine class and homework assignments, classroom interaction during question-and-answer sessions, recitations, discussions, oral reading, problem-solving at the chalkboard, special projects, presentations, and reports. Teachers act upon a great deal of data that they collect for themselves about their own students. Herman and Dorr-Bremme's survey reveals that a teacher's own observations and classwork are more important than other types of testing for providing information for classroom decision making; and that teachers' opinions, judgments, and recommendations are more important than any type of testing for school decision making. Moreover, both teachers and administrators view teacher-made tests as more important sources than district and state-mandated tests for making a variety of decisions in schools and classrooms.

However, as Stiggins and colleagues (Stiggins, 1985; Stiggins & Bridgeford, 1985; Stiggins, Conklin, & Bridgeford, 1986) have observed, we have a very limited understanding of classroom assessment practices. Teachers rely on their own sources of information about their students, yet the quality of that information is variable, and we do not know if such information leads to good classroom decisions. Moreover, the broad base of information on students available to teachers in the classroom is not available to anyone else in the school.

Classroom teachers, in relying on their observations and memories of student behavior, may make mistakes. Reviewing the literature related to the information that teachers collect on student performance by means other than testing, Rudman et al. (1980) conclude that, "in contrast to teachers' perceptions of their students' test scores there is some evidence that teachers' reporting of their students' classroom interpersonal behavior is neither stable nor accurate (Elmore & Beggs, 1972; Barnhard, Zimbardo, & Sarason, 1968; Openshaw, 1967; Feshbach, 1969; Tolor, Scarpetti, and Lane, 1967)" and that "teachers seem not to be accurate observers of pupils' academic behavior" (p. 58).

There are several ways to view teachers' assessments of student performance. Egan and Archer (1985) observe that examining teacher appraisals of students using experimental models of prejudice borrowed from social psychology (e.g., Rosenthal & Jacobson, 1968) can be contrasted with studying diagnosis in other professions, where the accuracy and rationality of the appraisal are assumed and interest is directed to the strategy of the appraisal process. Egan and Archer (1985) compare teacher appraisals of student ability in mathematics and English with appraisals inferred from standardized tests. They conclude that

> there is little basis for a claim that teachers' ratings are inaccurate — not because their ratings can be shown to be accurate, by reference to some predetermined measure of true ability, but because we cannot produce a rational strategy of classification that is similar to theirs and that gives substantially better results. [p. 32]

It thus may be useful to consider the ways teachers utilize the information they collect on students and their performance and behavior.

Three strategies for improving upon the information collected and used by teachers should be considered. First, in view of the amount of time teachers spend assessing student performance, teachers should be trained appropriately in the collection and use of such information. With the growth in the size of the disadvantaged population, waiting for specialists to diagnose the learning and social problems of students will become impractical. Each teacher must be equipped with the skills to assess student performance and behavior and understand the contributing factors. Stiggins (1985) notes that resources must be allocated for providing technical assistance to teachers, if we want them to develop their classroom assessment skills. With the appropriate assistance, teachers should be able to develop systematic approaches to gathering information on students and linking that information to decisions about instruction.

Second, schools should take the information each teacher collects about students and use it beyond that teacher's classroom. This will be a difficult process, as teachers must work to produce information on students that can be shared with other teachers and rendered sufficiently valid and reliable to be passed on to others in the school. Stiggins (1985) recommends that teachers be provided with resources for collaborating on assessments. This might lead to common assessment practices within a school and shared understanding about the meaning of information gathered on students.

Third, schools and districts should enable and encourage teachers to make use of data collected at other levels to develop a better understanding of the students in their own classes. School- and district-level data systems might be used to provide data on the actual students in a teacher's classes. This often happens now for standardized test data, but it happens less often for data on students' backgrounds, and it very seldom happens for data on students' school experiences. For example, teachers seldom have a clear understanding of the academic histories of the students in their classes (Garet & DeLany, 1985). State- and national-level data might also be used to provide teachers with a sense of how their students compare to others in the state and nation.

School and district staff will need to devote time and attention to preparing the information presented to teachers in a manner that is readily interpretable. Teachers do not have and are unlikely to take the time necessary to examine data on students and their performance in order to extract the implications for their classes. Schools must insure that the data made available to teachers are not misinterpreted.

The time and effort required of teachers to collect, maintain, and interpret data on their students can be a deterrent to the widespread use of strategies such as curriculum-based progress-monitoring procedures. As Fuchs, Fuchs, Hamlett, and Hasselbring (1987) describe it,

With curriculum-based progress-monitoring procedures, teachers select long-term curricular goals, design measurement systems that correspond to those curricular goals, routinely monitor student progress toward goals using those measurement systems, use the database to evaluate the effectiveness of the educational program, and modify instruction as needed to insure goal attainment. [p. 14]

Keeping in mind the problem of limited teacher time, let us look at an example of a curriculum-based progress-monitoring approach. A good one is provided by the data-based special education delivery system utilized by the Pine County Minnesota Special Education System (Tindal, Wesson, & German, 1982). The system collects data on four academic areas (reading, spelling, written expression, and math) and four social behavior areas (noise, out-of-place movement, unacceptable physical contact with another person or another person's property, and off-task activity). This data base is used for decisions in seven areas: identification, initial assessment, eligibility determination, individualized educational program (IEP) selection, IEP development, IEP implementation review, and program review. For each decision, a student support team is convened to review the data and make the decision.

This strategy, developed for use with special education students, could be used to monitor the progress of all students and make appropriate decisions about educational programs. However, as noted, such systems are likely to meet with teacher resistance, since even computer-based systems of progress monitoring are likely to place considerable time demands on already busy schedules. There is some evidence to suggest, though, that teachers are more satisfied with computer-based systems than with paper-and-pencil systems (Fuchs et al., 1987).

There are also examples of classroom-level data collection on students that might be used beyond the confines of a single teacher and classroom. Natriello (1982) reports on a school district in which the English teachers in four high schools took on the challenge of making one of the most complex assessment processes, the assessment of student writing, more consistent and uniform. To accomplish this, they developed what they called a "general rubric," a grading standard for themes. It specified the various levels of student performance in terms of six distinct dimensions: grasp of subject, thesis, paragraphing, explanation and justification of specifics, style, and mechanics. The common grading standard allowed teachers to have a better understanding of and greater confidence in the grades given by their colleagues. It also had the effect of conveying a consistent set of standards for writing to students as they moved through high school.

CONCLUSIONS

The needs of students, particularly disadvantaged students are multi-faceted and complex. The resources of schools must be similarly multifaceted and complex. Moreover, if the appropriate school resources are to be delivered effectively to students, each level of the educational system must have the capacity to collect systematic data on students and their needs. Wherever educational decisions are made, if we wish to utilize resources most effectively, we must have as complete and as accurate information on students as possible. The strategies outlined in this chapter provide some initial directions for enhancing our data-gathering efforts to benefit disadvantaged students. Still, understanding the needs of disadvantaged students does not guarantee that schools will be able to respond to those needs. In the next chapter we consider some structural changes in schools that might permit them to be more responsive to disadvantaged students.

8

Restructuring Schools to Meet the Needs of Disadvantaged Students

The programs for meeting the educational needs of disadvantaged students discussed in Part II have been designed to operate in conjunction with schools as they currently exist. A more comprehensive approach to dealing with this challenge would be to rethink the basic design of elementary and secondary schools. This could lead to a major restructuring of schools as we know them.

To consider the need for restructuring we must understand the current organization of most elementary and secondary schools in the United States. Schools are organized as bureaucracies that process students in batches (Bidwell, 1965). To continue to organize schools in this way and believe that they will succeed in educating most students requires that we accept certain tenuous assumptions about students. First, we must assume that most of the students served by a school have fairly uniform middle-class characteristics, which include developed academic skills, predictable learning needs, and habits of prosocial behavior. Second, we must assume that the schools can serve students effectively by focusing upon a rather limited range of the events that comprise the lives of students. We must assume that schools need only be concerned with the immediate lives of students and with only a narrow band of school-related activities. These assumptions probably work fairly well for middle-class students living in communities and families able to provide for their developmental and career-related needs and able to monitor their out-of-school activities. They may have applied to most Americans in an earlier era when society was dominated by local leaders and institutions that shared fairly homogeneous values (Comer, 1981). These assumptions also served reasonably well when the U.S. economy provided large numbers of positions for those who were unable to succeed in traditional schools.

But such assumptions almost certainly cannot apply to disadvantaged students in our complex modern society. Disadvantaged students present the school with exceptional diversity as well as with patterns of performance and behavior that traditional schools operated by middle-class professionals do not anticipate. Moreover, disadvantaged students come with histories of deficiencies and futures of even less promise. Finally, disadvantaged students enjoy few of the out-of-school social and economic resources that sustain middle-class students, and they do not benefit from the local support system that sustained earlier, more geographically stable generations of disadvantaged youngsters. The diverse, unfamiliar, and unpredictable backgrounds and characteristics of disadvantaged students confront the school with great uncertainty and the need to learn a great deal about the student in order to move quickly to marshal the appropriate resources.

If a school is unequipped to ascertain the needs of its disadvantaged students, and if a school has too few resources available to help them, then the only choice left to management and staff is to adopt a custodial mode of operation in which the goal is simply for the school to survive as an organization, regardless of its effects on its clients. For schools serving disadvantaged students to become more than custodial institutions, they must develop the capacity (1) to deal with the diversity and uncertainty presented by disadvantaged students in contemporary society, (2) to understand the prior and future conditions that affect such students, (3) to realize the coexisting conditions in nonschool segments of the students' lives, and (4) to provide such students with the appropriate academic and nonacademic resources that are prerequisites for learning. In this chapter we take a fresh look at the organization of elementary and secondary schools as they attempt to meet the needs of disadvantaged students.

CONCEPTUAL FRAMEWORK

A number of strategies for restructuring schools have been suggested (Cohen, 1988; Task Force on Teaching as a Profession, 1986), and there are a growing number of restructuring attempts (David, 1989; Maine Department of Educational and Cultural Services, 1988; Public School Forum of North Carolina, 1988; Seattle Public Schools, 1988; Spady, 1988). Our purpose here is not to catalog these approaches to restructuring, but rather to develop a framework within which to examine the restructuring efforts of schools, for their capacity to meet the needs of disadvantaged students.

The basic premise of this framework is that, if schools are to succeed with disadvantaged students, and to some extent with all students, they must become more responsive to their various needs. Schools must be able to develop a wide array of services and deliver them at the time they are needed. This kind of responsiveness requires that schools be able to acquire and quickly process a great deal of information about students and their ongoing performance and behavior. If schools were able to concentrate on one student at a time, it would not be very difficult to be responsive, but schools must deal with hundreds and thousands of students simultaneously.

There are three factors that together make the task of meeting the educational needs of disadvantaged students in schools particularly challenging.[1] First, all students, but particularly disadvantaged students, present schools with a diverse set of needs that require schools to be able to bring to bear a variety of resources in order to mount appropriate and ultimately successful responses. The typical secondary school has long had a highly differentiated staff responsible for a wide range of educational treatments. The typical elementary school, while not having a staff as differentiated as the secondary school, has come to include an enlarged set of instructional specialists; and the middle school or junior high school that has grown out of the higher grades of the elementary school has moved toward greater differentiation. Schools serve increasingly diverse bodies of students with differing background characteristics, skills, and abilities. Moreover, schools must command and employ an even wider array of resources to meet the needs of disadvantaged students. These may include drug and alcohol counseling, pregnancy prevention, services for adolescent mothers, preparation for work, intervention in troubled family situations, and more.

Second, public schools in the United States have been charged with producing a wide range of products, from math and electronics specialists to educated prospective parents and safe drivers; from learning-disabled students who can function in adult society to students capable of performing in dramatic roles, winning music awards, and achieving athletic scholarships. Indeed, it is central to the notion of the comprehensive school that it produces many different kinds of graduates. Moreover, schools are also charged with preparing well-adjusted functioning individuals able to participate in society as responsible citizens of a democracy. The diversity of these outcomes makes the process of schooling extremely complex.

Third, our society is demanding that students' achievement be higher than it ever has been before. In an earlier era, it did not matter so much if students failed to achieve in school or dropped out, as the economy could accommodate individuals lacking literacy and numeracy skills. The evolving U.S. economy will no longer have places for those who are not able to perform well in school and graduate.

These three factors—the diversity of student needs and the resources required to meet them, the diversity of goals for schooling, and the increasing level of performance necessary for success—have all strained the capacity of traditional schools, which have organizational forms that evolved under much less challenging conditions. Most school reforms over the past 20 years, with the notable exceptions of school desegregation and PL 94-142 (which mandated the mainstreaming of handicapped youngsters), have been directed at reducing the impact of these three factors, not at enhancing the capacity of schools to deal with them.

For example, several policies have been designed to reduce the diversity of students and resource needs that confront schools. Magnet-school programs are designed to reduce the diversity of students in a school by assembling groups of students with similar interests in the same building. Special programs such as those for teen mothers, for drug-dependent students, and for disruptive youth attempt to reduce diversity in two ways: first by removing students with certain characteristics from the regular school program, and second by grouping them together, often in separate facilities. Calls for schools to be involved only with academic concerns also represent an attempt to curtail the diversity of resources that must be managed by schools. Various proposals for enhancing student and parental choice in selecting schools may have similar effects in reducing the diversity of students present in individual schools.

A number of policies have also been designed to reduce the diversity of goals or outcomes pursued by schools. The growth of standardized testing in the 1970s had the effect of constricting the range of outcomes for which schools were held responsible. The "back-to-basics" movement that began in the 1970s continued into the reforms of the 1980s in the form of the "New Basics" recommended by the National Commission on Excellence in Education (1983), again narrowing the range of educational outcomes to which attention was directed.

Finally, there have also been policies that had the effect of reducing the level of performance expected of schools. The minimal-competency testing programs implemented by a number of states have served to focus the attention of educators and the public on student performance at relatively low levels. This ignores the needs of higher-achieving students and is far different from holding schools responsible for the academic and social growth of all students.

The foregoing discussion serves to illustrate a fundamental difference between prior reform efforts and our approach to restructuring schools. Rather than attempting to reduce the challenges presented by the diversity of students, the diversity of resources and goals, and the high levels of performance expected of schools, we argue for changes in the organization of schools to meet these challenges. A major focus is the reduction of uncertainty.

Like other organizations, schools must deal with uncertainty in executing their tasks; that is, they must attempt to improve the matching of resources with needs in working to produce desired outcomes. Schools need information on current student performance and behavior and on barriers to improved performance and behavior. They also need information on educational processes and their impact on students. If uncertainty is viewed as the gap between the information required to respond most appropriately to student needs and the information that is actually available, then there are two basic ways to reduce uncertainty (Galbraith, 1973): (1) by reducing the school's need to process information, and (2) by increasing the capacity of the school to process information. The restructuring strategies that we propose in the next sections are aimed at these ends.

STRATEGIES FOR REDUCING THE SCHOOL'S NEED TO PROCESS INFORMATION

As schools have grown in size and the control of the educational process has become more centralized, the demands of schools and school systems for information on student needs and performance have increased dramatically. As decision making about the educational program has become far removed from students and classrooms, the need to provide decision makers with information on students has become more pressing. For example, if decisions about curriculum are to be made at the school district level instead of at the classroom level, then district decision makers need detailed information on past patterns of student performance and the impact of any new curricular offerings. Unfortunately, the capacity of schools and districts to gather and process such information has often not kept pace with the centralization of decision making. As a result, decisions about the school program are often made without adequate information. This problem has become even more severe as more and more decisions about the educational program have moved to the state level as a result of the recent wave of school reforms.

One way to correct the problem of centralized decision making in the absence of adequate information is to move decision making closer to the source of the information—the students and those who teach them. We recommend four strategies for moving decisions to levels where information on student performance and behavior is available: (1) revising rules and programs to promote flexibility; (2) using goal setting to enhance the discretion of local educators; (3) creating self-contained teaching/learning units, to allow educators to make decisions about deploying resources to meet student needs; and (4) providing educational resources above those thought minimally necessary, thus allowing educators some discretion in addressing emerging needs. We discuss each of these strategies in turn.

Flexible Rules and Programs

Rules, procedures, and programs are all devices designed to increase the ability of an organization to plan activities. They are common in all types of schools and embody certain assumptions about the way tasks will be performed. Schools adopt and utilize a variety of procedures, or sequences of rule-governed behavior, such as those connected with scheduling classes, recording attendance, accounting for "dropouts," reporting student performance, and hiring and assigning teachers. Schools also employ a great variety of programs, ranging from the standard curriculum guidelines to the programs of study to which students are assigned, to special instructional programs to meet special needs of students. Indeed, efforts to address the needs of disadvantaged students typically take the form of programs, and these have often been implemented at the insistence of external funding agents concerned that resources be targeted appropriately. Schools have relied upon rules, programs, and procedures to organize many of their activities. In general, rules solve a number of problems for schools and enable them to create order out of uncertainty. In some areas, such as student misbehavior, research has demonstrated that well-developed systems of rules reduce problems (Gottfredson & Gottfredson, 1985).

However, rules, programs, and procedures work only when the exceptions or deviations are relatively few in number. In schools confronting the wide sociocultural diversity characteristic of disadvantaged populations, the number of exceptions and deviations is often large. As a result, the rules fail to serve the function of reducing uncertainty and often cause a redirection of the energies of staff toward rule enforcement and away from the educational processes that rules are supposed to permit. Even in suburban schools with middle-class students, the number of exceptions and deviations may make the use of strict systems of rules difficult (Natriello, 1982). Programs may suffer when school officials spend unnecessary time deciding which students are eligible for program resources when all students in the school might profit from such resources. For example, students in urban schools often participate in a variety of pull-out programs that may do more to disrupt the regular class, composed primarily of students who nearly qualify for such programs, than to target educational resources effectively. As the numbers and proportions of disadvantaged students increase in our elementary and secondary schools, special programs will become a less effective strategy for responding to their needs. As we discussed in Part II, when disadvantaged students return to the regular school environment after being served by a special program, their performance deteriorates below the level of their more advantaged peers.

Rules designed with one set of conditions in mind are often counterproductive when actual conditions in schools are quite different. Thus, restructuring efforts may seek to modify or eliminate rules or shift decisions regarding the creation of rules from outside the school to the school level. For example, planners of the Schools for the Twenty-First Century project in Seattle (Seattle Public Schools, 1988) proposed to have one day a week with flexible scheduling, to permit student contact time devoted to activities such as self-directed study; large-group instruction; and community service and staff activities such as planning, training, and curriculum development. Such scheduling might allow the staff to meet the needs of students more effectively. Other restructuring efforts have granted relief from inappropriate rules and regulations. The Lead Teacher Project in North Carolina (Public School Forum of North Carolina, 1988) granted schools relief from state statutes and policies in exchange for accountability for results. A restructuring effort in Maine included provisions for waivers for current state requirements (Maine Department of Educational and Cultural Services, 1988).

As a general principle, rules, procedures, and programs should be developed, specified, and controlled at those levels in the school system that have access to the best information on the impact of those rules, procedures, and programs. For example, it may make sense to have a "no pass, no play" rule to govern student participation in interscholastic athletics, but the rule should be specified at a level where adequate information is available on the impact of the rule. If state legislators decide to enact such a rule, they should be willing (1) to invest in the data-collection effort to monitor its impact continuously, (2) to establish a mechanism by which to consider appropriate exceptions to the rule, and (3) to certify to the public that the rule is having a positive effect on the education of students. If lawmakers are not able or willing to engage in these activities, then perhaps a rule of this sort is best left to individual schools or districts, where the same requirements might be more easily met. Those who promulgate rules, procedures, and programs should assume responsibility for their effects.

Using Goal Setting and Monitoring to Increase Individual Autonomy

Goal setting is a strategy designed to increase the flexibility of an organization to adapt to the inability to plan for all events. Goal setting makes it possible for individuals at various points in the school to respond to novel situations without referring to superiors in the hierarchy. If the goals of the organization are understood, individuals can exercise considerable discretion, as long as their actions are consistent with the overall goals. Thus, in theory, goal setting is a mechanism for decentralized decision making.

In the last 25 years schools have increasingly come to rely upon targeting or goal setting in the form of instructional objectives (Mager, 1962). Federal initiatives for management by objectives and program evaluation (Rivlin, 1971), state emphases on program structure and assessment such as Florida's and North Carolina's public reporting, court rulings such as New Jersey's "Thorough and Efficient" mandate (Wise, 1979), and the popularization of research such as Edmonds's "Five Effectiveness Factors" have all pushed schools toward rational goal setting. Some have even suggested that schools have relied on such devices to too great an extent (Callahan, 1962; Natriello, 1984; Wise, 1979).

But the implementation of goal setting in many schools has resulted in less rather than more flexibility. When goals are linked to highly specified behavioral expectations for performers, they serve to deprive individuals of discretion and rob organizations of flexibility. Moreover, the setting of goals and objectives can become a ritual designed to please those in power, while having either no effect or a constraining effect on the performance of key tasks. For schools serving the disadvantaged, inappropriately implemented goal setting systems can have serious negative consequences, since they curtail the ability of schools to respond quickly to student needs.

Moreover, schools serving diverse populations may have special difficulties in implementing a goal-setting process. Resolution of tensions among conflicting programmatic priorities remains a social policy issue for most schools. This may be particularly true for those serving disadvantaged populations, where agreement on goals may be difficult to reach and where goals, once agreed upon, may be difficult to achieve. Thus, a strategy with the potential to enhance the flexibility and effectiveness of the organization may actually impede it.

The involvement of all relevant participants — administrators, teachers, parents, students — in the goal setting process can be a method of achieving the consensus necessary for schools to function effectively. Comer (1980) argues that consensus about where the school needs to go and what it is trying to accomplish is the most important element in making schools work. Once consensus is achieved through a participatory process, the articulated goals and objectives of a school should function as a liberating force by defining broad limits within which teachers and administrators can work to meet the needs of students.

A number of districts utilize goal setting and monitoring of results at the school level. The North Carolina Lead Teacher Project includes school-based accountability teams that develop models tailored to the school goals determined by the faculty of each school (Public School Forum of North Carolina, 1988). A 1989 overview of the project states that, "once faculties have been involved in determining accountability goals and setting strategies to meet their goals, measurable improvement is the result" (Public School Forum of North Carolina, 1989, p. 3). Similarly, the Seattle Public Schools' (1988) School Focused Leadership is a "process by which each school community defines its unique needs and participates in formulating the district-wide vision, goals, and objectives" (p. 51).

Clune and White (1988) found that school-based management councils are fundamental elements of districts engaged in school-based management.

The principal, teachers, parents, community members, and, sometimes, students serve on these councils. They make decisions for individual schools regarding matters such as textbook selection, curriculum, and hiring. These councils can develop goals for individual schools and monitor progress toward achieving those goals.

Systems for goal setting, including instructional and behavioral objectives, should be used to permit and enhance the discretion of local educators, as well as facilitate students' access to appropriate educational resources. Once in place, goals should also be used to guide accountability efforts.

Creating Self-Contained Teaching/Learning Units

Organizing around self-contained tasks is a strategy designed to allow organizations to adapt more readily to their inability to anticipate needs; it also helps them to plan by placing all relevant resources — and the authority to employ them — in close proximity to the clients who need them. Such a strategy reduces the need to plan and allocate particular resources prior to the time when client conditions actually become apparent.

Schools have often organized around self-contained tasks. This strategy is the dominant form of organization at the elementary school level, where teachers and students are placed together in self-contained classrooms in which many of the necessary instructional resources are present. This form has been severely threatened, however, as special pull-out programs, typically federally funded, have disrupted this arrangement.

At the secondary school level, the dominant form of organization has not been self-contained tasks. Instead, there is a functional division of labor as a student moves among a series of teachers, each of whom is thought to possess one kind of learning resource (e.g., English, mathematics, science, social studies, etc.). Unfortunately, in most secondary schools, there is little communication among these teachers and little coordination of the overall student program (Garet & DeLany, 1985; Natriello, 1982). While it is generally assumed that this process is managed by the guidance staff responsible for developing student schedules, there is considerable evidence that most guidance counselors do not have sufficient time or information to coordinate student programs in a meaningful way.

This lack can lead to serious difficulties for students, at the very least placing a premium upon the ability of students to manage their own programs. Some students become very astute managers of their programs, while others, among them the disadvantaged, never quite understand the subtleties of selecting courses that maximize their performance. This exacerbates the existing performance differentials between students of different ability levels. It also presents a situation in which most of the important instructional management is being done by students themselves, sometimes in conjunction with astute parents. Administrators, guidance counselors, and teachers have insufficient information to plan coherent academic programs for students initially, and have almost no information in sufficient time to make adjustments to those programs as problems develop and re-planning is required.

When these problems become severe and inescapable, secondary schools often resort to the strategy of self-contained tasks. This pattern of organization, in which designated learning resources are available to a work group of teachers and students organized around outputs, is evident in special programs for students with clear academic problems, such as dropouts, teenage mothers, and learning disabled students. The important point to note is that this form of organization makes information on the performance of the system more readily available to those who have access to the resources necessary to overcome any performance problems. Earlier reforms calling for "house plans," schools within a school, middle school modules, and "alternatives" reflect efforts to influence schools in this direction.

An example of the strategy of self-contained tasks is evident in David's (1989) description of middle schools in the Jefferson County Public Schools in Louisville, Kentucky:

> Middle schools are organized into mini-schools, each with roughly 150 students run by a team of five teachers, one of whom plays the role of "team leader." Each team makes its own decisions about instructional methods, curriculum, scheduling, and materials; as one teacher described: "The schedule is entirely up to the team; we don't ring any bells. There was a time when we believed only counselors could do that." [p. 5]

These teaching teams have most of the resources needed to respond quickly to the educational needs of their students.

While secondary schools have sometimes organized around self-contained tasks, in general they have retained the functional task division in which a single student receives instruction from multiple teachers, each of whom is a specialist in some segment of the curriculum. There is little reason to expect most secondary schools to depart from this dominant and traditional pattern of organization, in spite of articulate calls from Sizer (1984) and others for more cohesive programs. Of course, it is just this form of organization that presents the most difficulty for providing decision makers with information on the performance of complex and unprogrammable tasks. While all students are served less well by this lack of information, disadvantaged students have the fewest nonschool resources to compensate for this situation, so they suffer the most.

Entrenched patterns notwithstanding, schools can be organized around self-contained teaching/learning teams to a greater extent than they are currently. Schools can establish teams to serve groups of students, so professional staff members familiar with the needs of students can diagnose educational problems, make decisions about the educational resources they require, and see to it that students receive the appropriate resources. Such forms of organization should not be reserved for students with very severe problems, but used to serve all students, to help prevent problems from developing.

Providing Schools with Slack in Staff Resources

Perfect planning would allow schools always to have just the appropriate level and mix of resources to meet student needs. Both staff and students would be optimally engaged in the educational enterprise, and neither would have excess time on their hands. Unfortunately, organizations as large and complex as schools cannot plan perfectly, and they must therefore decide whether the "slack" that arises when resources and needs are not balanced should occur among staff or students, either by deliberately providing extra staff resources for peak demand periods or by allowing students to be unengaged in the educational enterprise whenever student needs exceed staff capacity. Each option has its consequences: On the one hand, "slack" staff resources means providing additional personnel who may be unengaged during periods of lower demand, and this in turn inevitably has an impact on budgets. On the other hand, "slack" student resources means allowing students to be idle, which results in lowered performance of individual students and of the school overall.

A simple example from the world of retail merchandising demonstrates this phenomenon. A store manager attempts to plan staffing patterns so that there are sufficient staff to meet customer demands. However, since customer demands ebb and flow in unpredictable ways, at times the staff outnumber customers and are not directly engaged in service, while at other times the customers greatly outnumber the staff and must wait unserved until a staff member becomes available. In either case there are resources that are unengaged, sometimes those of the retailer, sometimes those of the customer. An organization may attempt to balance its resources against the demands of customers or clients; it may decide to have additional staff on hand in order that clients must seldom if ever be unengaged; or it may decide to have minimal staff and thereby cause clients or customers to be unengaged a good deal of the time. Of course, the latter strategy involves a risk that customers or clients will take their business elsewhere.

The strategy of slack student resources has always played a role in the organization of schools, but it is only most recently that we have become more keenly aware of the costs associated with this strategy. There are a number of obvious troubling examples. Jackson's (1967) point that students spend a good deal of their time waiting was made following observations of an elementary school classroom, and Goodlad (1984) noted the same phenomenon to an even greater extent among secondary school students. Students spend a good deal of time unengaged in learning activities because they are simply waiting for instruction to commence. This is true of the time spent passing between classes or subjects, the time spent waiting for a class to be brought to order, the time spent while a teacher disciplines other students, and so on. Until recently we have not thought of student time as a resource, but concern with how time on task affects student learning (Karweit, 1984) is evidence that educational researchers and practitioners have come to realize the importance of this type of resource.

But student waiting time is not the only example of slack student resources in American schools. Other forms include the assignment of students to classes that are overcrowded or inappropriate for their learning needs, the lapse in time between when a teacher or student discovers that a misassignment has occurred and when a student can be reassigned to a more appropriate class, the unproductive transitions between sequential classes whose contents are not coordinated, and the inordinate and unnecessary difficulties experienced by teachers and students when students' programs have not been constructed to provide them with appropriate skills to master a course to which they have been assigned (e.g., chemistry students who have not been advised to take appropriate math courses). Schools with high levels of slack student resources often become nothing more than custodial institutions.

Finally, perhaps the most insidious form of slack student resources is the series of implicit decisions on the part of administrators, teachers, and students to settle for less than the highest possible standards and less than excellent performance. In the past several years there has been more than a little evidence that standards for performance in U.S. schools have been seriously compromised (National Commission on Excellence in Education, 1983; Natriello & Dornbusch, 1984; Resnick & Resnick, 1985). While it is possible to attribute this type of decline to a general lowering of standards in society at large, it is also possible to interpret it as the result of schools being forced to accommodate an increasingly diverse and unpredictable group of students and to provide for them an increasingly diverse set of outcomes. The important point is not that increasing diversity leads to lower standards, but that increasing diversity leads to a more challenging set of tasks for those charged with managing schools. This is particularly true for schools serving disadvantaged populations. When school administrators fail to come to grips with such increased diversity, the result by default is an increase in slack resources in the form of student disengagement, lower standards, and poorer performance.

Significant slack is also generated when resource allocation patterns continue unchanged, even after significant shifts in need; and when resources are dependent upon external events, as opposed to assessments of internal needs. An example of the failure to reallocate resources appropriately might be the heavy investment in school security in lieu of services made during days of student rebellion that continues during days of student apathy. An example of resource allocations that are overly dependent on external events as opposed to internal needs is the all-too-common establishment of dropout prevention programs to signal to the community that the school is addressing the dropout problem when the system lacks the capacity internally to identify potential dropouts and assign them to prevention programs that actually meet their needs. This is particularly a problem in communities where the public is most critical of the schools, those very communities where disadvantaged students are most likely to be concentrated.

In restructuring schools it is important to move from a condition of slack student resources to one of slack staff resources. A key component of restructuring efforts is the provision of time for staff to "reflect, plan, and discuss teaching innovations and problems with their colleagues" (Task Force on Teaching as a Profession, 1986, p. 60). As Elmore (1988) notes, "Participation and concerted action require time away from regular school duties and time to develop and implement new ideas" (p. 11). Yet, as Cohen (1988) observes, "At present, schedules for teachers largely match the school day of students (though the teaching day is generally somewhat longer) and, despite the allotment of preparation time for teachers, rarely are there significant blocks of time during which teachers can interact with one another or with small numbers of students" (p. 13).

Strategies have been developed to make more time available for teachers. The use of support staff such as technicians, assistants, clerical aides, teaching interns, and community volunteers may provide some relief for the time constraints under which teachers operate (Task Force on Teaching as a Profession, 1986). Increasing reliance on paraprofessionals may permit teachers to engage in essential planning and collaborative activities (Pickett, 1989). One school in the North Carolina Lead Teacher Project used a schedule adjustment to provide all teachers with a duty-free lunch as well as daily planning time for teams (Public School Forum of North Carolina, 1988). Whatever the strategy, schools must be restructured such that teachers have sufficient slack time to engage in the new tasks envisioned for them.

Schools should be encouraged and enabled to shift from a situation of slack student resources to a situation of slack staff resources. Schools should be organized and supported so that there are back-up systems, reserve personnel, and other extra resources that can be used when problems arise, as they inevitably will when dealing with at-risk students. Teachers and administrators must have appropriate alternative courses of action if we do not want them to adopt a custodial mode of operation when faced with the problems of disadvantaged students. Conversely, students must have access to a surfeit of educational resources.

Providing appropriate slack staff resources will require a basic and profound rethinking of our approach to the support of educational systems. We must stop applying criteria of efficiency to educational institutions, for they are inherently inefficient systems. They require large amounts of slack staff resources to be able to respond to the unpredictable problems presented by disadvantaged students.

STRATEGIES FOR ENHANCING THE SCHOOL'S CAPACITY TO PROCESS INFORMATION

The second set of strategies for reducing uncertainty and improving the performance of schools operates by enhancing the capacity of school organizations to gather, process, and use information about student performance and behavior and the impact of educational resources on that performance and behavior. Earlier we referred to the movement of the locus of educational decision making away from the sources of information pertinent to those decisions, and we offered four strategies for reversing this trend. It is also possible to improve the movement of information within the educational system, so that it can more readily reach decision makers at levels further from the sources of the information. This is the subject of this section, and we offer three strategies for achieving this end: (1) structuring more effective hierarchies, (2) creating bridging or lateral relationships that cut across organizational subunits, and (3) investing in the development of more sophisticated vertical information systems. We discuss each of these in turn.

Structuring More Effective Hierarchies

Galbraith (1973) points out that hierarchies originate to provide a way of dealing with exceptions to rules, programs, and procedures. When an event arises that was not anticipated, performers at one level in the organization can ask individuals higher in the hierarchy for a decision about how to respond. Presumably individuals further up the hierarchy can assemble more complete information and formulate an appropriate response. Hierarchy is one of the strategies that allows organizations to adapt to their inability to plan for all conditions. Hierarchy has played a key role in the organization of schools. The administrative ranks have long played a primary role in the organization and management of schools (Tyack, 1974).

Recently the notion of having a strong principal to direct operations has been cited as an element of an "effective" school for urban disadvantaged youngsters (Edmonds, 1984). A number of theorists, however, have developed perspectives that call into question the role of the principal. Weick (1976) and Meyer and Rowan (1978) have observed that schools tend to be only loosely coupled, with principals often disconnected from the instructional work of the teachers. External factors also mitigate against strong administrative leadership. As Kirst (1984) and others have noted, the authority relations involving federal, state, and central district officers; program and project officers; and union officers; together with the school principal and administrative staff, create a complex hierarchical pattern that often belies the public notion of a "strong principal." Nevertheless, emerging perspectives suggest that it is possible for the principal to operate through both weak bureaucratic and cultural linkages to have a positive effect on the instructional program (Firestone & Wilson, 1985).

One difficulty with the emphasis on the leadership of the principal is that no single individual can respond to the number of exceptions that may be generated when large numbers of students come into contact with the school rules, programs, and procedures. While it is true that teachers also handle exceptions and deviations, they generally do so in the context of the classroom, where they must interrupt the instructional process. As a result, teachers often ignore exceptions and deviations in order to continue with the original instructional plan. Once again, this may be satisfactory when the number of exceptions and deviations is relatively small. In schools serving the disadvantaged, where the number is large, teachers must choose between responding to infractions themselves, ignoring infractions and pursuing instructional plans, or referring the infractions to the principal or assistant principal and continuing with instruction. When many teachers refer exceptions to administrators, the administrative staff becomes overloaded. The result is the same for counseling staff, when they are the targets of referrals.

What is missing in schools is a more differentiated hierarchy in which actors at different levels might be equipped to deal with different kinds of exceptions. While there have been a number of suggestions for career-ladder plans for teachers, most of these have evolved as ways of making teaching a more attractive career. What is needed is an examination of the roles that need to be filled in dealing effectively with the exceptions generated by all students, and especially by disadvantaged students, as they present so many. Current staff arrangements for responding to exceptions (e.g., special services) are not well connected to any hierarchy in schools and are particularly poorly connected to classroom teachers. This results in long delays before appropriate resources can be brought to bear upon problems presented by students. Supervising teachers, with professional positions between classroom teachers and building administrators, could fill an important role as managers of instructional resources. Individuals in such positions could be equipped with specialized knowledge of various student problems (e.g., learning disabilities, precursors of dropping out) or educational resources (e.g., techniques of writing instruction, peer counseling). Problems referred to them would receive timely and expert treatment.

The Task Force on Teaching as a Profession (1986) recommended the creation of the position of a "lead teacher," who would provide leadership in the school and help colleagues to maintain high standards of teaching and learning. The Lead Teacher Program in North Carolina, which began simply as an attempt to create a new and attractive role for teachers, has grown into a much larger effort to restructure schools so they improve outcomes for students (Public School Forum of North Carolina, 1988). Lead teachers head teaching teams that plan together and exercise growing latitude over resources, scheduling, and instructional decisions. By creating a new level in the hierarchy, the program has actually moved decision making closer to the classroom and made the schools more responsive to the needs of students.

Other organizational arrangements might also provide needed relief for overburdened school hierarchies. For example, Comer (1980) describes the effective involvement of multiple participants in a school advisory committee that reinforced and supplemented the regular school hierarchy:

> By bringing people together into a governing/managing group that was made up of parents, teachers, administrators, aides, and everybody in that program — and if we had been in a high school it would have included students — by having that group share in identifying the problems in the school, of planning to address those problems, implementing the program that was developed, evaluating the program, and then modifying that program, and having all those people responsible for doing that, and involved in doing that, you restored that sense of trust, that sense of community that existed naturally before. [p. 5]

By involving parents in the governance process, Comer and colleagues were able to reintegrate two hierarchical authority systems — the school and the family — that had grown apart with the transition from a society of small towns and rural areas to our present society in which those who staff our schools, particularly our urban schools, often live outside the community. Not only did the governance committee involve more individuals in responding to the needs of students, it also unified the authority systems to which students were exposed. Elements of this approach have been noted in other effective schools for disadvantaged students. Wehlage and Smith (1986) cite participatory decision making by staff in governance as a common feature of effective programs for disadvantaged students being studied by the National Center for Effective Secondary Schools. Levin (1987) also stresses the importance of involving teachers, administrators, students, and parents in the governance of accelerated schools for disadvantaged students.

Attention should be directed to the development of more elaborate hierarchies oriented around educational problems. A single strong administrator may be fine in a very small school. For larger schools and most schools serving disadvantaged and diverse students, a more elaborate hierarchy involving supervisory teachers able to deploy and redeploy educational resources quickly is required. Staff positions in such hierarchies could be supplemented by a variety of other individuals concerned with the educational and social development of students. Such additions to the inadequate hierarchical arrangements found in most schools could enhance their capacity to receive information on exceptions and special cases, process that information, and develop rapid responses to the problems of students. Rapid responses to student problems from those with expertise would make teachers more willing to refer problems for action and would offer more support for the work of teachers in classrooms.

Creating Bridging or Lateral Relationships

The development of lateral relationships (i.e., relations that cut across organizational subunits) among individuals in different hierarchies in a school or school district is a strategy for increasing the flexibility of the school to adapt to the inability to plan for all events. By relying on bridging or lateral relationships in arriving at decisions, a school could increase its ability to react to exceptions and deviations from previously developed plans. Lateral relationships allow individuals closer to the task being performed to consult, reach decisions, and redeploy resources in response to changing conditions.

The development of lateral relationships has not been a frequently employed strategy in U.S. schools. Interaction among classroom teachers is a case in point. Despite its demonstrated value, the creation of truly collegial environments in which teachers can exchange information related to instruction is rare. While some schools form coordinating groups *within* curriculum areas, the use of such liaisons *across* curriculum areas has been less common, with the exception of some staffing patterns in alternative schools. It is possible to conceive of a liaison role for coordinating the program of study for a particular grade level or a particular subset of students (e.g., students enrolled in advanced-placement science and mathematics courses), but the practice seems rare. Even more rare is the involvement of such lateral processes in decisions to alter plans in response to emerging conditions.

In a study of four public high schools, Natriello (1982) found that there was little communication among different subject-matter departments regarding the total curriculum. The absence of such coordination resulted in teachers being unaware of the workload assigned to students by other teachers. Natriello concluded that this lack of information about the total student workload made individual teachers somewhat reluctant to place heavy demands upon students in their subject areas. In curriculum terms, such lack of coordination leads to perennial internal debates about which teachers are to be responsible for the reading, writing, and spelling performance of students. For example, does the social studies teacher teach and/or monitor competencies in written composition? Does the English teacher teach reading? In the absence of explicit coordination, students experience a disjointed program of instruction. Once again, while middle-class students may have other sources of educational experiences, disadvantaged students are particularly vulnerable to any limitations of the schools.

One strategy for creating bridging roles is that suggested by David (1989). She points out how districts involved in school restructuring delegate responsibilities previously held by district staff. For example, curriculum development may become the task of teachers, with district staff playing a coordinating, as opposed to directing, role. This is an instance in which central office staff are shifted from a place in the hierarchy to act as bridges between hierarchies.

Schools should provide mechanisms and opportunities for the development of lateral relationships among staff in different departments, so they can make decisions regarding the entire educational program in a timely way. Individuals in bridging roles can bring together the necessary information and resources to respond to problems without requiring information to move further up the hierarchy. If teachers had direct contact with district-level specialists through liaisons, they would be able to receive more rapid responses to their requests for special assistance for students.

Developing More Sophisticated Vertical Information Systems

A vertical information system is a strategy designed to increase the capacity of an organization to plan. It is intended to function such that information on the performance of the organization is moved quickly up the hierarchy to those who have the authority to plan for the organization and subsequently to change overall plans and redeploy resources as needs become apparent.

Vertical information systems have begun to develop in school districts across the country in the past 20 years (Kean, 1983). In addition to teacher employment and attendance data, such systems typically collect information on student performance on standardized tests and attempt to make it available to school personnel. More sophisticated systems involve a wider variety of information on student performance and instructional treatments in the form of an instructional information system (Williams & Bank, 1987). The growth of such activities in school districts has been accompanied by the adoption of formal organizational units to manage such research-and-evaluation activities (Kean, 1983; Williams, Lyon, Doscher, Walker, & Cullian, 1979). Theorists have articulated plans for the full development and utilization of such systems. Several examples of such systems were discussed in Chapter 7.

Nevertheless, few schools appear to have vertical information systems that can provide useful data in a timely fashion, thus permitting the rational deployment and redeployment of resources. In the absence of such information, the decisions of school leaders are likely to be influenced more by external factors than by needs internal to the system. For example, amidst the wave of interest in programs to prevent or reduce dropping out, few districts are even in a position to analyze the status of their programs and understand which parts of their current programs appear to be related to early school leaving. However, this has not prevented district leaders from adopting new programs by way of demonstrating an interest in the plight of potential dropouts.

Even when schools have the technical capacity to operate vertical information systems, it is often the case that the information in these systems is not used or not fully used by educators (Sproull & Larkey, 1979). The development of systems that could and would be used by educators might have a substantial benefit for disadvantaged students, if the information could be used to provide more timely and more complete information on student educational performance and lead to subsequent modifications in educational programs. This type of information is essential for the early identification of student learning problems and problems with school programs.

The need for a good vertical information system in restructured schools is evident in the interim report of the North Carolina Lead Teacher project (Public School Forum of North Carolina, 1988):

> The existing information structures in schools will not support a comprehensive and defensible accountability model. The absence of clerical assistants for teachers, inadequate computing capabilities and the lack of criterion-referenced tests for diagnosing, placing and monitoring student performance are just three

of the deficiencies that need to be addressed to make school accountability a reality. [p. 7]

The report goes on to explain how school staff overcame these problems,

> by assigning clerical assistants to instructional teams, purchasing computers, analysing existing norm-referenced tests and matching the contents to the prescribed curriculum, identifying alternatives to help them diagnose and place students and monitor their performance, and buying multi-level instructional materials. At one site, a sophisticated computer-assisted and computer-managed instructional program was implemented. The results were significant gains in student performance. [p. 7]

Because accountability for results is essential for gaining the latitude to restructure schools, vertical information systems become important components of restructuring efforts.

School districts should be encouraged and assisted to develop comprehensive vertical information systems for collecting data on students and the range of educational services delivered in the district. In the absence of such systems, school leaders are in a poor position to make informed decisions about the educational program. Vertical information systems are a key device for moving information from the level of the student in the classroom to the level of school and district leaders. Particular attention should be devoted to developing systems that provide the information needed to permit the frequent redeployment of school resources to meet changing student needs.

THE APPLICATION OF RESTRUCTURING STRATEGIES

The seven strategies for restructuring schools discussed in the previous two sections are all designed to enhance the certainty with which schools develop and deliver educational resources to students, particularly disadvantaged students. The reduction of uncertainty in the operation of schools should lead to improvements in student performance and behavior. Each of the seven strategies will reduce uncertainty, the first four by decreasing the need to process information at higher levels in the school organization, the last three by enhancing the capacity of the school system to process information.

Not all seven strategies have to be employed for improvements to result. Indeed, employing certain of these strategies may make it less necessary to employ others. For example, to the extent that schools create self-contained teaching/learning teams, it may become less important to invest in vertical information systems. In some sense then, these strategies are functionally equivalent.

It seems, however, that each of these strategies has certain limitations. For example, it is not likely that creating self-contained teaching/learning teams will enable all educational decisions to be made at the teacher level and remove the need for a vertical information system or an elaborated hierarchy. It is equally unlikely that a vertical information system can be made sophisticated enough, no matter how much of an investment is made, to move all educational decisions above the classroom or school levels. Thus, the application process is one of developing an appropriate mix of these strategies in the effective restructuring of schools.

OTHER APPROACHES TO RESTRUCTURING SCHOOLS

Some discussions of restructuring schools have focused attention on the creation of working environments for teachers that would support the development of teaching as a profession (e.g., Task Force on Teaching as a Profession, 1986; Tucker & Mandel, 1986). The assumption is that, if the work environment of schools for teachers is improved, we will be able to attract more capable individuals into teaching and that, if capable professionals are granted sufficient autonomy, they will organize instruction to improve student learning. The rationale behind such restructuring discussions begins with the working conditions of teachers. The aim is to allow schools to compete for scarce talent with other professions by creating professional working conditions (Task Force on Teaching as a Profession, 1986).

Our own approach to restructuring is somewhat different. We begin with the needs of students, particularly disadvantaged students, and ask what changes in the formal organizational properties of schools will lead to improved learning for disadvantaged youngsters. Our approach is closer to that of Cohen (1988), who argues that "the primary rationale for restructuring schools lies in the need to improve the productivity of the educational system in general, and, in particular, student acquisition of higher order thinking skills" (p. 7). We therefore do not assume that the working conditions of teachers must automatically be made more professional. That our suggestions for restructuring schools may lead to the creation of more professional working environments for teachers is a by-product of our analysis of the needs of disadvantaged youth and the structure of organizations, not a function of our initial assumptions. Those who advocate restructuring schools primarily to make them more attractive workplaces for teachers may attack us for ignoring the needs of teachers except as they relate to the provision of better instruction for students, or they may take comfort in the fact that our conclusions are only subtly different from their own. We call for a system that permits greater discretion for teachers in classrooms *and* for a system that permits better informed and more rapid decision-making at higher levels.

One example will suffice to illustrate how our approach differs from some widely held views on restructuring. Some proponents of restructuring schools have observed that teaching, unlike other professions, relies on the "undifferentiated staffing model that characterizes most schools" (Tucker & Mandel, 1986, p. 24). This is viewed as placing schools at a disadvantage as they compete with other organizations for the most talented individuals, since it is often the responsibility and the challenge of doing the most difficult work that hold individuals in a field. The solution to this problem, from the viewpoint of the Task Force on Teaching as a Profession (1986), is the development of a staffing structure headed by lead teachers who would coordinate and be accountable for the educational activities in a school.

Our analysis of the problems of students in schools suggests the need for greater coordination of the educational activities of the school if we are to be truly able to respond to the quickly changing circumstances of disadvantaged youth. It further suggests that too little such coordination is currently occurring and that current staffing configurations provide insufficient levels and numbers of coordinating personnel to do the job that needs to be done. One solution to this problem is the creation of differentiated school staffing arrangements, in which teachers, individually or collectively, would assume greater responsibility for assessing student needs and coordinating the delivery of appropriate services. Obviously, the lead teachers envisioned by other proponents of restructuring could perform this function, and if that had the additional benefit of making teaching more attractive, all the better. But for us, the key consideration is the provision of better educational services to students.

EDUCATIONAL REFORM AND THE
RESTRUCTURING OF SCHOOLS

Our recommendations for restructuring schools imply a critique of some current school reform efforts. The present analysis suggests that efforts stemming from the "excellence" movement may be detrimental to the interests of disadvantaged youngsters. For example, the primary direction of curricular reform suggested in this movement is a narrowing of the school curriculum along traditional academic lines. The curriculum of choice for the reformers (National Commission on Excellence in Education, 1983) resembles nothing so much as the college preparatory program. The diversity represented by the vocational program and the general program would be restricted.

The proponents of school reform are correct in perceiving the diverse curricula of many schools as unmanaged, but they offer little in the way of suggestions for developing the capacity of schools to process information and direct diverse educational services to students in appropriate ways. Thus, instead of enhancing the capacity of schools to respond to the information needs created by a diverse student population with needs for diverse educational resources, the school reform movement would have us reduce the variety and flexibility available in the current school curriculum. The same impact is implied by the "choice" movement, which envisions different kinds of schools among which students and parents would choose. This strategy relocates outside the school those choices that are available within the comprehensive school, presumably leaving each school less diverse.

The emphasis of the reformers on a "strong principal" who runs a "tight ship" may also be misplaced and/or improperly described. This perspective places too much emphasis on a single individual and too little emphasis on the way in which administrators who offer leadership to faculty members can facilitate their appropriate involvement, through increased lateral relationships across classrooms and departments and through the delegation of tasks to informal faculty leaders and teaching/learning teams.

The second wave of reforms — those that have sought to provide assistance to students likely to be adversely affected — may also be counterproductive. Attempts to address the needs of at-risk students have typically taken the form of special programs or services targeted at certain groups of students. The potential exists that these special efforts will expend resources without developing the organizational capacity of schools. For example, one dilemma for schools wishing to establish dropout-prevention efforts is that they often lack the basic student information systems that would enable them to identify students and their problems properly, in order to understand the quality and extent of programming necessary in the district.

We may be ready to move on to a third wave of school reform, which would involve a serious reexamination and restructuring of the organization of schools. Our analysis carries a number of implications to guide such a restructuring. The seven strategies for dealing with uncertainty identified earlier represent new ways for analyzing and redesigning the organization of schools to enable them to address more effectively the needs of all students, but in particular the needs of disadvantaged students. Not all schools serving disadvantaged students should be expected to employ all of the strategies; however, individual schools may find it useful to explore alterations in their structure and operations along these lines.

CONCLUSIONS

In this chapter we have developed a conceptual framework for a broad-based approach to restructuring schools so that they will be able to meet the needs of all students, including disadvantaged students. Where appropriate, we have discussed some particular instances in which elements of our restructuring strategy are currently in operation. The emphasis, however, is not on providing specific suggestions but on developing a general understanding of ways in which restructured educational organizations might better serve disadvantaged students. This conceptual approach may disappoint those readers who are eager for quick solutions, but restructuring schooling requires a basic rethinking of the way we operate schools. While all students present school organizations with the challenge of meeting their educational needs, disadvantaged students present schools with needs that are particularly difficult to address within the structure of the typical school in this country. Indeed, for many disadvantaged students, the typical school presents an incompatible environment (Comer, 1980).

We believe that the strategies for restructuring outlined here will enable schools to meet the needs of disadvantaged students more effectively. In the process, they will also improve schools for teachers and for students who are not considered disadvantaged. Approaching the problems of disadvantaged students through the restructuring of school organizations may be both the most effective and the most politically viable choice since such a strategy offers benefits to all students and their parents, and hence to the society.

9

Implications for Educational Policy

In the course of this book, we have discussed the nature of the educationally disadvantaged population, the history of strategies to educate this group, and some emerging notions about how to make schools more responsive to the educationally disadvantaged children they serve. In this chapter, we develop recommendations for how our society might better educate disadvantaged children, a group that has typically been ill served by our educating institutions. We begin by restating our view of the problem of the educationally disadvantaged, including our definition of disadvantage and a statement specifying the dimensions of the problem; and we follow this by critiquing two of the current educational strategies that states and districts are contemplating or implementing. We conclude by sketching our own recommendations for educating the disadvantaged, focusing on the "new three R's": resources, restructuring, and research.

At the outset we noted that schooling and education are not synonymous. Like Cremin (1988), we define education quite broadly as a process of acquiring the knowledge, skills, and values necessary for individuals to function as competent adults and citizens in society. Industrialized societies rely on their social institutions to educate their young people. Although schools are the primary institution that these societies have charged with the task of educating their children, they certainly are not the only such institutions. In particular, we have highlighted the family and the community as key educating institutions.

Our definition of *educational disadvantage* maintains that children may be disadvantaged by exposure to inadequate educational experiences in the school, the family, and/or the community. By inadequate experiences we mean experiences that prevent young people from acquiring the knowledge, skills, attitudes, and values that society demands of all adults, so that they may participate fully in social, political, and economic life.

CURRENT STRATEGIES FOR EDUCATING DISADVANTAGED CHILDREN

We have shown that the United States has tried a great many strategies for educating disadvantaged children, unhappily with quite limited success.

Social critics, politicians, and political pundits are constantly on the lookout for new directions to test, as the press to educate the disadvantaged becomes more apparent. Some approaches clearly hold more promise than others, judging by the theories that underpin them and the current accumulation of evidence. In this section we critique two of the most prominent approaches currently in vogue: school choice, and raising standards for performance.

School Choice

Looming as a principal new bandwagon for educational reform is the concept of school choice. The press for public school choice has emerged from states, local districts, and the federal government, with President Bush now a major proponent of the concept. Choice plans take a variety of forms, varying along at least three dimensions:

1. The geographic scope, including statewide or interdistrict choice, districtwide choice, and within-district choice options
2. The kinds of schools among which students and parents might choose, with some highlighting alternative schools and others focusing on magnet schools (sometimes called "theme," "educational option," or specialty schools)
3. The means by which choice is exercised, whether by open enrollment or "controlled choice." In controlled-choice systems, parents typically rank all of the schools in the district according to their preferences, and the school system assigns the child to a school, simultaneously attempting to preserve desired racial/ethnic composition goals and meet capacity limits, on the one hand, while satisfying the preferences of parents, on the other.

The strategy of school choice appears to derive from an evolutionary model of schools as organizations (e.g., Aldrich, 1979). Through a process of natural selection, schools adapt to meet the needs of their environments, or they fail. In choice plans, "survival of the fittest" insures that schools are constantly changing to match the demands of their environments. Thus, proponents of choice argue that allowing parents and children to choose their schools creates a healthy competition among schools, spurring innovation and diversity.

There are several stages by which school choice is thought to work:

1. The competition among schools for students implies that schools will strive to appeal to students and parents, perhaps through innovative curricular programs, teaching techniques, or variations in other facets of school organization.

2. Information about these variations will be disseminated to parents and students, in order that they might choose among schools based on which school offers a program best suited to a given student's needs.
3. Parents will make such an informed selection among schools.
4. By exercising this choice, parents will move their children from poor schools, which are not responsive to their children's needs, to good schools, which do respond to what their children require.
5. Parents and children who choose their schools will be more involved in the educational process.
6. The movement of students is correlated with the resources available to schools, so that poor schools either adapt and become more responsive to student needs and desires, or they wither and close; and good schools, which already have adapted, survive and flourish.

While this model is appealing, we seriously doubt that its operation will have the desired effect of appreciably raising the educational achievement of disadvantaged children. This is because for each of the stages we have just outlined, we are skeptical that the processes implied are effective in the case of disadvantaged children.

Innovation and Variation. We question the extent to which school choice programs spur variations among schools in the way the educationally disadvantaged are served. Our reservations stem in part from our recognition of the remarkable resilience of the organizational structure of elementary and secondary schools in this country. In spite of wide variations in the environments in which U.S. schools operate, the vast majority look very much alike. Our belief is that choice plans create largely cosmetic differences among schools in the way they serve their clients. Even the different curricular emphases among magnet schools strike us as mainly superficial, as low-achieving students typically are still taught basic skills in the conventional manner. In your local convenience store, "freedom of choice" means the freedom to choose Coke or Pepsi. We see school choice much the same way.

Magnet schools are an exemplar of how choice plans tend to overlook the disadvantaged. Most magnet programs are somewhat selective, admitting students who are more motivated and talented than students who either do not apply at all or are not accepted into these programs. Evidence for this is provided by Blank, Dentler, Baltzell, and Chabotar (1983), who found that 89% of the magnet schools that they surveyed had admissions criteria used to screen out students who were performing below grade level or were seen as behavior problems. Even in settings where there are explicit attempts to draw students from the full range of the achievement distribution, selectivity comes into play. In New York City's Educational Options high school program, for instance, one-sixth of the selected students are required to be below-average readers, based on an annual standardized reading test (Gampert & Blank, 1988). But anecdotal evidence suggests that the low-achieving students selected typically have attendance records that are much better than average, indicating a degree of persistence or dependability that distinguishes them from other students.

One model for examining the possible effects of choice programs on the disadvantaged is curriculum tracking within high schools. Tracking frequently entails specialized instructional programs, although perhaps not as differentiated as the typical magnet program. Nevertheless, tracking (or at least curricular choice) is the most prominent choice mechanism within American secondary schools (Raywid, 1985), and the allocation of children to curricular tracks often involves the same academic performance criteria that are used in allocating children to magnet programs.

If we extrapolate from the evidence on the effects of tracking to the likely effects of other public school choice programs, we cannot be very optimistic about their effects on disadvantaged students. The tracking literature strongly suggests that low-track students receive a poorer quality of instruction than higher-track students, with lower expectations for performance, slow-paced instruction, and dull curricular materials and instructional techniques (Hallinan, 1987; Oakes, 1985). By implication, the students who are not enrolled in the more glamorous magnet programs will be relegated to the educational landfill and subjected to ineffective traditional instructional methods and materials. Thus it is hard to see how low-achieving, disadvantaged students would benefit from most choice plans.

Access to High-Quality Information Regarding Choice. We are dubious about the quality of the information describing the differences among schools that will be accessible to the parents of disadvantaged children. Parents will require appropriate knowledge of the various educational options available if they are to make informed choices, yet proponents of choice programs have relatively little to say about how such information will be gathered and disseminated (Riddle & Stedman, 1989). As we noted in Chapter 7, there are few districts in which even school leaders have detailed information on the performance of individual schools. Most accounts of choice programs suggest that parents will make choices based on relatively superficial knowledge of school characteristics. For example, the school district might report schools' average achievement test scores. But similar scores could result from schools that do moderately well with all students or from those that do very well with some students and quite poorly with other students, leading parents of disadvantaged children to select among schools on the basis of averages that say little about those schools' abilities to educate their children.

If parental choice can be affected by relatively unsophisticated information about schools, then schools will have an incentive to engage in misleading public relations campaigns to attract parents and students. Such misleading campaigns might be especially effective with relatively less-informed parents. The negative impact of such public relations can be seen in the proprietary school industry, where subway signs, matchbook covers, and television commercials extol the virtues of various vocational schools to unsuspecting, often disadvantaged, young adults. Proprietary vocational schools claim to train large numbers of disadvantaged citizens, especially welfare recipients, and the competition among them is fierce, as the stakes are high. In the 1987–1988 academic year in New York State, for instance, private for-profit vocational schools received more than $500 million dollars in federal and state financial aid awarded to their students (Interface, 1989).

Because the competition among such schools is so keen, proprietary schools frequently exaggerate their completion and placement success rates, and students are often subject to rude awakenings when the programs and classroom conditions fail to live up to their billing. Consequently, attrition and loan default rates are very high, much higher than for students from other kinds of postsecondary institutions (Interface, 1989).

While we acknowledge the singular nature of for-profit institutions, we fear that the sharp competition over students at the elementary and secondary levels produced by choice plans may create the same press in the public sector that exists in the private sector. It is at least possible that expanded school choice would be accompanied by the same deceptive advertising, lack of accountability, and broken dreams of the disadvantaged that we observe in the proprietary schools.

Basis of Choice. We are skeptical that parents of disadvantaged children will make decisions based on which schools provide programs that best serve their children. Schools' reputations rest far more on the quality of their students than on the quality of their programs. High-achieving students equal good schools, while low-achieving students equal bad schools. There are only two ways to get high-achieving students: recruit them, or transform low achievers into high achievers. Currently it is easier to recruit high achievers than to create them. For this reason, most school choice plans emphasize variations designed to recruit high-achieving students. There may be some schools dominated by a teaching or service ethic that influences them to seek out disadvantaged students, but it is not clear that they can survive in a competitive marketplace. We doubt whether many parents will want to send their children to schools that are known for attracting and retaining disadvantaged students.

Ability to Exercise Choice. We doubt that the parents of disadvantaged children will be able to move their children from bad schools to good schools. Beyond transportation problems and the difficulty of gaining access to the "good" schools, they may not wish to uproot their children. Choice programs assume that parents, when confronted with an unsatisfactory school situation, will move their children to another school. This might be fine for middle-class students, but it might introduce additional damaging instability into the already unstable lives of disadvantaged youngsters. Disruptions in family life and residential mobility already cause problems for disadvantaged children. The school may be a source of stability in their lives. Parents seeking to provide a stable environment for their children may choose to put up with unsatisfactory schools to maintain whatever stability they can muster.

Family Involvement. We also are skeptical that choice programs will be successful in increasing the involvement of parents of the disadvantaged. As we noted in Chapter 2, parents of disadvantaged students typically are not effective managers of their children's school careers. They frequently have had unpleasant experiences with the schools and may not have the knowledge to make informed choices about their children's schooling. As Riddle and Stedman (1989) claim,

> the net effect of greater choice could be self-selection into certain schools or districts, leaving primarily the children of parents who are unable or unwilling to become actively involved attending other schools. Benefitting from the availability of choice may require a degree of free time, energy and knowledge that many parents do not possess. [p. 18]

Survival of the Fittest. We believe that the likely result of school choice programs — survival of the "fittest" schools — will have the unintended consequence of weakening the bonds among families, schools, and communities, thereby curtailing our ability to educate disadvantaged children successfully. For example, the movement of students away from their neighborhood schools can have just such an effect. As Riddle and Stedman (1989) have written, "Neighborhood schools may be said to have a 'natural constituency' that might be threatened by expansion of districtwide school choice. Enabling families to 'escape' from institutions perceived to be in decline may simply make those institutions more deficient" (p. 17).

Also, competition among schools may produce the unintended consequence of weakening all schools. While it is conceivable that competition among schools might have beneficial effects for consumers, much as it does in competitive markets for goods and services, it must be remembered that schooling is not the same type of commodity as are goods and services. In particular, there may be grave consequences associated with the closing of schools. We rarely view the success or failure of a restaurant as a matter of public concern. But schools, unlike restaurants, are fundamental social institutions on which rest the core of society's commitment to educate its young people. The constant threat of closure necessarily weakens the ability of schools to fulfill their mandate, because institutions that can close so quickly are universally viewed as transient and unimportant.

In addition to our misgivings about the presumed stages of choice, there is the matter of uncertainty discussed at length in Chapter 8. If school choice creates uncertainty about who will attend a particular school, and this produces further uncertainty about the level of fiscal and other resources that will be available to a school to serve its students, then school choice may effectively limit a school's (or a district's) ability to plan for the future and allocate resources where they are needed (Riddle & Stedman, 1989). The seriousness of this problem can scarcely be overstated, especially in light of our earlier discussion of the pernicious effects of uncertainty.

In spite of our reservations about the possible effects of choice on the disadvantaged, there is little concrete evidence available about the actual effects of choice programs on students. Most attempts to make sense of such programs are stymied by the inability to control analytically for self-selection. That is, students and their parents select themselves into the available options in a school or a district, and the reasons why students and parents select particular programs may be correlated with students' success in school. In the absence of explicit models of the choice process, it is well-nigh impossible to isolate the effects of choice.

Consider the best-known "success story" in public school choice, Community School District 4 in East Harlem, New York City. This district, predominantly nonwhite and low income, in the early 1970s began open enrollment in all of its junior high schools, many of which house multiple specialized instructional programs. The district also has several elementary schools that accept students who live throughout the district. Since the onset of open enrollment in District 4, the academic performance of district students has increased dramatically, relative to other districts in the city.

While the performance gains observed in District 4 are impressive, it is not clear to what extent these gains can be attributed to the district choice plan. As with most such plans, it is extremely difficult to isolate the independent effects of choice from other contemporaneous changes in schools, or from the self-selection of talented students into schools or districts (Riddle & Stedman, 1989). For example, about 25% of the students attending junior high school in District 4 in the 1985–1986 school year lived outside of the community school district (Riddle & Stedman, 1989). The presence of these students, who presumably were more capable academically than the district residents, may partially account for the district's high achievement level.

The idea of choice is tremendously appealing to politicians for several reasons, but surely one of the most attractive is the belief that it is a relatively cheap way to improve American schools. We are extremely wary of this claim, however. While actually implementing some form of choice plan may not cost much, making it work for disadvantaged children may have substantial unanticipated costs.

Raising Standards

Perhaps the foremost strategy of educational reform in recent years has been raising standards for performance in secondary schools (and, to a lesser extent, in elementary and middle schools). Following on the heels of the National Commission on Excellence in Education's (1983) report, *A Nation at Risk,* states and local school districts began to implement a variety of reforms, many of which were focused on improving student performance by using strategies such as strengthening curricular content; imposing exit requirements; raising the academic expectations of children, teachers, and administrators; and increasing the length of the school day and year.

The Commission's report and the reforms that followed it were largely silent on the implications of these reforms for disadvantaged or "at-risk" students. Our analyses of the potential consequences of raising standards for disadvantaged populations are reported elsewhere (McDill et al., 1985, 1986; Natriello, McDill, & Pallas, 1985; Natriello, Pallas, & McDill, 1986b; Pallas, Natriello, & McDill, 1987). Briefly, we concluded that, while raising standards for performance might produce higher achievement in some cases, this strategy, in the absence of substantial additional help for at-risk students, might have the unintended consequences of (1) making schools less flexible in the curricular options they present to students, (2) creating conflict between the demands imposed by schools and other demands that young people face, and (3) increasing the likelihood that low-achieving students might fail in school and ultimately drop out.

It still is too early to evaluate the consequences of this aspect of the reform movement, but preliminary evidence is beginning to trickle in, largely based on the subjective impressions of students, teachers, and administrators. It may be some years before there is conclusive evidence on the effects of the reforms, as only very recent cohorts of children entering school will be exposed to these reforms throughout their school careers (Pallas, 1989; Pallas et al., 1987). In spite of this very important caveat, the emerging evidence does provide a guide to the shape of the reforms. In particular, we can glean some knowledge about how, if at all, the current wave of reforms is responding to the needs of educationally disadvantaged students.

Clune (1989) reports on a six-state study of the implementation and effects of increased course-taking requirements for high school graduation. He concludes that there is evidence that the reform has been implemented, given the observed increase in math and science course-taking. The districts Clune and his colleagues surveyed reported that most of these additions consisted of basic, general, or remedial courses, leading Clune to conclude that, "evidently, the reforms amounted to a national experiment in offering lower-level academic courses to middle- and low-achieving students who previously took something else (vocational courses, various electives)" (p. 15).

The respondents observed the usual advantages and disadvantages of increased course-taking, with better college preparation as the most commonly cited advantage, and a reduction in the number of electives available to students the most commonly cited disadvantage of the reform. Clune (1989) found that the respondents felt that the state-level reforms were not sensitive to local districts' needs. He noted,

The overriding opinion of school-level people (including principals, counselors, and teachers) was that the new requirements did not address the districts' real needs. Respondents indicated that different students had different needs and the requirements did not address divergent needs, especially not the needs of the disadvantaged students, minority students, or the non-college-bound students. [pp. 23–24]

In spite of the rhetoric, then, there is little evidence that the reform strategy of raising standards has been sensitive to the needs of disadvantaged students. Policy makers instituting changes in graduation requirements have been conspicuously silent about the content of the curriculum, and most states have given rather little guidance to local districts on how to implement the intended reforms. Consequently there is great uncertainty regarding the extent to which the newly implemented reforms constitute an advance over existing practice, especially for low-achieving students.

As we have noted, a major criticism of the movement to raise standards is that, in the absence of additional help for low-achieving students, simply increasing academic performance standards might have the pernicious effect of pushing marginal students out of school. Clune (1989) argues, we believe correctly, that the data needed to resolve the issue of the effects that raising standards has had on dropout rates simply are not yet available, although here, too, there is suggestive evidence from a different corner.

Catterall (1989) analyzed the effects that minimum-competency tests — especially high school exit tests that students must pass before receiving a high school diploma — have on low-achieving high school students. He interviewed a sample of test coordinators, school principals, and school counselors and surveyed over 700 high school students. Although the educators largely reported that (lacking concrete information) they believed that the exit tests were too simple to pose a significant barrier to graduation even for low achievers, the students' responses argued that failing the exit tests might lead them to drop out. Catterall developed a careful analytic model predicting students' self-reported likelihood of finishing high school, as a function of family background, school context, and in-school performance. He found that failing a required graduation test significantly lowered students' confidence about whether they would finish high school. The fact that this effect persists in the face of substantial controls for academic performance, including high school track, self-reported grades, and grade retention, implies that whether or not a student fails a high school exit test may have an independent effect on students' self-perceptions, and ultimately on their chances for finishing high school.

Of course, direct evidence of the effects that failing such minimum-competency tests have on the risk of dropping out would clearly be preferable, but in the absence of such data, Catterall's (1989) analysis does raise concern. Perhaps most damning to the notion that raising standards is an effective strategy for educating disadvantaged youth is Catterall's discussion of what happens when a child fails a required high school exit test. He found little evidence that test failure moved schools to mobilize resources to serve poorly performing students. In other words, most schools did not have well-articulated or coherent strategies for responding to test failure. It is hard to envision how raising standards for disadvantaged students might succeed when schools lack an institutional response to the failures of the disadvantaged to meet those standards.

Just as raising standards for academic performance may simply place additional barriers in the paths of disadvantaged students, so are choice programs unlikely to lead to the development of schools designed to serve the needs of the disadvantaged. The incentives under choice programs are to attract the best students, those who are most developed academically and socially upon admission and who will most readily continue to develop academically and socially and reflect well on the school. The notion of an institutional response to the disadvantaged is one of the keys to our recommendations for more successfully educating this group. While choice and raising standards are strategies with limited potential for serving the disadvantaged, there are other ways and means to attack the problem. After reviewing the massive literature on educational programs for the disadvantaged, and developing our own theory-based framework for analyzing the issues, we now present our own recommendations for how our society can best serve the educationally disadvantaged.

THE NEW THREE R'S: RESOURCES, RESTRUCTURING, AND RESEARCH

In this section we discuss what we refer to as the "new three R's": resources, restructuring, and research. In particular, we consider the resources necessary to educate the disadvantaged, the restructuring of the educating institutions to which the disadvantaged are exposed, and the type of research needed to make those institutions more effective in serving this population.

We have organized our discussion to consider resources, restructuring, and research separately. For some of our recommendations, the choice of heading is arbitrary, as the recommendations may pertain to more than one of these topics simultaneously. Some of our suggestions for restructuring, for example, are dependent on sufficient resources to carry out the organizational transformations for which we call. Similarly, successful restructuring may depend on the availability of adequate research on programmatic strategies and high quality data on individual students. Moreover, the availability of resources may hinge on adequate research and data that properly frame the extent and nature of the problem of serving the educationally disadvantaged. Thus, resources, restructuring, and research are intertwined.

Resources

Our assessment in the area of resources is quite blunt: Successfully educating the disadvantaged will require a substantial influx of new resources. Virtually all of the evidence we have reviewed points in this direction. Many programs for the disadvantaged are reaching only a small fraction of the number of children and their families who could benefit from them. Head Start and WIC are examples of programs with demonstrable effects that are unable to serve their entire target populations. Additional resources are needed to enable such programs to serve all of the disadvantaged children who need them.

Moreover, even those programs that are effective must often dilute the intensity of the social and educational services they provide, in order to serve as many children and families as possible. We believe that a primary explanation for why a great many well-intentioned and plausible educational programs for the disadvantaged have only small positive impacts is that they are not intensive enough. A high school dropout-prevention program that doubles the number of guidance counselors, for example, may be a step in the right direction, but may not alter an at-risk student's school experience sufficiently to make a difference, if the net result is that each counselor is responsible for 350 students instead of 700.

In spite of a great deal of rhetoric to the contrary, there are no quick fixes to educating the disadvantaged. We believe that the quantity of resources needed to give these students a real chance for educational success is very large, dramatically larger than either previous critics or existing practice would suggest. Resources, of course, come in many forms, including human, material, and financial. Human and material resources carry costs, although often these costs are hard to estimate. Even recent proposals for increased voluntarism and service by American youth and adults have real costs associated with them — at the least, the costs of foregoing other types of leisure or work activities. Because of these and other ambiguities, we cannot hazard a guess as to the dollar costs of the new resources for which we call.

The contention that disadvantaged students need greater resources for education does not originate with us. In fact, expenditure inequities across richer and poorer school districts are frequently the basis for suits filed by the poorer districts against the state. Although these cases typically turn on wording in the state constitution, the defendants frequently invoke the argument that the level of school expenditures is not associated with the level of school achievement. Economist Eric Hanushek (1981, 1986, 1989) is the most prominent proponent of this position. While there are a variety of critiques of Hanushek's argument, one is particularly telling. The empirical evidence on which he and others rely does not consist of examining achievement changes in impoverished school districts where massive increases in resources have been made available to serve poor and otherwise disadvantaged children. It may seem odd that the evidence relied upon in these debates would be anything else, since this seems to be the crux of the matter. Most of the research, however, reports "snapshot" analyses capturing the variations in achievement and expenditures among school districts at a single point in time. The fact is that there is virtually no evidence of the consequences of colossal increases in the educational resources to which disadvantaged children are exposed, because this strategy has never been systematically adopted.

Even raising the level of resources expended by poor districts to that of wealthier districts would represent a massive investment in poorer districts.

But the schooling of disadvantaged children probably requires even more resources than the schooling of middle-class or otherwise advantaged children. There surely are no widely publicized examples of poor districts that devote a greater quantity of resources to their schools than similarly sized wealthy districts.

We pose three additional arguments about resources. First, the sheer volume of resources for which we call greatly exceeds this society's historical commitment to education in general, and educating the disadvantaged in particular. The level of resources devoted to educating the disadvantaged is unlikely to increase substantially without a major change in the attitudes, beliefs, and knowledge about the extent and seriousness of the problem held by educators, parents, policy makers, and legislators. While blue-ribbon panels issue new reports on at-risk children almost like clockwork, somehow the message has not yet sunk in. We frankly do not know what it will take to mobilize American society to devote the level of resources to educating the disadvantaged that we believe is necessary to serve them successfully.

Second, there are hard choices to be made about how to allocate current resources and whatever incremental gains might be achieved in the near future. We strongly believe that resources must be targeted first at the very young, in the form of prenatal, neonatal, and infant care programs. There simply is no excuse in our society for malnourished, low-birthweight, or otherwise unhealthy babies and young children. If these early problems are not checked, they grow, and redressing them requires more resources and more complex service delivery systems in schools and communities. Even with these later resources, there is no guarantee of success.

Third, the evidence is quite clear that resources must be devoted to the disadvantaged throughout their educational careers. It simply is not sufficient to target young, disadvantaged children for special resources for a year or two, and thereby expect their educational problems to be over forever. The school, the family, and the community each is a persistent influence on the lives of children, and the disadvantaging features of each of these institutions may persist throughout a child's educational career. The educational resources that society devotes to such children to offset the effects of their environments must parallel our understanding of how and when families, communities, and schools impede children's development. We believe, for instance, that the disappointing "fade-out" effects observed in early childhood education programs are largely due to discontinuities in the level of resources to which educationally disadvantaged children are exposed.

There is an obvious tension in our belief that resources must be targeted at the earliest points in children's development and also sustained throughout disadvantaged children's educational careers. This strain would be obviated if there were enough educational resources to serve all of the educationally disadvantaged all of the time. At present, we are far, far away from such a state. Rather, we serve some of the disadvantaged some of the time, and we don't even do that very well.

Of course, simply throwing money at schools is not going to solve any problems, but large sums of money have never been committed to schools serving disadvantaged youth. Resources must be used wisely. Indeed, with the growing numbers of disadvantaged youngsters, even a substantial increase in the level of resources available to schools is not likely to be sufficient to address these students' educational needs. There appears to be a growing gap between the level of resources society is willing and able to commit to educating the disadvantaged and the accumulating needs of that population of students. We do not know if it is possible to close that gap in the near future or even in the next generation; however, we propose two additional recommendations that might offer this country some hope of adequately addressing the needs of its disadvantaged students. These are to restructure the schools and to conduct research into the educational process. Resources must be used prudently, and our recommendations regarding restructuring and research provide some guidance about sensible uses of resources so that they might make a difference in the lives of disadvantaged children.

Restructuring

Our recommendations for restructuring include both the restructuring of our major educating institutions and, also important, the restructuring of linkages among these institutions. The educating institutions we have emphasized throughout this book are the school, the family, and the community.

Restructuring the School, the Family, and the Community. Our analysis of the restructuring of schools consumed the whole of Chapter 8. We drew several conclusions from that analysis. First, we argued that schools should decrease their need for processing information about the performance of students, by shifting decision making to levels closer to students. Decisions made at the school and classroom level are likely to be more responsive to the needs of disadvantaged students. Second, we argued that, because some decisions will always need to be made at higher levels in the system, investments should be made in improving the capacity of the educational system to process information on students and their performance and behavior. We discussed specific strategies for accomplishing both of these necessary changes in schools. Finally, we recommended that educational decisions be made at the levels where the best information could be used to inform a particular decision and that educators and policy makers accept responsibility for the impact of educational policies.

We have relatively little to say about the restructuring of families to better educate the disadvantaged. In fact, we are quite wary of governmental attempts to intervene in the inner workings of families. The family tradition-ally has been viewed as a private institution, operating without fear of government intervention. While the state has encroached a bit, the United States has never had a family policy, and it seems unlikely to us that manipu-lating family composition and characteristics through governmental incen-tives will be a prominent strategy in the future.

We also do not have much to offer regarding community restructuring *per se*. We believe that what Wilson (1987) has described as the social dis-location characteristic of our urban centers is arguably this country's most severe social problem. The root of this problem is persistent and prolonged poverty that spans generations and consumes entire communities. We see poverty as a "predisposing factor," in that it makes families, schools, and communities vulnerable to decay, thereby weakening the bonds these institu-tions forge between children and society. Eliminating or reducing the extent of poverty in the inner city cannot by itself solve the problem of successfully educating the disadvantaged, but removing this predisposing factor should bolster the key educating institutions.

Many of the current ideas about community restructuring focus on the reindustrialization and revitalization of our urban centers (Wilson, 1987). While not denying the potential of such approaches, our own vision high-lights the restructuring of community services. Many of the ideas we have developed about schools apply equally well to community agencies. Most prominent among these is the adoption of a case-management approach to serving the educationally disadvantaged.

Of course, many community social service agencies employ a case-management approach to service delivery, but there are several weaknesses in the traditional implementation of this strategy. First, the services typically are reactive rather than proactive. The major consequence is that agencies intervene late rather than early and are forced to confront more complex, severe problems. With respect to community services, an ounce of preven-tion truly is worth a pound of cure. Our consideration of maternal and infant health care in Chapter 4 is perhaps the best example of this principle.

Second, the traditional case-management orientation of community so-cial services lacks coordination across agencies. Different agencies may be responsible to different parts of state and local government. Coordination among agencies is difficult even when there is a single funding source, but much more so when agencies are responsible to different masters and differ-ent missions.

One of the consequences of lack of coordination is the dilution of the array of services that disadvantaged children might receive. Most case-management approaches to service delivery are more intensive than the antithetical systemic approach, but the number of individuals eligible for services (or the number that might benefit from them, a different concept) almost always exceeds the number for whom there are adequate resources. Consequently, relatively few children receive the intensity of services that may be necessary for them to overcome the educational disadvantages they face. This is both a resource and a restructuring problem.

Moreover, in the absence of explicit coordination of services, the management of services is often left to the client, who may not have the information necessary to understand the available options, and hence may not make good choices among those options. Coordination of services facilitates their accessibility and ease of use, a point Schorr (1988) notes.

Finally, we point out the need within communities to develop comprehensive, clear plans for delivering services to the disadvantaged. Most communities lack a coherent policy on what services are needed, who should be receiving them, and who is responsible for delivering them. An explicit policy with clearly stated goals, that takes into account the bureaucratic and administrative complexities characteristic of contemporary social service delivery, can help insure that individuals do not fall through the cracks in the social machinery.

Restructuring Linkages among Schools, Families, and Communities. Our primary recommendation for restructuring the ties among schools, families, and communities is simply stated: The bonds among these educating institutions must be strengthened and aligned, if these institutions are to be successful in educating the disadvantaged. Possible strategies for reinforcing these bonds include greater family involvement in the schools and making the school more prominent in the life of the community.

In order for the linkages among these educating institutions to tighten, two changes in social policy must occur. First, there must be incentives for the establishment of stronger ties among families, schools, and communities. Second, the disincentives or barriers that stand in the way of these bonds must be abolished.

Examples of incentives for stronger linkages include making the school a more central community and family resource through extended-day and weekend programs; developing community-based education/learning settings in museums, community agencies, and businesses; promoting corporate support for family involvement in schools, through flexible work schedules and more direct business involvement in child care; and providing financial and technical support for parental involvement strategies (Epstein & Scott-Jones, 1988; McLaughlin & Shields, 1987).

Examples of ways to remove barriers to connections among families, schools, and communities include locating community services so that they are accessible at schools and the workplace (Levy, 1989); using community media such as radio, television, and newspapers to inform families about the schools; and insuring that schools and community agencies have liaisons who can communicate with language minority students and their families (Epstein, 1986; Epstein & Scott-Jones, 1988).

These examples of establishing incentives and removing barriers are merely illustrative of a much wider range of strategies for strengthening the bonds among families, schools, and communities. As the notion of linkages, partnerships, and collaborations becomes more central to our strategies for restructuring the services we deliver to the educationally disadvantaged, the number of examples will skyrocket. There is, we believe, a largely untapped arena for linkages that will spur some very creative and exciting proposals.

Our recommendations for restructuring schools have called for greater coordination of educational resources and their delivery to students. Restructuring schools must lead to improved management of the educational experiences of students, whether at the classroom, school, district, state, or federal level. Restructuring the relationships among schools, families, and communities must result in the same type of improved management of the educational and social resources delivered to disadvantaged youth. At a time when the gap between available resources and needs is growing, we must obtain as much leverage as possible from all of the resources at our command. The coherent, mutually reinforcing mobilization of school, family, and community resources may be our best hope for addressing the problems of disadvantaged students. We simply cannot afford duplication, lack of coordination, and piecemeal approaches if we wish to have an impact on the problem.

Research

Schools and other educating institutions are commonly thought to produce a product. In fact, schools have been described as factories, translating raw materials (i.e., children) into products (i.e., citizens with certain knowledge, skills and values). The metaphor is weak on the technology of production, as there probably is greater consensus on how to produce a radial tire than there is on how to educate a child. This should surprise no one. After all, there is much greater variability among children, who are the "raw materials" of schooling, than there is among, say, batches of rubber.

Moreover, there is widespread agreement on the characteristics of good tires, but considerable disagreement on what sorts of young people schools should produce.

Economists describe the relationship between inputs and outputs in a production process as a *production function* (Hanushek, 1979). Schooling, in particular, as well as the broader process of education, has a poorly specified production function. Put simply, there is a great deal we do not know about how to educate disadvantaged children successfully. Throughout this book we have strived to summarize what we do know, based on the last two decades of research and practice, but the inescapable conclusion is that, at this time, there are more questions than there are answers.

Research is the primary tool for answering these persistent questions about what works for the disadvantaged. Only careful research can tell us the essential elements in local preschool programs; the keys to dropout prevention at the high school level; the school restructuring strategies that improve the academic performance of disadvantaged youth; the ways that families and communities influence children's performance in school; or how to replicate a pilot program successfully in other sites.

Our call for increased research on the education of the disadvantaged is both broad and deep. We believe that research should be conducted at each of the levels that we discussed in Chapter 7, that is, by the federal government, states, and local school districts, as well as at the school and classroom levels. The scope of needed research ranges from quite broad, fundamental questions concerning how disadvantaged and other children learn, to comparatively narrow questions about the relative effectiveness of specific educational treatments and interventions.

One of the threads that runs through our beliefs about the need for research is the importance of program evaluation. It is senseless to implement and run educational programs without systematically assessing their effects on the intended beneficiaries. Nevertheless, our review of the current educational literature shows quite convincingly that only a small fraction of the current crop of educational innovations has been rigorously evaluated. It is absolutely essential that evaluation be built into the design of educational experiments and innovations. If we hope to transfer our knowledge of what particular educational intervention works for the disadvantaged, and under what conditions, we must have thorough controls and information on the population being served, the nature of the treatment, both the expected and unanticipated outcomes of the treatment, and the social and political factors that facilitated or obstructed successful implementation of the program.

Gathering these kinds of data is never easy, but there is a particular design that is generally superior to the others. Controlled experiments with the random assignment of some students to a treatment group and others to a control group, as a rule, provide much more secure conclusions about the relative effectiveness of the educational treatment under study than alternative designs. Unfortunately, a variety of social and political forces frequently conspire to block randomization, yielding results that are tentative at best and simply wrong at worst. Probably the most common reason why programs championed as successful fail to replicate their positive effects in other settings is that the evaluations of such programs were not able to isolate the true effects of the programs from other confounding factors.

As we noted earlier, the resources for serving disadvantaged children are far below the level we believe necessary for educating these children successfully. It is very likely, therefore, that resources that should be devoted to research are in fact being diverted to programs themselves, as resources are in such short supply. We need to strengthen our commitment both to the resources available for serving educationally disadvantaged children and to the resources available for educational research and development.

Diverting research resources to programs, while understandable, is particularly unwise at a time when the gap between available resources and the needs of the disadvantaged is growing. Our review of educational programs suggests that previous and current programmatic efforts bring modest improvements of short duration in the educational performance of disadvantaged students. This is true of even the best-funded programs. More resources for programs will bring improvements, but, unless we develop new, more cost-effective strategies for educating the disadvantaged, our society is unlikely ever to be in a position to deal with this problem. We need both more resources and more effective ways of using those resources. Educational research and development offer the only hope for improving the situation. Indeed, our current educational problems may be the result of long-term severe underinvestment in educational research and development.

Precise figures on the extent of the national commitment to educational research and development are hard to come by. There are, however, estimates of federal expenditures on educational research and development. In fiscal year 1987, for example, the U.S. Department of Education spent $123 million on educational research and development (Finn, 1988). In contrast, federal funds authorized for medical research and development in 1986 totaled $5.1 billion (National Science Board, 1985). In other words, the federal government spends more than 40 times as much on medical research and development as it does on educational research and development.

We do not, of course, wish to demean the importance of medical research. An efficient and effective health care system is essential to the maintenance of individuals' and society's well-being. In addition, when we look at total expenditures, the amount allocated for health in the United States is about 50% higher than total spending on elementary, secondary, and higher education (U.S. Bureau of the Census, 1987). But the disparity in the area of research is too great to shrug off. In 1986 the federal government allocated 25 times more money for space research and technology ($3.1 billion) than for educational research and development, and in the same year it allocated more than seven times as much for transportation research and development ($905 million). The federal government also planned to spend more than six times as much money on agricultural research ($778 million) as on educational research and development.

Finn (1988) and others have argued that the federal government should play a minimal role in education in the United States, as education is primarily the responsibility of states and local governments. The most extreme form of this argument is that the sole legitimate federal role in education is in the gathering and dissemination of educational statistics reporting on the condition of education in the United States. But we are hard pressed to see how education should be held to a different standard than health, transportation, or agriculture.

Education is the responsibility of *everyone:* the federal government, the states, and local communities and the families who reside in them. In calling for federal leadership both in resources and research, we do not intend to absolve states and communities of their responsibility to support education to the fullest extent that they can.

A CRUELER, HARSHER NATION

We have argued strongly that successfully educating the population of disadvantaged children will demand a monumental increase in the level of resources that this country devotes to this task. Reluctantly, we see little evidence that our society is prepared to make the necessary commitment to its children. What, then, will happen?

One distinctly unpleasant scenario revolves around the notion of educational triage (Hess, 1986). This image derives from medicine, wherein health care practitioners sometimes must make difficult decisions about which patients are most likely to benefit from the treatments available, and which ones cannot. When resources are scarce, health care practitioners typically try to apply these limited resources where they believe they will do the most good.

But educational resources are more wanting than health care resources. Without the requisite resources, society cannot educate all of its children. We envision the possibility of a future where schools and communities try to serve the population of "survivors," that is, where society's scarce educational resources are devoted to nurturing those children seen as having the greatest potential to succeed. The remaining children will be ignored, left largely to founder on the rocks of society's indifference and hardened neglect.

It is an ugly vision, but it could happen. We are already nearer to it than we care to admit. The question before us is whether we have time to reverse the present course and make substantial improvements in the education of disadvantaged youth. Our nation has faced and overcome more severe crises in the past, and there is reason to believe that, if we became committed to educating the disadvantaged, we could overcome the current bleak picture. However, in recent years we have become a society unwilling to make sacrifices and particularly unwilling to place the interests of others above our own interests. Thus whether we as a society act to improve the education of the disadvantaged may hinge upon leadership that understands and communicates that failing to make sacrifices now condemns us to a declining national standard of living in the future, and that the interests of the disadvantaged are increasingly intertwined with the self-interests of all of us. It is a message we may not want to hear, but it is one that we dismiss at our peril.

NOTES

REFERENCES

INDEX

ABOUT THE AUTHORS

Notes

CHAPTER 4

1. The CSR authors (McKey et al., 1985) define "educationally meaningful" as an average score on the criterion in question of .25 standard deviation units greater for the Head Start group than for the control group, a magnitude of difference which they believe accompanies "noticeable improvements in classroom performance" (p. 5).

2. If our understanding of DISTAR is accurate, Schweinhart et al. (1986b) mislabeled this second model, since DISTAR is a program designed for use in the early elementary grades. This view is reinforced by Gersten's (1986) critique of the study, in which he points out that DISTAR is indeed an elementary program. He emphasizes that "these students [those labeled as being in the 'DISTAR' program by Schweinhart et al., 1986b] were taught in a systematic way based on the principles outlined in *Teaching Disadvantaged Children in the Preschool* (Bereiter & Engelmann, 1966)" (pp. 293–294).

3. Remarkably, this debate was essentially repeated in an issue of *Educational Leadership* (Bereiter, 1986b; Brandt, 1986; Gersten & White, 1986; Schweinhart & Weikart, 1986a, 1986c).

4. The information on this 1966–1967 cohort was taken directly from Stallings and Stipek (1986, pp. 736–737), since Gordon's (1969) original assessment was unavailable. A summary of the theoretical rationale, implementation, and evaluation of the program involving three different intervention efforts by Gordon and colleagues in the greater Gainesville area between 1966 and 1977, in which they followed some of the students until age 11, is presented in Jester and Guinagh (1983). However, we find important parts of their presentation, such as sampling design and analysis of data, to be incomprehensible.

CHAPTER 5

1. Both House et al. (1978) and Bereiter and Kurland (1981–1982a) used local site means on various subtests of the Metropolitan Achievement Test (MAT) as their measures of achievement, in contrast to the Abt researchers, who used individual students at the sites as their units of analysis. However, in contrast to House et al., who used locally adjusted (via covariance analysis) site-level differences between Follow Through and non–Follow Through groups as the dependent variable, with covariance adjustments being calculated on an individual basis, Bereiter and

Kurland used site means for Follow Through groups as the dependent variables, with other site-level scores, such as socioeconomic status and achievement test scores at time of entry into the program (as a measure of academic readiness), as covariates. Bereiter and Kurland argue that their methodology provides a more powerful analysis than that of House et al. because, for example, their approach removes error variance associated with non–Follow Through groups.

2. House et al.'s (1978) rankings of models on achievement effects are, overall, similar to those of Bereiter and Kurland (1981–1982a); however, in the former analysis essentially no statistically significant differences were uncovered, whereas the latter analysis produced significant differences among models on all subtests of the MAT. Bereiter and Kurland's results and conclusions produced an acrimonious exchange with House, a discussion of which is beyond the scope of our presentation (see Bereiter & Kurland, 1981–1982b; House, 1981–1982).

CHAPTER 6

1. Stinchcombe argued that much psychological and behavioral nonconformity occur in school when adult status is perceived by adolescents as not being clearly linked to or articulated with present performance. This perspective was earlier expressed in the "subcultural" formulation of gang delinquency of Cohen (1955) and of Cloward and Ohlin (1960). However, neither of these sets of authors attempted to test their propositions systematically, using firsthand evidence.

2. Without doubt, the most ambitious example of such a community effort is the Community Action Program (CAP), a part of President Johnson's War on Poverty legislation enacted in 1964. CAP involved the concept of comprehensive, coordinated, and community-wide planning and implementation of programs focused on combating poverty. The local mechanism for coordination and implementation of efforts was "the community action agency—a public or private agency designed to pull a locality's existing institutional resources together and to develop . . . a functional agenda for its need in fighting poverty" (Levitan, 1969, p. 63). The program was intended to restructure social services to poverty-stricken citizens in several ways, including allowing extensive policy-making participation by clients served by the program and coordination of services at the local level.

CHAPTER 8

1. Our analysis is rooted primarily in the understanding of organizational operations provided by contingency theory (Perrow, 1979; Thompson, 1967) and, more specifically, the organizational design perspective advanced by Galbraith (1973). This framework was developed to aid in the analysis of organizations in general and reveals much about strategies for schools to use in responding to the needs of disadvantaged students. Briefly, this perspective suggests that in any enterprise there is no one best way to organize, but that not every way of organizing is equally

effective. The choice of an appropriate organizational form within a rational perspective will depend upon the predictability of the task being performed; that is, on management's ability to control means/ends relations. Thus, the most effective way to organize is contingent upon the uncertainty and diversity of the basic task being performed by the organizational unit.

Furthermore, the greater the uncertainty of the task, the greater the amount of information that has to be processed among decision makers during the execution of the task. If a task is well understood, either because of technical analysis or a stable tradition, much of the task can be planned prior to its actual execution; if a task is less well understood, then more knowledge, much of it acquired during the actual execution of the task, will be required to perform the task successfully. The basic effect of uncertainty is to limit the ability of the organization to plan or make decisions about activities in advance of their execution.

Task uncertainty is defined as the difference between the information required to perform a task and the information possessed by the organization. The amount of task uncertainty is a result of a combination of a specific task and a specific organization. Galbraith (1973) argues that the amount of information needed to perform a task in an organization is a function of three factors: (1) the diversity of the outputs provided; (2) the number of different input resources utilized; and (3) the level of goal difficulty or performance. The greater the diversity of outputs and resources and the higher the level of performance demanded, the greater the amount of information needed to perform a task.

References

Aldrich, H. E. (1979). *Organizations and Environments.* Englewood Cliffs, NJ: Prentice-Hall.

Alexander, J. F., & Malouf, R. E. (1983). Intervention with children experiencing problems in personality and social development. In E. M. Hetherington (Ed.), *Handbook of Child Psychology* (Vol. 4, pp. 914–981). New York: John Wiley.

Alexander, K. L., & Pallas, A. M. (1984). Curriculum reform and school performance: An evaluation of the "New Basics." *American Journal of Education, 92,* 391–420.

Anderson, R. B., St. Pierre, R. G., Proper, E. C., & Stebbins, L. B. (1978). Pardon us, but what was that question again? A response to the critique of the Follow Through evaluation. *Harvard Educational Review, 45,* 161–170.

Anson, R. (1980). Hispanics in the United States: Yesterday, today, and tomorrow. *The Futurist, 14*(4), 25–31.

Applebee, A. N., Langer, J. A., & Mullis, I. V. S. (1988). *Who Reads Best? Factors Related to Reading Achievement in Grades 3, 7, and 11.* Princeton, NJ: Educational Testing Service.

Ashley, W., Jones, J., Zahniser, G., & Inks, L. (1986). *Peer Tutoring: A Guide to Program Design* (Research and Development Series No. 260). Columbus, Ohio: Ohio State University Center for Research in Vocational Education.

Aspira. (1983). *Racial and Ethnic High School Dropout Rates in New York: A Summary Report.* New York: Aspira.

Atkeson, B. M., & Forehand, R. (1979). Home-based reinforcement programs designed to modify classroom behavior: A review and methodological evaluation. *Psychological Bulletin, 86,* 1298–1308.

Bailyn, B. (1960). *Education in the Forming of American Society.* Chapel Hill: University of North Carolina Press.

Baker, D. P., & Stevenson, D. L. (1986). Mothers' strategies for children's school achievement: Managing the transition to high school. *Sociology of Education, 59,* 156–166.

Baldwin, W., & Cain, V. S. (1981). The children of teenage parents. In F. Furstenberg, R. Lincoln, & J. Menken (Eds.), *Teenage Sexuality, Pregnancy, and Childbearing* (pp. 265–279). Philadelphia: University of Pennsylvania Press.

Baratz, S. S., & Baratz, J. C. (1970). Early childhood intervention: The social science basis of institutional racism. *Harvard Educational Review, 40,* 29–50.

Barber, D. N. (1977). *Trenton, New Jersey Follow Through: Behavior Analysis Approach. Proposal to the Joint Dissemination Review Panel, U.S. Department of Education.* Trenton, NJ: Trenton Board of Education.

Barker, R. G., & Gump, R. V. (1964). *Big School, Small School: High School Size and Student Behavior.* Stanford, CA: Stanford University Press.

Barnhard, J. W., Zimbardo, P. G., & Sarason, S. B. (1968). Teachers' ratings of student personality traits that relate to IQ and social desirability. *Journal of Educational Psychology, 59,* 128–132.

Barr, R., & Dreeben, R. (1983). *How Schools Work.* Chicago: University of Chicago Press.

Barro, S., & Kolstad, A. (1987). *Who Drops Out of High School? Findings from High School and Beyond* (Report No. CS 87–397c). Washington, DC: U.S. Department of Education, National Center for Education Statistics.

Bean, F. D., Swicegood, C. G., & King, A. G. (1985). Role incompatibility and the relationship between fertility and labor supply among Hispanic women. In G. J. Borjas & M. Tienda (Eds.), *Hispanics in the U.S. Economy* (pp. 221–242). Orlando, FL: Academic Press.

Beaton, A. E. (1986). *National Assessment of Educational Progress 1983–84: A Technical Report.* Princeton, NJ: Educational Testing Service.

Becker, H. J. (1986). The effects of computer use on children's learning: Limitations of past research and a working model for new research. *Peabody Journal of Education, 64,* 81–110.

Becker, W. C. (1978). The national evaluation of Follow Through: Behavior-theory-based programs come out on top. *Education and Urban Society, 10,* 431–458.

Becker, W. C., & Carnine, D. (1980). Direct instruction: An effective approach for educational intervention with disadvantaged and low performers. In B. J. Lekey & A. E. Kazden (Eds.), *Advances in Child Clinical Psychology* (pp. 429–473). New York: Plenum.

Becker, W. C., & Gersten, R. (1982). A follow-up of Follow Through: The later effects of the direct instruction model on children in fifth and sixth grades. *American Educational Research Journal, 19,* 75–92.

Bell, C. A., Casto, G., & Daniels, D. S. (1983). Ameliorating the impact of teen-age pregnancy on parent and child. *Child Welfare, 62,* 167–173.

Beller, E. K. (1973). Research on organized programs of early research. In R. M. W. Travers (Ed.), *Second Handbook of Research on Teaching* (pp. 530–600). Chicago: Rand McNally.

Bereiter, C. (1971). *An Academic Preschool for Disadvantaged Children: Conclusions from Evaluation Studies.* Paper presented at the Hyman Blumberg Memorial Symposium on Research in Early Childhood Education, Johns Hopkins University, Baltimore, MD.

Bereiter, C. (1986a). Does direct instruction cause delinquency? *Early Childhood Research Quarterly, 1,* 289–292.

Bereiter, C. (1986b). Does direct instruction cause delinquency? Response to Schweinhart and Weikart. *Educational Leadership, 44*(3), 20–21.

Bereiter, C., & Engelmann, S. (1966). *Teaching Disadvantaged Children in the Preschool.* Englewood Cliffs, NJ: Prentice-Hall.

Bereiter, C., & Kurland, M. (1981–1982a). A constructive look at Follow Through results. *Interchange, 12*(1), 1–22.

Bereiter, C., & Kurland, M. (1981–1982b). Response to House. *Interchange, 12*(1), 27–30.

Berger, J. (August 27, 1989). East Harlem Students Clutch a Dream. *New York Times,* sec. 1, pp. 1, 28.

Bernstein, B. (1960). Language and social class. *British Journal of Sociology, 11,* 271–276.

Bernstein, B. (1961). Social class and linguistic development: A theory of social learning. In A. H. Halsey, J. Floud, & C. A. Anderson (Eds.), *Education, Economy, and Society* (pp. 288–314). New York: The Free Press of Glencoe.

Bernstein, B. (1962). Social class, linguistic codes and grammatical elements. *Language and Speech, 5,* 221–240.

Bernstein, B. (1964). Elaborated and restricted codes: Their social origins and some consequences. *American Anthropologist, 66,* 55–69.

Berrueta-Clement, J. R., Schweinhart, L. J., Barnett, W. S., Epstein, A. S., & Weikart, D. P. (1984). *Changed Lives: The Effects of the Perry Preschool Program on Youths Through Age 19.* Ypsilanti, MI: High/Scope Press.

Betsey, C. L., Hollister, R. G., Jr., & Papageorgiou, M. R. (Eds.). (1985). *Youth Employment and Training Programs: The YEDPA Years.* Washington, DC: The National Academy Press.

Beyer, F. S., & Smey-Richman, B. (1988, April). *Addressing the "At-Risk" Challenge in the Nonurban Setting.* Paper presented at the annual meeting of the American Educational Research Association, New Orleans, LA.

Bianchi, S. M. (1984). Children's progress through school: A research note. *Sociology of Education, 57,* 184–192.

Bickel, W. E., & Cooley, W. W. (1985). Decision-oriented educational research in school districts: The role of dissemination processes. *Educational Evaluation, 11,* 183–203.

Bidwell, C. E. (1965). The school as a formal organization. In J. G. March (Ed.), *Handbook of Organizations* (pp. 972–1018). Chicago: Rand McNally.

Birman, B. F., Orland, M. E., Jung, R. K., Anson, R. J., & Garcia, G. N. (1987). *The Current Operation of the Chapter I Program.* Washington, DC: U.S. Government Printing Office.

Blank, R., Dentler, R. A., Baltzell, D. C., & Chabotar, K. (1983). *Survey of Magnet Schools—Final Report: Analyzing a Model for Quality Integrated Education.* Washington, DC: James H. Lowry & Associates.

Blau, P., & Shoenherr, R. (1971). *The Structure of Organizations.* New York: Basic Books.

Bloch, D. B. (n.d.) *Case Management—A Comprehensive Service Approach to Dropout Prevention.* New York: New York City Board of Education.

Bloom, B. (1964). *Stability and Change in Human Characteristics.* New York: John Wiley.

Bloom, B. (1984). The search for methods of group instruction as effective as one-to-one tutoring. *Educational Leadership, 41*(8), 4–17.

Blust, R. S., Coldiron, J. R., & Cica, J. T. (1985, April). *Are Effective Schools, Based on a Cognitive Definition, Effective in the Non-cognitive Area?* Paper presented at the annual meeting of the American Educational Research Association, Chicago, IL.

Bock, G., Stebbins, L. B., & Proper, E. C. (1977). *Education and Experimentation: A Planned Variation Model, Vol. 4-B. Effects of Follow Through Models.* Cambridge, MA: Abt.

Boocock, S. S. (1980). *Sociology of Education: An Introduction.* Boston: Houghton Mifflin.

Boruch, R. (1985). Implications of the youth employment experience for improving applied research and evaluation policy. In C. L. Betsey, R. G. Hollister, Jr., & M. R. Papageorgiou (Eds.), *Youth Employment and Training Programs: The YEDPA Years* (pp. 231–253). Washington, DC: National Academy Press.

Boston Compact Evaluation Subcommittee. (1988). *The Boston Compact: Measuring the Results.* Boston: Author.

Boston Compact Measurement Committee. (1989). *Memorandum to the Boston Compact Steering Committee Regarding Recommendations for Compact II Goals and Measures.* Boston: Author.

Bowles, S., & Gintis, H. (1976). *Schooling in Capitalist America.* New York: Basic Books.

Brandt, R. S. (1986). On long-term effects of early education: A conversation with Lawrence Schweinhart. *Educational Leadership, 44*(3), 15–18.

Broman, S. H. (1981). Long term development of children born to teenagers. In K. Scott, T. Field, & E. Robertson (Eds.), *Teenage Parents and Their Offspring.* New York: Grune & Stratton.

Broman, S. H., Nichols, D., & Kennedy, W. (1975). *Preschool IQ: Prenatal and Early Developmental Correlates.* Hillsdale, NJ: Lawrence Erlbaum.

Bronfenbrenner, U. (1975). Is early intervention effective? In M. Guttentag & E. L. Struening (Eds.), *Handbook of Evaluation Research* (Vol. 2, pp. 519–603). Beverly Hills, CA: Sage.

Brooks, C. (1966). Some approaches to teaching English as a second language. In S. W. Webster (Ed.), *The Disadvantaged Learner* (pp. 515–523). San Francisco: Chandler.

Brooks-Gunn, J., & Furstenberg, F. F., Jr. (1985). Antecedents and consequences of parenting: The case of adolescent motherhood. In A. D. Fogel & G. F. Nelson (Eds.), *The Origins of Nurturance* (pp. 233–258). Hillsdale, NJ: Lawrence Erlbaum.

Bruner, J. S. (1961). *The Process of Education.* Cambridge, MA: Harvard University Press.

Bruno, R. R. (1984). *Educational Attainment in the United States: March 1981 and 1980* (U.S. Bureau of the Census, Current Population Reports, Series P-20, No. 390). Washington, DC: U.S. Government Printing Office.

Bruno, R. R. (1988). *School Enrollment — Social and Economic Characteristics of Students: October 1986* (U.S. Bureau of the Census, Current Population Reports, Series P-20, No. 429). Washington, DC: U.S. Government Printing Office.

Bryk, A. S., & Thum, Y. M. (1989). *The Effects of High School Organization on*

Dropping Out: An Exploratory Investigation. New Brunswick, NJ: Center for Policy Research in Education.

Bullock, J. (1981). *Dade County, Florida Training for Turnabout Volunteers* (Proposal to the Joint Dissemination Review Panel, U.S. Department of Education). Miami, FL: Dade County Public Schools.

Burkheimer, G. J., French, A. M., Levinsohn, J. R., & Riccobono, J. A. (1977). *Evaluation Study of the Upward Bound Program: A First Follow-Up* (Final Report on Contract No. OEC-0-73-7052 to the U.S. Office of Education). Research Triangle Park, NC: Research Triangle Institute.

Burkheimer, G. J., Levinsohn, J. R., Koo, H. P., & French, A. M. (1976). *Evaluation Study of the Upward Bound Program* (Final Report on Contract No. OEC-0-73-7052 to the U.S. Office of Education). Research Triangle Park, NC: Research Triangle Institute.

Burkheimer, G. J., Riccobono, J. A., & Wisenbaker, J. M. (1979). *Evaluation Study of the Upward Bound Program: A Second Follow-Up* (Final Report on Contract No. HEW-300-78-0037 to the U.S. Office of Education). Research Triangle Park, NC: Research Triangle Institute.

Cahill, M., White, J. L., Lowe, D., & Jacobs, L. E. (1987). *In School Together: School-Based Child Care Serving Student Mothers.* New York: Academy for Educational Development.

California State Department of Education. (1984). *Performance Report for California Schools: Indicators of Quality.* Sacramento, CA: Author.

Callahan, R. (1962). *Education and the Cult of Efficiency.* Chicago: University of Chicago Press.

Campbell, D. T., & Boruch, R. F. (1975). Making the case for randomized assignment to treatments by considering the alternatives: Six ways in which quasi-experimental evaluations in compensatory education tend to underestimate effects. In C. A. Bennett & A. A. Lumsdaine (Eds.), *Evaluation and Experiment* (pp. 195–296). New York: Academic Press.

Campbell, D. T., & Erlebacher, A. (1970). How regression artifacts in quasi-experimental evaluations can mistakenly make compensatory education look harmful. In J. Hellmuth (Ed.), *Compensatory Education: A National Debate* (Vol. 3, pp. 185–233). New York: Brunner/Mazel.

Campbell, F. A., Breitmayer, B., & Ramey, C. T. (1986). Disadvantaged single teenage mothers and their children: Consequences of free educational day care. *Family Relations, 35*(1), 63–68.

Carnine, D., Carnine, L., Karp, J., & Weisberg, P. (1988). Kindergarten for economically disadvantaged children: The direct instruction component. In C. Warger (Ed.), *A Resource Guide to Public School Early Childhood Programs* (pp. 73–98). Alexandria, VA: Association for Supervision and Curriculum Development.

Carpenter, M. A., & Hopper, P. A. (1985). *Synthesis of State Chapter I Data, Summary Report.* Washington, DC: U.S. Department of Education.

Carter, L. (1984, August/September). The sustaining effects study of compensatory and elementary education. *Educational Researcher, 13,* 5–13.

Catterall, J. S. (1985). *On the Social Costs of Dropping Out of School.* Palo Alto, CA: Stanford Education Policy Institute.

Catterall, J. S. (1989). Standards and school dropouts: A national study of tests required for high school graduation. *American Journal of Education, 98,* 1–34.

Center for Statistics. (1986). *Plan for the Redesign of the Elementary and Secondary Data Collection Program.* Washington, DC: U.S. Department of Education.

Christoffel, P., & Celio, M. B. (1973). A benefit-cost analysis of the Upward Bound program: A comment. *Journal of Human Resources, 8,* 110–114.

Cicirelli, V. G. (1984). The misinterpretation of the Westinghouse study: A reply to Zigler and Berman. *American Psychologist, 39,* 915–916.

Clark, K. B. (1965). The cult of cultural deprivation: A complex social psychological phenomenon. In K. B. Clark (Ed.), *Environmental Deprivation and Enrichment* (pp. 41–42). New York: Ferkhauf Graduate School of Education, Yeshiva University.

Clark, K. B. (1972). Cultural deprivation theories: The social and psychological limitations. In K. B. Clark, M. Deutsch, A. Gartner, F. Keppel, H. Lewis, T. Pettigrew, L. Plotkin, & F. Riessman, *The Educationally Deprived: The Potential for Change* (pp. 3–12). New York: Metropolitan Applied Research Center.

Clark, R. (1985). Evidence for confounding in computer-based instruction studies: Analyzing the meta-analyses. *Educational Communication and Technology Journal, 33,* 249–262.

Clifford, G. J. (1985). The shifting relations between schools and nonschool education: An historical account. In M. D. Fantini & R. L. Sinclair (Eds.), *Education in School and Nonschool Settings: 84th Yearbook of the National Society for the Study of Education* (pp. 4–28). Chicago: University of Chicago Press.

Cloward, R. A., & Ohlin, L. E. (1960). *Delinquency and Opportunity: A Theory of Delinquent Gangs.* New York: Free Press.

Clune, W. H. (1989). *The Implementation and Effects of High School Graduation Requirements: First Steps Toward Curricular Reform* (Research Report Series RR-011). New Brunswick, NJ: Center for Policy Research in Education.

Clune, W. H., & White, P. A. (1988). *School-Based Management: Institutional Variation, Implementation, and Issues for Further Research* (Research Report Series RR-008). New Brunswick, NJ: Center for Policy Research in Education.

Cohen, A. K. (1955). *Delinquent Boys.* Glencoe, IL: Free Press.

Cohen, E. G. (1986). *Designing Groupwork: Strategies for the Heterogeneous Classroom.* New York: Teachers College Press.

Cohen, M. (1988). *Restructuring the Education System: Agenda for the 1990s.* Washington, DC: Center for Policy Research, National Governors' Association.

Cohen, P. A., Kulik, J. A., & Kulik, C. (1982). Educational outcomes of tutoring: A meta-analysis of findings. *American Educational Research Journal, 19,* 237–248.

Coleman, J. S. (1981). Quality and inequality in American education: Public and Catholic schools. *Phi Delta Kappan, 63,* 159–164.

Coleman, J. S., Bremner, R. H., Clark, B. R., Davis, J. B., Eichorn, D. H., Griliches, Z., Kett, J. F., Ryder, N. B., & Doering, Z. B. (1974). *Youth: Transition to Adulthood.* Chicago: University of Chicago Press.

Coleman, J. S., Campbell, E. Q., Hobson, C. J., McPartland, J., Mood, A., Weinfeld, F. D., & York, R. L. (1966). *Equality of Educational Opportunity.* Washington, DC: U.S. Government Printing Office.

Coleman, J. S., & Hoffer, T. (1987). *Public and Private High Schools: The Impact of Communities.* New York: Basic Books.

Coleman, J. S., & Husen, T. (1985). *Becoming Adult in a Changing Society.* Paris: Organisation for Economic Co-Operation and Development.

Comer, J. (1980). *The New Haven School Intervention Project.* Paper presented at the Strategies for Urban School Improvement Workshop Series, Horace Mann Learning Center, Washington, DC.

Comer, J. (1981). *Societal Change: Implications for School Management.* Washington, DC: National Institute of Education.

Committee asks New York State to offer high-quality preschool to all 4-year-olds. (1989, January 11). *Education Week,* p. 18.

Committee for Economic Development. (1985). *Investing in Our Children. A Statement by the Research and Policy Committee of the Committee for Economic Development.* New York: Author.

Committee for Economic Development. (1987). *Children in Need: Investment Strategies for the Educationally Disadvantaged.* New York: Author.

Condry, S. (1983). History and background of preschool intervention programs and the Consortium for Longitudinal Studies. In Consortium for Longitudinal Studies (Ed.), *As the Twig Is Bent . . . Lasting Effects of Preschool Programs* (pp. 1–31). Hillsdale, NJ: Lawrence Erlbaum.

Consortium for Longitudinal Studies. (Ed.). (1983). *As the Twig Is Bent . . . Lasting Effects of Preschool Programs.* Hillsdale, NJ: Lawrence Erlbaum.

Cooke, C., Ginsburg, A., & Smith, M. (1985). The sorry state of education statistics. *Basic Education, 29*(5), 3–8.

Cooley, W. W. (1983). Improving the performance of an educational system. *Educational Researcher, 12*(6), 4–12.

Council of Chief State School Officers. (1988). *School Success for Students at Risk.* Orlando, FL: Harcourt Brace Jovanovich.

Cremin, L. A. (1976). *Public Education.* New York: Basic Books.

Cremin, L. A. (1988). *American Education: The Metropolitan Experience, 1876–1980.* New York: Harper & Row.

Cronbach, L. J. (1982). *Designing Evaluations of Educational and Social Programs.* San Francisco: Jossey-Bass.

Cusick, P. (1983). *The Egalitarian Ideal and the American High School.* New York: Longman.

David, J. L. (1989). *Restructuring in Progress: Lessons from Pioneering Districts.* Washington, DC: Center for Policy Research, National Governors' Association.

Davis, J. A., & Kenyon, C. A. (1976). *Review of the Literature Relevant to the Upward Bound and Talent Search Programs* (Contract No. OEC-0-73-7052). Research Triangle Park, NC: Research Triangle Institute.

Davis, K. (1977). A decade of policy developments in providing health care for low-income families. In R. H. Haveman (Ed.), *A Decade of Federal Antipoverty Programs: Achievements, Failures, and Lessons* (pp. 197–240). New York: Academic Press.

Delatte, J. G., Orgeron, K., & Preis, J. (1985). Project SCAN: Counseling teen-age parents in a school setting. *Journal of School Health, 55,* 24–26.

Deutsch, M. (1960). *Minority Group and Class Status as Related to Social and Personality Factors in Scholastic Achievement.* Ithaca, NY: Society for Applied Anthropology.

Deutsch, M. (1963). The disadvantaged child and the learning process. In A. H. Passow (Ed.), *Education and Depressed Areas* (pp. 163–179). New York: Teachers College Press.

Deutsch, M. (1967). *The Disadvantaged Child.* New York: Basic Books.

Devin-Sheehan, L., Feldman, R. S., & Allen, V. L. (1976). Research on children tutoring children: A critical review. *Review of Educational Research, 46,* 355–385.

Diprete, T. A. (1982). *Discipline and Order in American High Schools.* Washington, DC: U.S. Government Printing Office.

Dornbusch, S. M. (1974, Fall/Winter). To try or not to try. *Stanford Magazine, 2,* 50–54.

Dossey, J. A., Mullis, I. V. S., Lindquist, M. M., & Chambers, D. L. (1988). *The Mathematics Report Card: Are We Measuring Up?* Princeton, NJ: Educational Testing Service.

Downs, A. (1966). Up and down with ecology—The "issue attention" cycle. *The Public Interest, 1*(Fall), 38–50.

Edmonds, R. (1979). Effective schools for the urban poor. *Educational Leadership, 37*(1), 5–24.

Edmonds, R. (1984). Effective schools for the urban poor. In M. R. Barnett & C. C. Harrington (Eds.), *Readings on Equal Education* (Vol. 7, pp. 283–297). New York: AMS Press.

Edson, C. H. (1984). Risking the nation: Historical dimensions on survival and educational reform. *Issues in Education, 1,* 171–184.

Edwards, L. N., & Grossman, M. (1979). The relationship between children's health and intellectual development. In S. Mushkin (Ed.), *Health: What Is It Worth?* (pp. 84–103). Elmsford, NY: Pergamon Press.

Egan, O., & Archer, P. (1985). The accuracy of teachers' ratings of ability: A regression model. *American Educational Research Journal, 22,* 25–34.

Ehly, S. W., & Larsen, S. C. (1980). *Peer Tutoring for Individualized Instruction.* Boston: Allyn & Bacon.

Eisman, H. (Ed.). (1986). *Alternative High Schools and Programs: 1986 Annual Report.* New York: New York City Board of Education.

Ekstrom, R. B., Goertz, M. E., Pollack, J. M., & Rock, D. A. (1987). Who drops out of high school and why? Findings from a national study. In G. Natriello (Ed.), *School Dropouts: Patterns and Policies* (pp. 52–69). New York: Teachers College Press.

Elkind, D. (1986). Formal education and early education: An essential difference. *Phi Delta Kappan, 67,* 631–636.

Ellson, D. G. (1976). Tutoring. In N. L. Gage (Ed.), *The Psychology of Teaching Methods* (pp. 130–165). Chicago: University of Chicago Press.

Ellwood, D. T. (1988). *Poor Support: Poverty in the American Family.* New York: Basic Books.

Elmore, P., & Beggs, D. L. (1972, March). *Stability of Teacher Ratings of Pupil Behavior in a Classroom Setting.* Paper presented at the annual meeting of the American Personnel and Guidance Association, Chicago, IL.

Elmore, R. F. (1985). Knowledge development under the Youth Employment and Demonstration Projects Act. In C. L. Betsey, R. G. Hollister, Jr., & M. R. Papageorgiou (Eds.), *Youth Employment and Training Programs: The YEDPA Years* (pp. 281–347). Washington, DC: National Academy Press.

Elmore, R. F. (1988). *Early Experiences in Restructuring Schools: Voices from the Field.* Washington, DC: Center for Policy Research, National Governors' Association.

Emmer, E. T., Evertson, C. M., Sanford, J. P., Clements, B. S., & Worsham, M. E. (1984). *Classroom Management for Secondary Teachers.* Englewood Cliffs, NJ: Prentice-Hall.

Empey, L. T. (1978). *American Delinquency: Its Meaning and Construction.* Homewood, IL: Dorsey Press.

Engelmann, S., & Engelmann, T. (1981). *Give Your Child a Superior Mind.* New York: Simon & Schuster.

Englund, W. (1986, April 22). Preschool academic push linked to later social problems. *Baltimore Sun,* p. 1a.

Entwisle, D. R., Alexander, K. L., Cadigan, D., & Pallas, A. M. (1987). Kindergarten experiences: Cognitive effects or socialization? *American Educational Research Journal, 24,* 337–364.

Epstein, J. L. (Ed.). (1981). *The Quality of School Life.* Lexington, MA: Lexington Books.

Epstein, J. L. (1986). Parent involvement: Implications for limited-English-proficient parents. *Proceedings of the Symposium on Issues of Parent Involvement and Literacy.* Washington, DC: Trinity College.

Epstein, J. L., & McPartland, J. M. (1976). The concept and measurement of the quality of school life. *American Educational Research Journal, 13,* 15–30.

Epstein, J. L., & Scott-Jones, D. (1988, November). *School-Family-Community Connections for Accelerating Student Progress in the Elementary and Middle Grades.* Paper presented at Stanford University Centennial Conference on Accelerating the Education of At-Risk Students, Stanford, CA.

Exum, H. A., & Young, E. D. (1981). A longitudinal assessment of academic development in an Upward Bound summer program. *Community/Junior College Research Quarterly, 5,* 339–350.

Fantini, M. D., & Weinstein, G. (1968). *The Disadvantaged: Challenge to Education.* New York: Harper & Row.

Farrington, D. P. (1987). Schools and delinquency prevention. *Today's Delinquent,* *6*(2), 71–86.

Fay, R. E., Passel, J. S., & Robinson, J. G. (1988). *The Coverage of Population in the 1980 Census* (Report No. PHC80-E4). Washington, DC: U.S. Government Printing Office.

Feshbach, N. D. (1969). Student teacher preferences for elementary school pupils varying in personality characteristics. *Journal of Educational Psychology, 60,* 126–132.

Fine, M. (1987). Why urban adolescents drop into and out of public high school. In G. Natriello (Ed.), *School Dropouts: Patterns and Policies* (pp. 89–105). New York: Teachers College Press.

Finn, C. E., Jr. (1988, October). Lessons learned: Federal policy making and the educational research community. *Phi Delta Kappan, 70,* 127–133.

Firestone, W. A., & Wilson, B. L. (1985). Using bureaucratic and cultural linkages to improve instruction: The principal's contribution. *Educational Administration Quarterly, 21,* 7–30.

Fitz-Gibbon, C. T. (1977). *An Analysis of the Literature on Cross-Age Tutoring.* Washington, DC: National Institute of Education.

Flax, E. (1987, April 29). Three-year study of E.D. statistics branch planned. *Education Week,* p. 4.

Fordham, S., & Ogbu, J. (1986). Black students' school success: Coping with the burden of "acting white." *The Urban Review, 18,* 176–206.

Freedberg, L. (February 22, 1987). The risks of labeling kids "at risk." *Baltimore Sun,* p. 5M.

Friedman, N. L. (1970). Cultural deprivation: A commentary in the sociology of knowledge. In J. L. Frost & G. R. Hawkes (Eds.), *The Disadvantaged Child: Issues and Innovations* (pp. 5–17). Boston: Houghton Mifflin Company.

Fuchs, L. S., Fuchs, D., Hamlett, C. L., & Hasselbring, T. S. (1987). Using computers with curriculum-based monitoring: Effects on teacher efficiency and satisfaction. *Journal of Special Education Technology, 8,* 14–27.

Fullan, M., Miles, M., & Taylor, G. (1980). Organization development in the schools: The state of the art. *Review of Educational Research, 50,* 121–184.

Fuller, B. (1981). Educational evaluation and shifting youth policy. *Evaluation Review, 5,* 167–188.

Furstenberg, F. F., & Brooks-Gunn, J. (1985). Teenage childbearing: Causes, consequences and remedies. In L. H. Aiken & D. Mechanic (Eds.), *Applications of Social Science to Clinical Medicine and Health Policy* (pp. 307–334). New Brunswick, NJ: Rutgers University Press.

Furstenberg, F., & Condran, G. (1987). *Family Change and the Decline of Adolescent Well-Being: Getting the Facts Straight.* Unpublished manuscript. University of Pennsylvania, Department of Sociology, Philadelphia.

Galbraith, J. (1973). *Organizational Design.* Reading, MA: Addison-Wesley.

Gallegos, G. E., & Kahn, M. W. (1986). Factors predicting success of underprivileged youths in Job Corps training. *The Vocational Guidance Quarterly, 34,* 171–177.

Gamble, T. J., & Zigler, E. (in press). The Head Start synthesis project: A critique. *Journal of Applied Developmental Psychology.*

Gamoran, A. (1987). The stratification of high school learning opportunities. *Sociology of Education, 60,* 135–155.

Gamoran, A., & Berends, M. (1987). The effects of stratification in secondary schools: Synthesis of survey and ethnographic research. *Review of Educational Research, 57,* 415–435.

Gampert, R. D., & Blank, R. (1988). *Educational Options High Schools Admissions Policy Study.* New York: New York City Board of Education.

Garbarino, J. (1978). The human ecology of school crime: A case for small schools. In E. Wenk & N. Harlow (Eds.), *School Crime and Disruption: Prevention Models* (pp. 123–133). Washington, DC: National Institute of Education.

Garbarino, J. (1980). Some thoughts on school size and its effects on adolescent development. *Journal of Youth and Adolescence, 9,* 19–31.

Garet, M. S., & DeLany, B. (1985). *Decisions and Random Draws: Course Choice in Math and Science.* Unpublished manuscript. Stanford University, School of Education. Stanford, CA.

Garms, W. I. (1971). A benefit-cost analysis of the Upward Bound Program. *Journal of Human Resources, 6,* 206–220.

Garms, W. I. (1973). Reply to a benefit-cost analysis of the Upward Bound program. *Journal of Human Resources, 8,* 115–118.

Gersten, R. (1986). Response to "Consequences of three preschool curriculum models through age 15." *Early Childhood Research Quarterly, 1,* 292–302.

Gersten, R., & Carnine, D. (1984). Direct instruction mathematics: A longitudinal evaluation of low-income elementary school students. *The Elementary School Journal, 84,* 395–407

Gersten, R., Darch, C., & Gleason, M. (1988). Effectiveness of a direct-instruction academic kindergarten for low-income students. *The Elementary School Journal, 89,* 227–240.

Gersten, R., & White, W. A. T. (1986). Castles in the sand: Response to Schweinhart and Weikart. *Educational Leadership, 44*(3), 19–20.

Glass, G. V. (1970). *Data Analysis of the 1968–69 Survey of Compensatory Education (Title I)* (Final Report on Grant OEG 8-8-9618604003-0587). Washington, DC: U.S. Office of Education.

Glass, G. V., & Smith, M. L. (1977). *"Pull Out" in Compensatory Education.* Boulder: Laboratory of Educational Research, University of Colorado.

Gold, M., & Mann, D. (1984). *Expelled to a Friendlier Place: A Study of Effective Alternative Schools.* Ann Arbor: University of Michigan Press.

Goodlad, J. (1984). *A Place Called School.* New York: McGraw-Hill.

Gordon, I. J. (1969). *Early Child Stimulation Through Parent Education* [Report No. PHS-R-306(01)]. Washington, DC: U.S. Government Printing Office.

Gottfredson, D. C. (1986). An empirical test of school-based environmental and individual interventions to reduce the risks of delinquent behavior. *Criminology, 24,* 705–731.

Gottfredson, D. C. (1987). An evaluation of an organization development approach to reducing school disorder. *Evaluation Review, 11,* 739–763.

Gottfredson, G. D. (1984). A theory-ridden approach to program evaluation. *American Psychologist, 39,* 1101–1112.

Gottfredson, G. D. (1985). *Effective School Battery: User's Manual.* Odessa, FL: Psychological Assessment Resources.

Gottfredson, G. D. (1987). American Education: American delinquency. *Today's Delinquent, 6*(2), 5–70.

Gottfredson, G. D. (1988). *Business Community/School Partnerships.* Baltimore, MD: Center for Research on Elementary and Middle Schools, Johns Hopkins University.

Gottfredson, G. D., & Gottfredson, D. C. (1985). *Victimization in Schools.* New York: Plenum Press.

Gottfredson, G. D., & Gottfredson, D. C. (1987). *Using Organization Development to Improve School Climate.* Baltimore, MD: Center for Research on Elementary and Middle Schools, Johns Hopkins University.

Gottfredson, G. D., Rickert, D. E., Jr., Gottfredson, D. C., & Advani, N. (1984). Standards for program development evaluation plans. *Psychological Documents, 14,* 32.

Granger, R. L., Cicirelli, V. G., Cooper, W. H., Rhode, W. E., & Maxey, E. J. (1969). *The Impact of Head Start: An Evaluation of the Effects of Head Start on Children's Cognitive and Affective Development* (Vol. 1). Athens, OH: Westinghouse Learning Corporation and Ohio University.

Grannis, J. (1975, July). Beyond labels: The significance of social class and ethnicity for education. *Equal Opportunity Review,* 1–5.

Grannis, J. (1979). *The Objective Environment, Environmental Press, and the Diversity of Learners and Teachers.* New York: Teachers College, Columbia University.

Grannis, J. (1989, April). Personal communication.

Grannis, J., Riehl, C., Pallas, A., Lerer, N., & Randolph, S. (1988). *Evaluation of the New York City Dropout Prevention Initiative: Final Report on the Middle Schools for Year Two, 1986–87.* New York: Institute for Urban and Minority Education, Teachers College, Columbia University.

Grannis, J., Riehl, C., Pallas, A. M., Lerer, N., Randolph, S., & Jewell, K. (1988). *Evaluation of the New York City Dropout Prevention Initiative: Final Report on the High Schools for Year Two, 1986–87.* New York: Institute for Urban and Minority Education, Teachers College, Columbia University.

Grant, W. V., & Snyder, T. D. (1986). *Digest of Education Statistics 1985–86.* Washington, DC: U.S. Government Printing Office.

Grant Foundation Commission on Work, Family and Citizenship. (1988). *The Forgotten Half: Pathways to Success for America's Youth and Young Families.* Washington, DC: William T. Grant Foundation.

Griswold, P. A., Cotton, K. J., & Hansen, J. B. (1986). *Effective Compensatory Education Sourcebook.* Washington, DC: U.S. Government Printing Office.

Hahn, A., & Danzberger, J. (1987). *Dropouts in America.* Washington, DC: Institute for Educational Leadership.

Hahn, A., & Lerman, R. (1985). *What Works in Youth Employment Policy.* Washington, DC: National Planning Association.

Hall, K. A. (1982). Computer-based education. In H. E. Mitzel (Ed.), *Encyclopedia of Educational Research* (Vol. 1, pp. 353–367). New York: Free Press.

Hallinan, M. (1987). Ability grouping and student learning. In M. Hallinan (Ed.), *The Social Organization of Schools: New Conceptualizations of the Learning Process* (pp. 41–69). New York: Plenum Press.

Hammack, F. M. (1987). Large school systems' dropout reports: An analysis of definitions, procedures, and findings. In G. Natriello (Ed.), *School Dropouts: Patterns and Policies* (pp. 20–37). New York: Teachers College Press.

Hanushek, E. A. (1979). Conceptual and empirical issues in the estimation of educational production functions. *Journal of Human Resources, 14,* 351–388.

Hanushek, E. A. (1981). Throwing money at schools. *Journal of Policy Analysis and Management, 1,* 19–41.

Hanushek, E. A. (1986). The economics of schooling: Production and efficiency in public schools. *Journal of Economic Literature, 24,* 1141–1177.

Hanushek, E. A. (1989). The impact of differential expenditures on school performance. *Educational Researcher, 18*(4), 45–51, 62.

Hargroves, J. S. (1986). The Boston Compact: A community response to school dropouts. *Urban Review, 18,* 207–217.

Hartle, T. W., & Bilson, A. (1986). *Increasing the Educational Achievement of Disadvantaged Children: Do Federal Programs Make a Difference?* Washington, DC: American Enterprise Institute.

Haveman, R. H. (1977). Introduction: Poverty and social policy in the 1960's and 1970's — An overview and some speculations. In R. H. Haveman (Ed.), *A Decade of Federal Antipoverty Programs: Achievements, Failures, and Lessons* (pp. 1–19). New York: Academic Press.

Havighurst, R. J. (1965). Who are the socially disadvantaged? *Journal of Negro Education, 40,* 210–217.

Hechinger, F. M. (1986, April 22). Preschool programs. *New York Times,* p. C8.

Hendrickson, G. L. (1977, April). *Review of Title I Education Services.* Paper presented at the annual meeting of the American Educational Research Association, New York.

Herman, J., & Dorr-Bremme, D. W. (1984). *Testing and Assessment in American Public Schools: Current Practices and Directions for Improvement.* Los Angeles: University of California at Los Angeles, Center for the Study of Evaluation.

Hertling, J. (1986, April 2). ED aides outline complete overhaul of data collection. *Education Week,* pp. 15–16.

Hess, G. A., Jr. (1986, Fall). Educational triage in an urban high school setting. *Metropolitan Education, 1,* 39–52.

Hindelang, M. J., Hirschi, T., & Weis, J. G. (1979). Correlates of delinquency: The illusion of discrepancy between self-report and official measures. *American Sociological Review, 44,* 995–1014.

Hirschi, T. (1969). *Causes of Delinquency.* Berkeley: University of California Press.

Hirschi, T., Hindelang, M. J., & Weis, J. (1982). Reply to "On the use of self-report data to determine the class distribution of criminal and delinquent behavior." *American Sociological Review, 47,* 433–435.

Horst, D. P., & Fagan, B. M. (1979). *Common Evaluation Hazards, ESEA Title I Evaluation and Reporting Systems.* Mountain View, CA: RMC Research Corporation.

House, E. R. (1979). Review of reports from the National Institute of Education on the Compensatory Education Study. *Proceedings of the National Academy of Education* (Vol. 6, pp. 358–424). Washington, DC: National Academy of Education.

House, E. R. (1981–1982). Response to Bereiter and Kurland: Changing lead into gold. *Interchange, 12*(1), 22–26.

House, E. R., Glass, G. V., McLean, L. D., & Walker, D. C. (1978). No simple answer: Critique of the Follow Through evaluation. *Harvard Educational Review, 46,* 128–160.

Howe, H. (1984). *Giving Equity a Chance in the Excellence Game.* Martin Buskin Memorial Lecture. Washington, DC: Education Writers Association.

Hughes, D., Johnson, K., Simons, J., & Rosenbaum, S. (1986). *Maternal and Child Health Data Book: The Health of America's Children.* Washington, DC: Children's Defense Fund.

Hunt, J. (1961). *Intelligence and Experience.* New York: Ronald Press.

Hunt, J. (1964). The psychological basis for using pre-school environment as an antidote for cultural deprivation. *Merrill Palmer Quarterly, 10,* 209–248.

Hurn, C. J. (1985). *The Limits and Possibilities of Schooling: An Introduction to the Sociology of Education.* Boston: Allyn & Bacon.

Inkeles, A. (1966). Social structure and the socialization of competence. *Harvard Educational Review, 36,* 265–283.

Institute of Medicine. (1985). *Preventing Low Birthweight.* Washington, DC: National Academy Press.

Interface. (1989). *Unfair at Any Price: Welfare Recipients at New York Proprietary Schools.* New York: Author.

Jackson, P. (1967). *Life in Classrooms.* New York: Holt, Rinehart & Winston.

Jencks, C., Bartlett, S., Corcoran, M., Crouse, J., Eaglesfield, D., Jackson, G., McClelland, K., Mueser, P., Olneck, M., Schwartz, J., Ward, S., & Williams, J. (1979). *Who Gets Ahead? The Determinants of Economic Success in America.* New York: Basic Books.

Jencks, C., & Brown, M. (1975). The effects of high schools on their students. *Harvard Educational Review, 45,* 273–324.

Jencks, C., & Mayer, S. (1988). *The Social Consequences of Growing Up in a Poor Neighborhood: A Review.* Unpublished manuscript. Northwestern University Center for Urban Affairs and Policy Research, Evanston, IL.

Jester, R. E., & Guinagh, B. J. (1983). The Gordon Parent Education Infant and

Toddler Program. In Consortium for Longitudinal Studies (Ed.), *As the Twig Is Bent . . . Lasting Effects of Preschool Programs* (pp. 103–132). Hillsdale, NJ: Lawrence Erlbaum.

Johnson, D., Maruyama, G., Johnson, R., & Nelson, D. (1981). Effects of cooperative, competitive, and individualistic goal structures on achievement: A meta-analysis. *Psychological Bulletin, 89,* 47–62.

Jung, S. H. (1984). *Reanalysis of High School and Beyond Data to Estimate the Impact of Upward Bound.* Washington, DC: Applied Systems Institute.

Karweit, N. (1984). Time-on-task reconsidered: A synthesis of research on time and learning. *Educational Leadership, 41*(8), 33–35.

Karweit, N. (1987a). Diversity, equity, and classroom processes. In M. Hallinan (Ed.), *The Social Organization of Schools: New Conceptualizations of the Learning Process* (pp. 71–102). New York: Plenum Press.

Karweit, N. (1987b). *Full or Half Day Kindergarten—Does It Matter?* (Report No. 11). Baltimore, MD: Johns Hopkins University, Center for Research on Elementary and Middle Schools.

Karweit, N. (1989). Effective kindergarten programs and practices for students at risk. In R. E. Slavin, N. L. Karweit, & N. A. Madden (Eds.), *Effective Programs for Students at Risk* (pp. 103–142). Boston: Allyn & Bacon.

Karweit, N., Gottfredson, D. C., & Gottfredson, G. D. (1988). *BTS: Behavior Tracking.* Baltimore, MD: Johns Hopkins University Center for Research on Elementary and Middle Schools.

Kean, M. H. (1983). Administrative uses of research and evaluation information. In E. W. Gordon (Ed.), *Review of Research in Education* (Vol. 10, pp. 361–414). Washington, DC: American Educational Research Association.

Kennedy, M. M. (1978, June). Findings from the Follow Through Planned Variation Study. *Educational Researcher, 7,* 3–11.

Kennedy, M. M., Birman B. F., & Demaline, R. E. (1986). *The Effectiveness of Chapter I Services.* Washington, DC: U.S. Government Printing Office.

Kennedy, M. M., Jung, R. K., & Orland, M. E. (1986). *Poverty, Achievement and the Distribution of Compensatory Education Services.* Washington, DC: U.S. Government Printing Office.

Kirst, M. (1984). *Who Controls Our Schools? American Schools in Conflict.* New York: Freeman.

Kirst, M. (1985). Policy and research issues in using data to promote school reforms. In Northwest Regional Educational Laboratory (Ed.), *Using Data and Information Systems to Support School Improvement and Accountability* (pp. 37–50). Portland, OR: Author.

Kleck, G. (1982). On the use of self-report data to determine the class distribution of criminal and delinquent behavior. *American Sociological Review, 47,* 427–433.

Klerman, L. V. (1979). Evaluating service programs for school age parents: Design problems. *Evaluation and the Health Professions, 1,* 55–70.

Kobrin, S. (1959). The Chicago Area Project—A 25 year assessment. *Annals of the American Academy of Political and Social Science, 322,* 19–29.

Korn, R. R., & McCorkle, L. W. (1965). *Criminology and Penology.* New York: Holt, Rinehart & Winston.

Larrivee, B. (1989). Effective strategies for academically handicapped students in the regular classroom. In R. E. Slavin, N. L. Karweit, & N. A. Madden (Eds.), *Effective Programs for Students at Risk* (pp. 291–319). Boston: Allyn & Bacon.

Lazar, I. (1983). Discussion and implications of the findings. In Consortium for Longitudinal Studies (Ed.), *As the Twig Is Bent . . . Lasting Effects of Preschool Programs* (pp. 461–466). Hillsdale, NJ: Lawrence Erlbaum.

Lazar, I., Hubbell, V. R., Murray, H., Rosche, M., & Royce, J. (1977). *The Persistence of Preschool Effects: A Long-Term Follow-Up of Fourteen Infant and Preschool Experiments.* Ithaca, NY: Consortium for Longitudinal Studies.

Leinhardt, G., & Pallay, A. (1982). Restrictive educational settings: Exile or haven? *Review of Educational Research, 52,* 557–578.

Lesser, A. J. (1985). The origin and development of maternal and child health programs in the United States. *American Journal of Public Health, 75,* 590–598.

Levin, H. (1972). *The Costs to the Nation of Inadequate Education.* Washington, DC: U.S. Government Printing Office.

Levin, H. (1977). A decade of policy developments in improving education and training for low-income populations. In R. R. Haveman (Ed.), *A Decade of Federal Antipoverty Programs: Achievements, Failures, and Lessons* (pp. 123–188). New York: Academic Press.

Levin, H. (1983). Reclaiming urban schools: A modest proposal. *IFG Policy Perspectives, 4,* 1–4.

Levin, H. (1985). *The Educationally Disadvantaged: A National Crisis* (Working Paper No. 6). Philadelphia: Public/Private Ventures.

Levin, H. (1986). *The Educationally Disadvantaged Are Still Among Us.* Unpublished manuscript. Stanford University, School of Education, Stanford, CA.

Levin, H. (1987). *Towards Accelerated Schools.* New Brunswick, NJ: Center for Policy Research in Education.

Levin, H., Glass, G. V., & Meister, G. R. (1984). *A Cost-Effectiveness Analysis of Four Educational Interventions* (Project Report No. 84-A11). Stanford, CA: Stanford University, Institute for Research on Educational Finance and Governance.

Levin, H., Glass, G. V., & Meister, G. R. (1986). The political arithmetic of cost-effectiveness analysis. *Phi Delta Kappan, 68,* 69–72.

Levin, H., & Meister, G. (1986). Is CAI cost-effective? *Phi Delta Kappan, 67,* 745–749.

Levine, D. E., & Havighurst, R. J. (1984). *Society and Education* (6th ed.). Boston: Allyn & Bacon.

Levine, D. E., & Havighurst, R. J. (1989). *Society and Education* (7th ed.). Boston: Allyn & Bacon.

Levitan, S. A. (1969). *The Great Society's Poor Law.* Baltimore, MD: Johns Hopkins Press.

Levitan, S. A., & Gallo, F. (1988). *A Second Chance: Training for Jobs.* Kalamazoo, MI: W. E. Upjohn Institute for Employment Research.

Levy, J. E. (1989). *Joining Forces: A Report from the First Year.* Alexandria, VA: National Association of State Boards of Education.

Lewis, O. (1966). The culture of poverty. *Scientific American, 215*(4), 19–25.

Lindesmith, A. L., & Strauss, A. L. (1950). A critique of culture-personality writings. *American Sociological Review, 15,* 587–600.

Littman, B., & Parmelee, A. H. (1978). Medical correlates of infant development. *Pediatrics, 61,* 470–474.

Lubchenco, L., Delivoria-Papadopoulos, M., & Searles, D. (1972). Long-term follow-up studies of prematurely born infants: II. Influence of birthweight and gestational age on sequelae. *Journal of Pediatrics, 80,* 509.

Lynn, L. E., Jr. (1973). *The Effectiveness of Compensatory Education: Summary and Review of the Evidence.* Washington DC: U.S. Department of Health, Education, and Welfare.

Madden, N. A., & Slavin, R. E. (1989). Effective pullout programs for students at risk. In R. E. Slavin, N. L. Karweit, & N. A. Madden (Eds.), *Effective Programs for Students At Risk* (pp. 52–72). Boston: Allyn & Bacon.

Mager, R. (1962). *Preparing Instructional Objectives.* Palo Alto, CA: Fearon.

Maine Department of Educational and Cultural Services. (1988). *Restructuring Schools in Maine.* Augusta, ME: Author.

Mallar, C., Kerachsky, S., Thornton, C., & Long, D. (1982). *Evaluation of the Economic Impact of the Job Corps Program. Third Follow-Up Report.* Princeton, NJ: Mathematica Policy Research.

Mann, D. (1987). Can we help dropouts? Thinking about the undoable. In G. Natriello (Ed.), *School Dropouts: Patterns and Policies* (pp. 3–19). New York: Teachers College Press.

Marecek, J. (1979). *Economic, Social, and Psychological Consequences of Adolescent Childbearing: An Analysis of Data from the Philadelphia Collaborative Perinatal Project.* Unpublished manuscript. Swarthmore College, Department of Psychology, Swarthmore, PA.

Mason, J., Wodarski, J. S., & Parham, T. M. J. (1985). Work and welfare: A reevaluation of AFDC. *Social Work, 3,* 197–203.

McCann, R. A., & Austin, S. (1988, April). *At-Risk Youth: Definitions, Dimensions, and Relationships.* Paper presented at the annual meeting of the American Educational Research Association, New Orleans, LA.

McCormick, M. C., Shapiro, S., & Starfield, B. (1984). High-risk young mothers: Infant mortality and morbidity in four areas in the United States, 1973–1978. *American Journal of Public Health, 74,* 18–23.

McDaniels, G. L. (1975). The evaluation of Follow Through. *Educational Researcher, 4*(11), 7–11.

McDill, E. L., Karweit, N. A., Natriello, G., & Pallas A. M. (1989, March). *The Growth of Kindergarten and Its Impact on Disadvantaged Students.* Paper presented at the annual meeting of the American Educational Research Association, San Francisco.

McDill, E. L., McDill, M. S., & Sprehe, J. T. (1969). *Strategies for Success in Compensatory Education: An Appraisal of Evaluation Research*. Baltimore, MD: Johns Hopkins University Press.

McDill, E. L., McDill, M. S., & Sprehe, J. T. (1972). Evaluation in practice: Compensatory education. In P. H. Rossi & W. Williams (Eds.), *Evaluating Social Programs* (pp. 141–185). New York: Seminar Press.

McDill, E. L., Natriello, G., & Pallas, A. M. (1985). Raising standards and retaining students: The impact of the reform recommendations on dropouts. *Review of Educational Research, 55,* 415–433.

McDill, E. L., Natriello, G., & Pallas, A. M. (1986). A population at risk: Potential consequences of tougher school standards for student dropouts. *American Journal of Education, 94,* 135–181.

McDill, E. L., & Rigsby, L. C. (1973). *Structure and Process in Secondary Schools: The Academic Impact of Educational Climates*. Baltimore, MD: Johns Hopkins University Press.

McDonough, S. C. (1984). Intervention programs for adolescent mothers and their offspring. *Journal of Children in Contemporary Society, 17*(1), 67–78.

McKey, R. H., Condelli, L., Ganson, H., Barrett, B. J., McConkey, C., & Plantz, M. C. (1985). *The Impact of Head Start on Children, Families, and Communities*. Washington, DC: CSR, Inc.

McLaughlin, D. H. (1977). *Title I, 1965–1975: A Synthesis of the Findings of Federal Studies*. Washington, DC: American Institutes for Research.

McLaughlin, M. W., & Shields, P. M. (1987). Involving low-income parents in the schools: A role for policy? *Phi Delta Kappan, 69,* 156–160.

McPartland, J. M., & McDill, E. L. (1977). Research on crime in schools. In J. M. McPartland & E. L. McDill (Eds.), *Violence in Schools: Perspectives, Programs, and Positions* (pp. 3–33). Lexington, MA: D. C. Heath.

Merton, R. K. (1948). Self-fulfilling prophecy. *Antioch Review, 8,* 193–210.

Meyer, J. W., & Rowan, B. (1978). The structure of educational organizations. In M. Meyer (Ed.), *Environments and Organizations* (pp. 78–109). San Francisco: Jossey-Bass.

Meyer, L. A. (1984). Long-term academic effects of the direct instruction Project Follow Through. *The Elementary School Journal, 84,* 380–394.

Miller, G. (1983). Children and Congress: A time to speak out. *American Psychologist, 38,* 70–76.

Miller, L. B., & Bissell, R. P. (1983). The Louisville Experiment: A comparison of four programs. In Consortium for Longitudinal Studies (Ed.), *As the Twig Is Bent . . . Lasting Effects of Preschool Programs* (pp. 171–200). Hillsdale, NJ: Lawrence Erlbaum.

Milne, A., & Gombert, J. (1983). Students with a primary language other than English: Distribution and service rates. In K. Baker & A. DeKanter (Eds.), *Bilingual Education* (pp. 113–138). Lexington, MA: D. C. Heath.

Milne, A. M., Myers, D. E., Rosenthal, A. S., & Ginsburg, A. (1986). Single parents, working mothers, and the educational achievement of school children. *Sociology of Education, 59,* 125–139.

Mims, G. L. (1985). Aspiration, expectation, and parental influences among Upward

Bound students in three institutions. *Educational and Psychological Research, 5,* 181–190.

Mincer, J. (1974). *Schooling, Experience, and Earnings.* New York: Columbia University Press.

Mirga, T. (1986, January 29). Radical overhaul offered for ED data collection. *Education Week,* pp. 1, 10–11.

Mirga, T., & Nienhuis, M. (1986, October 1). Statistics agency needs overhaul, panelists assert. *Education Week,* pp. 1, 17.

Morgan, D. L., & Alwin, D. E. (1980). When less is more: School size and student social participation. *Social Psychology Quarterly, 43,* 241–252.

Morrow, G. (1987). Standardizing practice in the analysis of school dropouts. In G. Natriello (Ed.), *School Dropouts: Patterns and Policies* (pp. 38–51). New York: Teachers College Press.

Mullin, S. P., & Summers, A. A. (1983). Is more better? The effectiveness of spending on compensatory education. *Phi Delta Kappan, 64,* 330–343.

Murphy, J. T. (1973). Title V of ESEA: The impact of discretionary funding on state education bureaucracies. *Harvard Educational Review, 43,* 362–385.

Murray, S. R., Murray, C., Gragg, F. E., & Kumi, L. M. (1982). *National Evaluation of the PUSH for Excellence Project: Final Report.* Washington, DC: American Institutes for Research.

Nathan, R. P. (1988). *Social Science in Government: Uses and Misuses.* New York: Basic Books.

National Assessment of Educational Progress. (1985). *The Reading Report Card.* Princeton, NJ: Educational Testing Service.

National Commission on Excellence in Education. (1983). *A Nation at Risk: The Imperative for Educational Reform.* Washington, DC: U.S. Government Printing Office.

National Diffusion Network. (1979). *Education Programs That Work* (6th ed.). San Francisco: Far West Laboratory for Educational Research and Development.

National Diffusion Network. (1986). *Education Programs That Work* (12th ed.). Longmont, CO: Sopris West.

National Diffusion Network. (1987). *Education Programs That Work* (13th ed.). Longmont, CO: Sopris West.

National Institute of Education. (1978). *Compensatory Education Study: A Final Report from the National Institute of Education.* Washington, DC: Author.

National Science Board. (1985). *Science Indicators: The 1985 Report.* Washington, DC: National Science Foundation.

Natriello, G. (1982). *Organizational Evaluation Systems and Student Disengagement in Secondary Schools* (Final Report to the National Institute of Education). St. Louis: Washington University.

Natriello, G. (1984). Managing the culture of the school. *Educational Leadership, 42*(2), 80–82.

Natriello, G. (1985). *Products and Processes of the National Center for Education Statistics: An Agenda for the Next Decade.* Washington, DC: National Center for Education Statistics.

Natriello, G. (1987a, April). *The Changing Context for Research and Policy on the*

Transition Between High School and Entry Level Positions in the Workplace. Paper presented at the annual meeting of the American Educational Research Association, Washington, DC.

Natriello, G. (Ed.). (1987b). *School Dropouts: Patterns and Policies.* New York: Teachers College Press.

Natriello, G., & Dornbusch, S. M. (1984). *Teacher Evaluative Standards and Student Effort.* New York: Longman.

Natriello, G., McDill, E. L., & Pallas, A. M. (1985). School reform and potential dropouts. *Educational Leadership, 43*(1), 10–14.

Natriello, G., & McPartland, J. (1987, April). *Adjustments in High School Teachers' Grading Criteria: Accommodation or Motivation?* Paper presented at the annual meeting of the American Educational Research Association, Washington, DC.

Natriello, G., Pallas, A. M., & McDill, E. L. (1986a). *Community Resources for Responding to the Dropout Problem.* New Brunswick, NJ: Rutgers University.

Natriello, G., Pallas, A. M., & McDill, E. L. (1986b). Taking stock: Renewing our research agenda on the causes and consequences of dropping out. *Teachers College Record, 87,* 430–440.

Neill, S. B. (1979). *Keeping Students in School: Problems and Solutions* (AASA Critical Issues Report). Arlington, VA: American Association of School Administrators.

Newmann, F. (1981). Reducing student alienation in high schools: Implications of theory. *Harvard Educational Review, 51,* 546–564.

Niemiec, R. P., Blackwell, M. C., & Walberg, H. J. (1986). CAI can be doubly effective. *Phi Delta Kappan, 67,* 750–751.

Nurss, J. R., & Hodges, W. L. (1982). Early childhood education. In H. E. Mitzel (Ed.), *Encyclopedia of Educational Research* (Vol. 1, pp. 489–513). New York: Free Press.

Oakes, J. (1985). *Keeping Track: How Schools Structure Inequality.* New Haven: Yale University Press.

Oakes, J. (1986). *Educational Indicators: A Guide for Policy Makers.* New Brunswick, NJ: Rutgers University, Center for Policy Research in Education.

OERI Urban Superintendents Network. (1987). *Dealing with Dropouts: The Urban Superintendents' Call to Action.* Washington, DC: U.S. Government Printing Office.

Ogbu, J. U. (1974). *The Next Generation: The Ethnography of Education in an Urban Neighborhood.* New York: Academic Press.

Olson, L. (1986, November 26). Data collection varies widely among states, study finds. *Education Week,* p. 13.

Olson, L. (1987, March 25). Bennett panel urges major expansion of NAEP. *Education Week,* pp. 1, 8–9.

Openshaw, K. (1967). A failure of the Minnesota Teacher Attitude Inventory to relate to teacher behavior. *Journal of Teacher Education, 18,* 233–239.

Pallas, A. M. (1987). School dropouts in the United States. In J. D. Stern & M. F. Williams (Eds.), *The Condition of Education* (1986 ed.; pp. 158–174). Washington, DC: U.S. Government Printing Office.

Pallas, A. M. (1989). Conceptual and measurement problems in the study of school dropouts. In R. G. Corwin & K. Namboodiri (Eds.), *Research in Sociology of Education and Socialization* (Vol. 8, pp. 87–116). Greenwich, CT: JAI Press.

Pallas, A. M., Natriello, G., & McDill, E. L. (1987). The high cost of high standards: School reform and dropouts. *Urban Education, 22,* 103–114.

Pallas, A. M., Natriello, G., & McDill, E. L. (1989, June/July). The changing nature of the disadvantaged population: Current dimensions and future trends. *Educational Researcher, 18*(5), 16–22.

Palmer, E. (1981). A community-based comprehensive approach to serving adolescent parents. *Child Welfare, 60,* 191–197.

Passow, A. H. (1970). Deprivation and disadvantage: Nature and manifestations. In A. H. Passow (Ed.), *Deprivation and Disadvantage: Nature and Manifestations* (International Studies in Education, 21; pp. 15–51). Hamburg, West Germany: Unesco Institute for Education.

Passow, A. H., & Elliott, D. L. (1967). The disadvantaged in depressed areas. In P. A. Witty (Ed.), *The Educationally Retarded and Disadvantaged: The Sixty-Sixth Yearbook of the National Society for the Study of Education,* Part I (pp. 20–39). Chicago: University of Chicago Press.

Pavuk, A. (1987, May 27). ED's statistics branch adopts guidelines for data collection. *Education Week,* p. 15.

Peng, S. S. (1983). *High School Dropouts: Descriptive Information from High School and Beyond* (Report No. 83-221b). Washington, DC: National Center for Education Statistics.

Pennsylvania Department of Education. (1984). *Educational Quality Assessment: Manual for Interpreting Intermediate School Results.* Harrisburg, PA: Division of Educational Testing and Evaluation, Pennsylvania Department of Education.

Pennsylvania Department of Education. (1985). *Educational Quality Assessment: Commentary.* Harrisburg, PA: Division of Educational Testing and Evaluation, Pennsylvania Department of Education.

Perlez, J. (1987, February 5). Dropout Figures to Include Data on Racial Basis. *New York Times,* p. A1.

Perpich, R. (1988). Minnesota plan expands options for public school students. *State Education Leader, 7*(2), 5.

Perrow, C. (1979). *Complex Organizations: A Critical Essay.* Glenview, IL: Scott, Foresman.

Phi Delta Kappa. (1980). *Why Some Urban Schools Succeed.* Bloomington, IN: Author.

Pickett, A. L. (1989). *Restructuring the Schools: The Role of Paraprofessionals.* Washington, DC: Center for Policy Research, National Governors' Association.

Portes, A., & Truelove, C. (1987). Making sense of diversity: Recent research on Hispanic minorities in the United States. *Annual Review of Sociology, 13,* 359–385.

Public School Forum of North Carolina. (1988). *North Carolina's Lead Teacher/Restructured School Pilot Project: An Interim Report.* Raleigh, NC: Author.

Public School Forum of North Carolina. (1989). *Lead Teacher/Restructured School Project Overview.* Raleigh, NC: Author.

Quay, H. C., & Allen, L. B. (1982). Truants and dropouts. In H. E. Mitzel (Ed.), *Encyclopedia of Educational Research* (Vol. 5, pp. 1958–1962). New York: Free Press.

Ramey, C. T., & Bryant, D. M. (1982). Evidence for prevention of developmental retardation during infancy. *Journal for the Division of Early Childhood, 5,* 73–78.

Ramp, E. A., & Rhine, W. R. (1981). Behavior analysis model. In W. R. Rhine (Ed.), *Making Schools More Effective: New Directions from Follow Through* (pp. 155–200). New York: Academic.

Ramsey, R. S. (1986). Taking the practicum beyond the school door. *Adolescence, 21,* 547–552.

Rantakallio, P. (1979). Social background of mothers who smoke during pregnancy and influence of these factors on the offspring. *Social Science and Medicine, 13A,* 423–429.

Rantakallio, P. (1983). A follow-up study up to the age of 14 of children whose mothers smoked during pregnancy. *Acta Paediatr Scand, 72,* 747–753.

Raywid, M. A. (1985). Family choice arrangements in public schools: A review of the literature. *Review of Educational Research, 55,* 435–467.

Resnick, D. P., & Resnick, L. B. (1985, April). Standards, curriculum, and performance: A historical and comparative perspective. *Educational Researcher, 14,* 5–21.

Riddle, W., & Stedman, J. B. (1989). *Public School Choice: Recent Developments and Analysis of Issues* (Report No. 89-219 EPW). Washington, DC: Congressional Research Service.

Riessman, F. (1962). *The Culturally Deprived Child.* New York: Harper & Row.

Riessman, F. (1963). The culturally deprived child: A new view. In U.S. Department of Health, Education, and Welfare, U.S. Office of Education, *Programs for the Educationally Disadvantaged* (pp. 3–10). Washington, DC: U.S. Government Printing Office.

Rist, R. C. (1970). Student social class and teacher expectations: The self-fulfilling prophecy in ghetto education. *Harvard Educational Review, 40,* 411–451.

Rivlin, A. (1971). *Systematic Thinking for Social Action.* Washington, DC: Brookings Institution.

Rosenholtz, S. B. (1977). *The Multiple Ability Classroom: An Intervention Against the Self-Fulfilling Prophecy.* Unpublished doctoral dissertation, Stanford University.

Rosenshine, B. (1979). The third cycle of research on teacher effects: Content covered, academic engaged time, and direct instruction. In P. Peterson & H. Walberg (Eds.), *Research on Teaching: Concepts, Findings, and Implications* (pp. 28–56). Berkeley, CA: McCutchan.

Rosenshine, B., & Furst, N. (1969). *The Effects of Tutoring upon Pupil Achievement: A Research Review.* Washington, DC: Office of Education. (ERIC Document Reproduction Service No. ED 064 462)

Rosenthal, R., & Jacobson, L. (1968). *Pygmalion in the Classroom*. New York: Holt, Rinehart & Winston.

Royce, J. R., Darlington, R. B., & Murray, H. W. (1983). Pooled analyses: Findings across studies. In Consortium for Longitudinal Studies (Ed.), *As the Twig Is Bent . . . Lasting Effects of Preschool Programs* (pp. 411–459). Hillsdale, NJ: Lawrence Erlbaum.

Rudman, H. C., Kelly, J. L., Wanous, D. S., Mehrens, W. A., Clark, D. C., & Porter, A. C. (1980). *Integrating Assessment with Instruction: A Review (1922–1980)*. East Lansing: Michigan State University, Institute for Research on Teaching.

Rumberger, R. W. (1987). High school dropouts: A review of issues and evidence. *Review of Educational Research, 57,* 101–121.

Saks, D. H. (1984). *A Legacy for the 21st Century: Investment Opportunities in Our Children's Schooling. Report Prepared for the Subcommittee on Business and the Schools, Committee for Economic Development*. Nashville, TN: Peabody College, Vanderbilt University.

Salganik, L., & Celebuski, C. (1987). *Educational Attainment Study: Preliminary Tables*. Washington, DC: Pelavin Associates.

Schools urged to develop wider set of assessments. (1988, September 14). *Education Week*, p. 5.

Schorr, L. B. (1988). *Within Our Reach: Breaking the Cycle of Disadvantage*. New York: Anchor Press/Doubleday.

Schramm, W. F. (1985). WIC prenatal participation and its relationship to newborn Medicaid costs in Missouri: A cost/benefit analysis. *American Journal of Public Health, 75,* 851–857.

Schwartz, R., & Hargroves, J. (1986–1987). The Boston compact. *Metropolitan Education, 3,* 14–24.

Schweinhart, L. J., & Weikart, D. P. (1980). *Young Children Grow Up: The Effects of the Perry Preschool Program on Youths Through Age 15*. Ypsilanti, MI: High/Scope Press.

Schweinhart, L. J., & Weikart, D. P. (1986a). Early childhood development programs: A public investment opportunity. *Educational Leadership, 44*(3), 4–12.

Schweinhart, L. J., & Weikart, D. P. (1986b, November). *Evidence of Problem Presentation by Early Childhood Education*. Paper presented at the Symposium on Social Prevention and Intervention in the Analytical Perspective of Guidance, Control, and Impact, Bielefeld, West Germany.

Schweinhart, L. J., & Weikart, D. P. (1986c). Schweinhart and Weikart reply. *Educational Leadership, 44*(3), 22.

Schweinhart, L. J., Weikart, D. P., & Larner, M. B. (1986a). Child-initiated activities in early childhood programs may help prevent delinquency. *Early Childhood Research Quarterly, 1,* 303–312.

Schweinhart, L. J., Weikart, D. P., & Larner, M. B. (1986b). Consequences of three preschool curriculum models through age 15. *Early Childhood Research Quarterly, 1,* 15–45.

Seattle Public Schools. (1988). *Twenty-One Seattle Schools for the 21st Century.* Seattle, WA: Author.

Sebring, P., Campbell, B., Glusberg, M., Spencer, B., Singleton, M., & Turner, M. (1987). *High School and Beyond 1980 Sophomore Cohort Third Follow-Up (1986) Data File User's Manual.* Chicago: National Opinion Research Center, University of Chicago.

Seitz, V., Rosenbaum, L. K., & Apfel, N. H. (1985). Effects of family support intervention: A ten-year follow-up. *Child Development, 56,* 376–391.

Sherman, J. D. (1987). *Dropping out of School: Causes and Consequences for Male and Female Youth.* Washington, DC: Pelavin Associates.

Shinn, M. (1978). Father absence and children's cognitive development. *Psychological Bulletin, 85,* 295–324.

Silverman, L. J., & Taeuber, R. C. (1985). *Synthesis of Invited Papers: Elementary/Secondary Education Data Redesign Project: A Public Discussion Draft.* Washington, DC: National Center for Education Statistics.

Sipe, C. L., Grossman, J. B., & Milliner, J. A. (1987). *Summer Training and Education Program (STEP): Report on the 1986 Experience-Executive Summary.* Philadelphia: Public/Private Ventures.

Sipe, C. L., Grossman, J. B., & Milliner, J. A. (1988). *Summer Training and Education Program (STEP) Report on the 1987 Experience.* Philadelphia: Public/Private Ventures.

Sirkin, J. R. (1985, November 27). Nation's school chiefs complete plans to gauge states, students. *Education Week,* pp. 1, 14–15.

Sirkin, J. R. (1986, March 5). "Report Card" out, alternatives eyed. *Education Week,* pp. 1, 10, 16.

Sizer, T. (1984). *Horace's Compromise: The Dilemma of the American High School.* Boston: Houghton Mifflin.

Slavin, R. E. (1983a). *Cooperative Learning.* New York: Longman.

Slavin, R. E. (1983b). *Student Team Learning.* Washington, DC: National Education Association.

Slavin, R. E. (1985). Team-assisted individualization: A cooperative learning solution for adaptive instruction in mathematics. In M. C. Wang & H. J. Walberg (Eds.), *Adapting Instruction to Individual Differences* (pp. 236–253). Berkeley, CA: McCutchan.

Slavin, R. E. (1986a). *Educational Psychology: Theory into Practice.* Englewood Cliffs, NJ: Prentice-Hall.

Slavin, R. E. (1986b, October). Meta-analysis in education: How has it been used? *Educational Researcher, 13,* 6–15.

Slavin, R. E. (1987a). *Effective Compensatory Programs for At-Risk Elementary School Students.* Talk presented at a meeting of the Council for Educational Development and Research, Orlando, Florida.

Slavin, R. E. (1987b). Making Chapter I make a difference. *Phi Delta Kappan, 69,* 110–119.

Slavin, R. E. (1989). Students at risk of school failure: The problem and its dimensions. In R. E. Slavin, N. L. Karweit, & N. A. Madden (Eds.), *Effective Programs for Students at Risk* (pp. 1–20). Boston: Allyn & Bacon.

Slavin, R. E., & Karweit, N. L. (1985). Effects of whole class, ability grouped, and individualized instruction on mathematics achievement. *American Educational Research Journal, 22,* 351-367.

Slavin, R. E., Karweit, N. L., Madden, N. A., & Stevens, R. (1986, September). *Effective Elementary Schools Program* (Grant No. OERI-G-86-0006). Baltimore, MD: Johns Hopkins University, Center for Research on Elementary and Middle Schools.

Slavin, R. E., Leavey, M. B., & Madden, N. A. (1984). Combining cooperative learning and individualized instruction: Effects on student mathematics achievement, attitudes, and behaviors. *The Elementary School Journal, 84,* 409-422.

Slavin, R. E., & Madden, N. A. (1989). Effective classroom programs for students at risk. In R. E. Slavin, N. L. Karweit, & N. A. Madden (Eds.), *Effective Programs for Students at Risk* (pp. 23-51). Boston: Allyn & Bacon.

Slavin, R. E., Madden, N. A., & Karweit, N. L. (1989). Effective programs for students at risk: Conclusions for practice and policy. In R. E. Slavin, N. L. Karweit, & N. A. Madden (Eds.), *Effective Programs for Students at Risk* (pp. 355-372). Boston: Allyn & Bacon.

Slavin, R. E., & Oickle, E. (1981). Effects of cooperative learning teams on student achievement and race relations: Treatment by race interactions. *Sociology of Education, 54,* 174-180.

Spady, W. G. (1988). Organizing for results: The basis of authentic restructuring and reform. *Educational Leadership, 46*(2), 4-8.

Spencer, G. (1986). *Projections of the Hispanic Population: 1983 to 2080* (U.S. Bureau of the Census, Current Population Reports, Series P-25, No. 995). Washington, DC: U.S. Government Printing Office.

Spencer, G. (1989). *Projections of the Population of the United States, by Age, Sex, and Race: 1988-2080* (U.S. Bureau of the Census, Current Population Reports, Series P-25, No. 1018). Washington, DC: U.S. Government Printing Office.

Spodek, B. (1985). Kindergarten. In T. Husen & T. N. Postlethwaite (Eds.), *International Encyclopedia of Education* (pp. 2812-2814). New York: Pergamon.

Spring, W. J. (1987, March/April). Youth unemployment and the transition from school to work: Programs in Boston, Frankfurt, and London. *New England Economic Review,* pp. 3-16.

Sproull, L. S., & Larkey, P. (1979). Managerial behavior and evaluator effectiveness. In H. C. Schulberg & J. M. Jerrell (Eds.), *The Evaluator and Management* (pp. 89-104). Beverly Hills, CA: Sage.

Stallings, J. (1975). *Implementations and Child Effects of Teaching Practices in Follow Through Classrooms* (Monograph of the Society for Research in Child Development, No. 40). Chicago: University of Chicago Press.

Stallings, J., & Kaskowitz, D. (1974). *Follow Through Classroom Observation Evaluation, 1972-73.* Menlo Park, CA: SRI International.

Stallings, J. A., & Stipek, D. (1986). Research on early childhood and elementary school teaching programs. In M. C. Wittrock (Ed.), *Handbook of Research on Teaching* (pp. 727-753). New York: Macmillan.

Stebbins, L. B., St. Pierre, R. G., Proper, E. C., Anderson, R. B., & Cerva, J. R. (1977). *Education As Experimentation: A Planned Variation Model: Vol. IV-A. An Evaluation of Follow Through.* Cambridge, MA: Abt.

Stedman, J. B., Salganik, L. H., & Celebuski, C. A. (1988). *Dropping Out: The Educational Vulnerability of At-Risk Youth.* Washington, DC: Congressional Research Service.

Stedman, L. C., & Smith, J. S. (1983). Recent reform proposals for American education. *Contemporary Education Review 2,* 85–104.

Steel, L., & Schubert, J. G. (1983, April). *The Effectiveness of Upward Bound in Preparing Disadvantaged Youth for Post-Secondary Education.* Paper presented at the annual meeting of the American Educational Research Association, Montreal, Canada.

Stein, M. K., Leinhardt, G., & Bickel, W. (1989). Instructional issues for teaching students at risk. In R. E. Slavin, N. L. Karweit, & N. A. Madden (Eds.), *Effective Programs for Students at Risk* (pp. 145–194). Boston: Allyn & Bacon.

Stern, J. D., & Williams, M. F. (1987). *The Condition of Education* (1986 Ed.). Washington, DC: U.S. Government Printing Office.

Stevens, R. J., Madden, N. A., Slavin, R. E., & Farnish, A. M. (1986). *Cooperative Integrated Reading and Composition: A Brief Overview of the CIRC Program.* Baltimore, MD: Johns Hopkins University, Center for Research on Elementary and Middle Schools.

Stevens, R. J., Madden, N. A., Slavin, R. E., & Farnish, A. M. (1987). Cooperative integrated reading and composition: Two field experiments. *Reading Research Quarterly, 22,* 433–454.

Stevenson, D. L., & Baker, D. P. (1987). The family-school relation and the child's school performance. *Child Development, 58,* 1348–1357.

Stiggins, R. J. (1985). Improving assessment where it means the most: In the classroom. *Educational Leadership, 43*(2), 69–74.

Stiggins, R. J., & Bridgeford, N. J. (1985). The ecology of classroom assessment. *Journal of Educational Measurement, 22,* 271–286.

Stiggins, R. J., Conklin, N. F., & Bridgeford, N. J. (1986). Classroom assessment: A key to effective education. *Educational Measurement: Issues and Practice, 5,* 5–17.

Stinchcombe, A. L. (1964). *Rebellion in a High School.* Chicago: Quadrangle Books.

Stodolsky, S., & Lesser, J. (1967). Learning patterns in the disadvantaged. *Harvard Educational Review, 37*(4), 546–593.

Stonehill, R. M. (1985, April). *The Sustained Achievement of Chapter I Students— A Summary of Findings.* Paper presented at the annual meeting of the American Educational Research Association, Chicago.

Strobino, D. N., Chase, G. A., Kim, Y. J., Crawley, B. E., Salim, J. H., & Baruffi, B. E. (1986). The impact of the Mississippi Improved Child Health Project on prenatal care and low birthweight. *American Journal of Public Health, 76,* 274–278.

Survey Research Center. (1981). *A Panel Study of Income Dynamics, Wave 14 (1981).* Ann Arbor: Institute for Social Research, University of Michigan.

Task Force on Teaching as a Profession. (1986). *A Nation Prepared: Teachers for the 21st Century.* New York: Carnegie Forum on Education and the Economy.

Thompson, J. (1967). *Organizations in Action.* New York: McGraw-Hill.

Tindal, G., Wesson, C., & German, G. (1982, April). *A Data-Based Special Education Delivery System: The Pine County Model.* Paper presented at the annual international convention of the Council for Exceptional Children, Houston, Texas.

Tittle, C. R., Villemez, W. J., & Smith, D. A. (1982). One step forward, two steps back: More on the class/criminality controversy. *American Sociological Review, 47,* 435–438.

Tolor, A., Scarpetti, W. L., & Lane, P. A. (1967). Teachers' attitudes toward children's behavior revisited. *Journal of Educational Psychology, 58,* 175–180.

Tucker, M., & Mandel, D. (1986). The Carnegie Report—A call for redesigning the schools. *Phi Delta Kappan, 20,* 24–27.

Tyack, D. (1974). *The One Best System.* Cambridge, MA: Harvard University Press.

Uhlenberg, P., & Eggebeen, D. (1986, Winter). The declining well-being of American adolescents. *The Public Interest, 82,* 25–38.

U.S. Bureau of the Census. (1983). *Lifetime Earnings Estimates for Men and Women in the United States: 1979.* Washington, DC: U.S. Government Printing Office.

U.S. Bureau of the Census. (1986a). *Household and Family Characteristics: March 1985* (Current Population Reports, Series P-20, No. 411). Washington, DC: U.S. Government Printing Office.

U.S. Bureau of the Census. (1986b). *State and Metropolitan Area Data Book, 1986.* Washington, DC: U.S. Government Printing Office.

U.S. Bureau of the Census. (1987). *Statistical Abstract of the United States: 1988.* Washington, DC: U.S. Government Printing Office.

U.S. Bureau of the Census. (1988a). *The Hispanic Population in the United States: March 1988 (Advance Report)* (Current Population Reports, Series P-20, No. 431). Washington, DC: U.S. Government Printing Office.

U.S. Bureau of the Census. (1988b). *Household and Family Characteristics: March 1987* (Current Population Reports, Series P-20, No. 424). Washington, DC: U.S. Government Printing Office.

U.S. Bureau of the Census. (1988c). *Money Income and Poverty Status in the United States: 1987 (Advance Data from the March 1988 Current Population Survey)* (Current Population Reports, Series P-60, No. 161). Washington, DC: U.S. Government Printing Office.

U.S. Bureau of the Census. (1989). *Marital Status and Living Arrangements: March 1988* (Current Population Reports, Series P-20, No. 433). Washington, DC: U.S. Government Printing Office.

U.S. Department of Education. (1981). *Annual Evaluation Report: Vol. 2. Fiscal Year 1981.* Washington, DC: U.S. Government Printing Office.

U.S. Department of Education. (1985). *Annual Evaluation Report: Vol. 6. Fiscal Year 1985.* Washington, DC: U.S. Government Printing Office.

U.S. Department of Education. (1988). *Annual Evaluation Report: Vol. 9. Fiscal Year 1988.* Washington, DC: U.S. Government Printing Office.

U.S. General Accounting Office. (1986a). *Job Corps: Its Costs, Employment Out-*

comes, and Service to the Public. Washington, DC: U.S. Government Printing Office.

U.S. General Accounting Office. (1986b). *School Dropouts: The Extent and Nature of the Problem.* Washington, DC: U.S. Government Printing Office.

U.S. General Accounting Office. (1987a). *Bilingual Education: Information on Limited English Proficient Students: Briefing Report to the Chairman, Committee on Labor and Human Resources, United States Senate.* Washington, DC: U.S. Government Printing Office.

U.S. General Accounting Office. (1987b). *Prenatal Care: Medicaid Recipients and Uninsured Women Obtain Insufficient Care.* Washington, DC: U.S. Government Printing Office.

U.S. General Accounting Office (1987c). *School Dropouts: Survey of Local Programs.* Washington, DC: U.S. Government Printing Office.

U.S. House of Representatives, Committee for Economic Development. (1985). *Job Corps Program: Its Benefits Outweigh the Costs.* Washington, DC: U.S. Government Printing Office.

U.S. House of Representatives, Committee on Ways and Means. (1985). *Children in Poverty.* Washington, DC: U.S. Government Printing Office.

U.S. House of Representatives, Select Committee on Children, Youth and Families (1988). *Opportunities for Success: Cost Effective Programs for Children, Update 1988.* Washington, DC: U.S. Government Printing Office.

Valentine, C. A. (1968). *Culture and Poverty.* Chicago: University of Chicago Press.

Valentine, C. A. (1971). Deficit, difference, and bicultural models of Afro-American behavior. *Harvard Educational Review, 41*(2), 137–157.

Wagenaar, T. C. (1987). What do we know about dropping out of high school? In R. G. Corwin (Ed.), *Research in the Sociology of Education and Socialization, Vol. 7* (pp. 161–190). Greenwich, CT: JAI.

Walters, P. B., & Rubinson, R. (1983). Educational expansion and economic output in the United States, 1890–1969: A production function analysis. *American Sociological Review, 48,* 480–493.

Wargo, M. J., Tallmadge, G. A., Michaels, D. D., Lipe, D., & Morris, S. J. (1972). *ESEA Title I: A Reanalysis and Synthesis of Evaluation Data from Fiscal Year 1965 Through 1970.* Palo Alto, CA: American Institute for Research.

Wehlage, G., & Rutter, R. (1987). Dropping out: How much do schools contribute to the problem? In G. Natriello (Ed.), *School Dropouts: Patterns and Policies* (pp. 70–88). New York: Teachers College Press.

Wehlage, G., & Smith, G. A. (1986). *Programs for At-Risk Students: A Research Agenda.* Madison: University of Wisconsin, National Center for Effective Secondary Schools.

Weick, K. (1976) Educational organizations as loosely coupled systems. *Administrative Science Quarterly, 21*(1), 1–19.

Weikart, D. P. (1971). *Early Childhood Special Education for Intellectually Subnormal and/or Culturally Different Children.* Ypsilanti, MI: High/Scope Educational Research Foundation.

Weitzman, M., Klerman, L. V., Lamb, G., Menary, J., & Alpert, J. J. (1982). School absence: A problem for the pediatrician. *Pediatrics, 69,* 739–746.

Werner, E. E., Bierman, J. M., & French, F. E. (1971). *The Children of Kauai.* Honolulu: University Press of Hawaii.

Wheeler, S. (1967). Review of "Rebellion in a high school" by Arthur Stinchcombe. *American Sociological Review, 32,* 1018–1021.

White, S. (1970). The national impact study of Head Start. In J. Hellmuth (Ed.), *Disadvantaged Child* (Vol. 3, pp. 163–184). New York: Brunner/Mazel.

Williams, R. C., & Bank, A. (1987). Realities and scenarios: Instructional information systems in classrooms of the future. In A. Bank & R. C. Williams (Eds.), *Information Systems and School Improvement: Inventing the Future* (pp. 145–151). New York: Teachers College Press.

Williams, R. C., Lyon, C. D., Doscher, L., Walker, C., & Cullian, L. (1979). *Evaluation Units in Small School Districts.* Los Angeles: University of California at Los Angeles, Center for the Study of Evaluation.

Williams, W., & Evans, J. W. (1969). The politics of evaluation: The case of Head Start. *Annals of the American Academy of Political and Social Sciences, 385,* 118–132.

Willis, P. (1977). Learning to Labor: How Working Class Kids Get Working Class Jobs. New York: Columbia University Press.

Wilson, W. J. (1987). *The Truly Disadvantaged: The Inner City, the Underclass, and Public Policy.* Chicago: University of Chicago Press.

Wise, A. (1979). *Legislated Learning.* Berkeley: University of California Press.

Wisler, C. E., Burns, G. P., Jr., & Iwamoto, D. (1978). Follow Through redux: A response to the critique by House, McLean, and Walker. *Harvard Educational Review, 45,* 171–185.

Wolfe, B. L. (1985). The influence of health on school outcomes. *Medical Care, 23,* 1127–1138.

Woodhead, M. (1988). When psychology informs public policy: The case of early childhood intervention. *American Psychologist, 43,* 443–454.

Wynn, R., & Wynn, J. L. (1988). *American Education* (9th Ed.). New York: Harper & Row.

Young, E. D., & Exum, H. A. (1982). Upward Bound and academic achievement: A successful intervention. *College Student Personnel, 23,* 291–299.

Zigler, E. (1973). Project Head Start: Success or failure? *Children Today, 2*(6), 2–71.

Zigler, E. (1987). Formal schooling for four-year-olds? No. *American Psychologist, 42,* 254–260.

Zigler, E., & Berman, W. (1983). Discerning the future of early childhood intervention. *American Psychologist, 38,* 894–906.

Zimiles, H. (1985, April). *The Role of Research in an Era of Expanding Preschool Education.* Paper presented at the annual meeting of the American Educational Research Association, Chicago, Illinois.

Index

About the Authors

GARY NATRIELLO is Associate Professor of Sociology and Education at Teachers College, Columbia University. He received his Ph.D. in the sociology of education from Stanford University. His interests include evaluation processes in schools and school organization, especially their implications for disadvantaged children.

EDWARD L. McDILL is Professor of Sociology and Co-Director of the Center for Research on Elementary and Middle Schools at The Johns Hopkins University. Professor McDill also serves on the staff of the Center for Research on Effective Schooling for Disadvantaged Students at Johns Hopkins. He has a longstanding interest in the evaluation of social and educational programs for the disadvantaged.

AARON M. PALLAS is Associate Professor of Sociology and Education at Teachers College, Columbia University. He received his Ph.D. in sociology from The Johns Hopkins University. He specializes in the study of education and social stratification, including school dropouts and the disadvantaged.